René Boux

Awake to love and work!
The lark is in the sky.

*"Morning Song"*

We bless thee for our creation,
preservation, and all the
blessings of this life. . . .

And we most humbly beseech
thee, of thy goodness, O Lord,
to comfort and succor all those
who, in this transitory life,
are in trouble, sorrow, need,
sickness, or any other adversity.

*The Book of*
*Common Prayer*

# TOUCHED WITH FIRE

**JOHN WHEELER**

# Touched with Fire

## THE FUTURE OF THE VIETNAM GENERATION

A GROLIER COMPANY

FRANKLIN WATTS, INC.
NEW YORK   TORONTO   1984

Library of Congress Cataloging in Publication Data

Wheeler, John, 1944–
Touched with fire.

Bibliography: p.
Includes index.
1. Vietnamese Conflict, 1961–1975—United States.
2. Vietnamese Conflict, 1961–1975—Influence and
results. 3. United States—History—1961–1969.
4. United States—History—1969–      I. Title.
DS558.W48 1984      959.70433'73      83-23586
ISBN 0-531-09832-X

Copyright © 1984 by John Wheeler
Printed in the United States of America
First U.S. publication 1984 by Franklin Watts, Inc.
387 Park Avenue South, New York, New York 10016
6   5   4   3   2   1

# CONTENTS

**PART III**
**TO COME**

# TOUCHED WITH FIRE

[We] cannot live in associations
with the past alone . . . if we
would be worthy of the past, we
must find new fields for action or
thought, and make for ourselves
new careers. But, nevertheless,
the generation that carried on
the war has been set apart by its
experience . . . in our youth our
hearts were touched with fire.

*Oliver Wendell Holmes, Jr.*
*Memorial Day, 1884*

# BEGINNING

For ten years, I have found myself wrestling with the question of how the events of the Vietnam era shape America. It seems clear to me that the war itself was both catalyst and fuel for the social, economic, and political change in America since 1960. It also seems clear that the events of the war years are interconnected, and they feed each other in their effects. Of course history did not begin in 1960, but so much happened so fast thereafter, that the decade bears special attention.

I am convinced that the events of the Vietnam War period will have more effect on America in the next twenty years than they have had in the last twenty years. The war especially affected the generation of sixty million Americans who came of age during the war years. Like the generation of Justice Holmes, each of us has been "touched with fire."

And we each have work to do. To do it, we need the counsel and prodding of those older and younger than we. The events of the war years created enduring divisions among the different groups within the generation, like the islands made by fracture lines when a brick hits a windshield. The fracture lines are caused by entrenched ideas, disillusionment, dashed expectations, and an unfortunate reluctance to discuss these divisions. The work is to be candid and specific in inventorying our past, assessing our present, and discussing the possible futures in which our generation contributes to America and the world. Our parents, employers, brothers and sisters, and teenage children have an objectivity and also a concern for us that can help us get the work done.

Our memories of the events of the Vietnam era still haunt us. They will shape the politics in our generation, certainly our attitudes on questions of war, peace, the draft, and the balance of domestic versus defense spending. In 1984, the memory is a predicate—implicit or explicit—of government and press pronouncements on El Salvador, Nicaragua, Afghanistan, Poland, Iran, Lebanon, and certainly Southeast Asia. These international issues are potential determinants in future presidential and other elective and appointive politics. The great issues in our time will be impenetrable if we do not sort out how our passage in the Vietnam War years is shaping each of us.

The future is what matters. It is in our collective hands. Books about the Vietnam era have not tied past to present and future. These books have dwelt heavily on the war zone, and not equally on America. The war's connections to the women's, environmental, and civil rights movements are not well explored. Before we can shape our future positively, we need to discuss these issues. Unspoken attitudes shape not only our lives, but our children's. (This gave me pause when I figured out that my children, entering kindergarten in September, 1983, will be in the college class of the year 2000.)

In the winter of 1982, I took these ideas to Ernest May, professor of history at Harvard University, then on sabbatical at the Wilson Center in Washington, D.C. He had taught Sam Williamson, my history teacher at West Point. My memory of Sam's esteem for May prompted me to call and arrange a luncheon meeting. May advises cabinet officers and presidents. He advised Kissinger.

I told him that I felt this tug to keep exploring the effects of the Vietnam War. I had found myself organizing the construction of the Southeast Asia Memorial at West Point by mobilizing the ten West Point classes of the sixties. The experience led to my service as chairman of the Vietnam Veterans Memorial Fund.

Professor May and I strolled down the Mall to the Vietnam Veterans Memorial. He liked the design, but he said little else. He was thinking. At lunch he began to talk. He referred me to a book that tends to confirm the picture I have in mind. It is George Fredrickson's *The Inner Civil War*, which explores how the Civil War shaped the generation of Americans who were young during its fighting. Fredrickson, trained at Harvard, is professor of history at Northwestern University. He writes, ''the collective trauma which polarized the nation's energies, thoughts and emotions . . . had consequences for the history of ideas which were comparable to its well-known political and economic effects.'' And the book discussed Holmes and his perception of having been ''touched with fire.'' I could only shake my head. Ask Ernest May a question, and you get an answer.

It took a century for a Fredrickson to address the Civil War in this way. I think the reason for the delay is that the social sciences had not developed the ideas of social bonding, structure, and communication necessary for the work. But in the 1980s, we have those tools at hand. The work can begin now, so that we can shape our own future with a depth of understanding unavailable to Holmes and his generation. The tasks are similar: both generations deal with a great war and subsequent events that sundered our country.

This book attempts to offer a coherent picture of where we have been and are now, and more importantly, the paths we can choose to go in our life together as a generation of Americans. Our work is to share our experiences of the Vietnam era. This dialogue will break down the divisions among men and women. It will lead to healing and a stronger country, one better able to give to the world. It will free the creativity that surges in our generation.

The point of this work is that if we understand how our past shapes us, we can govern how it shapes us.

## A PICTURE TO START WITH
The heart of the work is finding what we have in common. The Vietnam War lasted from 1959 to 1975, the longest in American history. The dates of the first and last casualties are engraved on the Vietnam Veterans Memorial in Washington. During that time, the largest generation in our history (the World War II ''baby boom'') reached twenty-one years of age, with all its young men subject to the military draft. Various estimates and assumptions differ, but in rough terms the generation includes about thirty million women and thirty million men, the total comprising about one hundredth of the people on our planet. Of the men, about ten million served in the armed forces; nearly three million served in the war zone.

Our generation shares the features of common experience, background, and power. We grew up in the 1950s and 1960s in a country united by electronics (radio, television, and the telephone) and many shared attitudes. For example, we watched and heard John Kennedy's inaugural address together. We watched "Disneyland," and "Davy Crockett" played by Fess Parker. We know what Conelrad and civil defense drills mean. We danced together. We turned rock 'n' roll into a cultural force. Such similarity was unique in history among so many young people at one time.

By around 1960, we were like wet clay, not loose sand that could be scattered by the winds of events. We were moldable, in our politically formative years. Cultural and electronic ties bound us together. Soon would come major forces to shape us and create cleavages. Because we are like clay, the effects do show. And because we are still young, we are supple and can mold a new unity.

We believed John Kennedy. We wanted to give to our country. We only dimly realized what it meant to be sent abroad to "pay any price, bear any burden . . . to assure the survival and the success of liberty."

This is fundamental American idealism. Matured by two decades of strife, that idealism is still our common strength as a generation. A mature idealism and shared experiences of youth create great potential for cohesion among our very large group. Because of our numbers and positions in the middle ranks of society, we are the inevitable source of leadership for our country's activities and institutions, from the mid-1980s through the turn of the century. We are the children of a wealthy country. We have come of age in a troubled world. We have the potential for supplying an influential (perhaps determinative) share of world leadership.

The events of the Vietnam War years caused three kinds of divisions. First, the man who wore the uniform was separated from the man who did not. Then, woman was separated from man, as the "all bets are off" attitude of the 1960s freed the women's movement, and as the factor of a despised war fed a feminization of the culture and disaffirmation of a distinctly masculine ideal. Finally, self has been separated from self, since

most of us suppress recognition of the memories and consequences of our choices made in the 1960s and early 1970s. These
separations alter the kind of attachments men and women make.
They can needlessly embitter political contests. And they leave
many of us harboring unnecessary hurts.

The need for restored unity, and at least honesty, make it
important to sort out the extent of and remedies for these divisions. The submerged, serious nature of the divisions within the
generation warrant particular attention now, especially in view
of the needless personal pain and disunity which they have perpetuated.

The lengthy formative effect of the war on such a key generation warrants attention. It was a slow-motion Antietam, Shi-
loh, and Gettysburg. The focus on our American generation is
not to diminish the truth that the armies and people of Southeast
Asia suffered in the war. Nor should we forget that the war's
American combat-casualty list (58,000 killed, 300,000 wounded)
is not of the same order as that of the Holocaust, the Russian
homeland defense of World War II, or that of the Gulag as
chronicled by Solzhenitsyn. Nevertheless, for our generation
Vietnam caused suffering, it had dramatic formative effects, and
the appreciation of these effects is essential to our national, and
therefore world, leadership.

Our work is to engage in a dialogue while we are still young,
to expose and examine our ideals and expectations as they were
actually shaped in the 1960s and 1970s. The individuals with
the interior strength to open this dialogue run all through the
generation. Exposed to light, the wounds and events of the era
will not be as hideous as we may think. This work is our generation's responsibility, and it is already begun. The appearance
of and interest in books on the narrower issue of the Vietnam
War itself supports this assertion.

Bonded by the heritage of World War II and the electronic
media and profoundly shaped and divided in freedom rides, the
Peace Corps, the women's movement, and the Vietnam War,
the sixty million Americans who came of age in the 1960s are
healing their divisions through remembrance and dialogue. This
work is vital, since we will be the leaders of our national institutions in the year 2000—we are the Century Generation.

## A PICTURE OF MYSELF

My need to explain how Vietnam era events shape us has to do with something I learned at West Point, and that is that the most important part of war is building the peace. The better you build the peace, the less imminent is the next war. This was never an explicit lesson at West Point, but it is built into the warp and woof of the study of war. You do not see it until you stand back a little and look. MacArthur's leadership in healing Japan after World War II is a clue that this is true. So is the European recovery plan of George Marshall.

The tug that brings me to *Touched with Fire* is my West Point classmates. Thomas Jay Hayes IV gave his life retrieving his wounded men. Matthew C. Harrison, Jr., was wounded twice under the same circumstances. He lived. So did Wesley K. Clark and Glenn F. ("Jeff") Rogers, Jr., who held their troops together despite agonizing exposure to enemy fire. Theirs is an example of giving that is spiritual in nature, and I cannot avert my eyes from it.

Paul Tillich and others teach that there are times when it takes courage to affirm that there are things worth living for. I think the more urgent question in the 1980s and 1990s is what things we hold to be worth dying for. You cannot blame America for withdrawing from that question after Vietnam. But we can look at that question now.

Anyone who stands up and affirms the Nicene Creed probably is obligated to disclose the habit. It can seem a little mad. I do it at Epiphany Episcopal Church in Washington. The Creed contains startling pronouncements. I believe God acts within us and loves this world, and I believe the brokenness and death about us is not the last word. And I believe in common sense. Given that the Creed is true, we can glimpse, sense God's presence. This occurs very often through other people, like Tommy Hayes, or the names on the Vietnam Veterans Memorial. If the Creed should not make sense to you, there are still the examples of love and hope people offer. I think it is often those examples that lead people to the Creed. They led me to it.

The effects on people of what we do is what ultimately matters. That is how to steer. The Creed affirms the Resurrection. I subscribe to C. S. Lewis on this:

It is a serious thing to live in a society of possible gods and goddesses, to remember that the dullest and most uninteresting person you talk to may one day be a creature which, if you saw it now, you would be strongly tempted to worship, or else a horror and corruption such as you now meet, if at all, only in a nightmare. All day long we are, in some degree, helping each other to one or the other of these destinations. It is in the light of these overwhelming possibilities, it is with the awe and the circumspection proper to them, that we should conduct all our dealings with one another, all friendships, all loves, all play, all politics. There are no *ordinary* people. You have never talked to a mere mortal. Nations, cultures, arts, civilizations [and Vietnam Veterans Memorials]—these are mortal and their life is to ours as the life of a gnat. But, it is immortals whom we joke with, work with, marry, snub, and exploit—immortal horrors or everlasting splendours. This does not mean that we are to be perpetually solemn. We must play. But, our merriment must be of the kind (and it is in fact the merriest kind) which exists between people who have, from the outset, taken each other seriously—no flippancy, no superiority, no presumption. And our charity must be real and costly love, with deep feeling for the sins in spite of which we love the sinner—no mere tolerance or indulgence which parodies love as flippancy parodies merriment.

The good news in all this is that God will not stop trying to bring us home, and with that I am certain Mr. Lewis agrees.

Especially when found in rare moments of rest on a battlefield, merriment is one of those glimpses that forces us to think. Perhaps that is the magic of *M*A*S*H*.

But these are ending kinds of things.

*The beginning for me was another kind of ending. It goes back to the day I left the Army, outprocessing at Fort Meyer in Washington in August of 1971. The Army had been my home for* twenty-six years. On an impulse I chose that day to explore what had been a fleeting thought. I went to Virginia Seminary in Alexandria, an Episcopal seminary, to see if I might spend a year there, studying, to sort out the question of my vocation. I felt alone and in need of repair. In fact, in a sandlot game the week before, a football had smashed into my right eye, causing bleeding all over the white of the eye. It was like a stoplight. Half a world-class hangover, one might have thought. Of all the days that summer, it was the one day that the dean, Cecil Woods, happened to be up from his Tennessee vacation home to check on things. Any other day and we would not have met. I told my story to Associate Dean Richard Reid. He asked Dean Woods to see me. The dean gave me a home, in that he admitted me as a special student for a year. At the time I felt needy because I needed a breather to sort out what work I should do.

Looking back, I see I was needy because I needed a way to start making sense of the ten years just then ended. The Seminary gave me a set of ideas and categories of thought with which to do that. And it taught me not to be afraid of priests, so that later when I met and married Elisa, who became an Episcopal priest, it was the most natural thing in the world. As with many Vietnam veterans, the love I found in marriage has been important to healing. So that spontaneous summer morning visit at Virginia Seminary was really a kind of prayer for healing, and I believe this book I find myself writing is part of the answer.

# PART I
# THEN

The process of living seems to con-
sist in coming to realize truths so
ancient and simple that, if stated,
they sound like barren platitudes.
They cannot sound otherwise to those
who have not had the relevant experience: that is why there is no real
teaching of such truths possible and
every generation starts from scratch. . . .

*C. S. Lewis*
**Letters**

# CHAPTER ONE

*Q. I am a thirty-year-old single woman who is expecting her first child. This child was planned, and I feel very celebratory about my pregnancy. My parents have a very different value system from my own, and while they are not going to disown me, they would not have agreed with my decision to have a child sans matrimony had they been consulted.*

*A. The times are with you, not only because others have chosen as you have, but because the idea of marriage as an irrevocable condition has been shattered among your parents' generation, as well as those younger. Even the most conventional of their friends will have learned by now that marriages are made and unmade with a speed that does not allow onlookers the luxury of analyzing them for the fun of placing blame. . . .*

Judith Martin
"Miss Manners" column
*Washington Post*
July 19, 1983

*"Lieutenant, this patrol. We might not make it back. We gotta go?"*

*"We gotta go, Corporal. We don't gotta make it back."*

Wartime conversation

# GOING

Great commitments are scary. They are more easily made by the young, who don't realize the implications. The young can more easily break them, too. But commitments made and kept are society's bone, the skeleton of the culture. The trembling and tears at weddings suggest that many sense that there is some truth in this view, since marriage is an example of a great commitment.

The idea of making and keeping a promise took a real beating in the 1960s and 1970s. For example, in my senior year of high school in 1962, the conventional wisdom was that two out of three new marriages stay unbroken. Twenty years later, it is one out of three. The point is not blame. The point is all the hurt. These hurts and unfulfilled promises and the convulsions of the 1960s and 1970s are so obviously parallel that it seems sensible to look for some possible connections among them.

Starting in the 1960s we all began a journey of great commitments. Then circumstances dissolved the commitments. The wound-up, unused energy spurted into new channels. An example was the go-go culture, both on Wall Street and the music scene.

Elisa DesPortes and I married on July 14, 1973, in Trinity Cathedral, Columbia, South Carolina. Trinity is an old church. It was there when Sherman's Union forces marched through the city. Elisa told me that night that she wept for an hour before the ceremony. In fact, the tears started when the black limousine arrived at her parents' home to take them all to the church. She said, for an instant, "The limousine looked like a hearse." There is a bit of relinquishing individual freedom and old habits for the new partners in a marriage. And there is the risky future.

We used the old-fashioned words "to have and to hold from this day forward, for better for worse, for richer for poorer, in sickness and in health, to love and to cherish, till death us do part." I was in a daze. The feeling was familiar. I tend to be dazed during the important passages in my life. I shift into automatic. I remember swearing in at West Point at sunset on July 2, 1962. I was seventeen. It was the end of the first day of Beast Barracks, the arduous summer-long introduction to the rigors of our new life as cadets. *"Is this happening to me?"*

I asked the same question before the first (and each subsequent) military parachute jump.

"STAND UP!" the jumpmaster says.

*"Is this happening to me?"*

"STAND IN THE DOOR!"

*Big doors open. Look at the horizon, the Army teaches. This will help you leap vigorously up and out, so that the slipstream will help the chute open. Gazing down is sloppy. It makes you tumble weakly out, twisting your risers. So you fix on the horizon, instead of the true destination.*

"GO!"

At the door by the altar, I saw Elisa coming down the aisle. Her eyes had a trace of tears, but she was beaming. My dad was best man. "Stand in the door!" I had whispered at the same moment to classmate John Bohuslar when he married Martha. My eyes were glazed. Dad's eyes were glazed. Shift to automatic.

We all subscribed to other great commitments when we were younger. At Kennedy's inaugural. The speech by Martin Luther King, Jr., at the Lincoln Memorial on August 28, 1963: "I have a dream that one day this nation will rise up and live out the true meaning of its creed: We hold these truths to be self-evident, that all men are created equal." A quarter of a million people were there. The media sent the word nationwide.

Betty Friedan, Germaine Greer, and Gloria Steinem galvanized women. The power of ideas of men like Buckminster Fuller led directly to Earth Day on April 22, 1970, the establishment of the environmental movement as a political determinant, and the creation of the Environmental Protection Agency.

And if I made a commitment at West Point, my friend Al-

bert W. ("Buster") Lewis Jr., made one on joining the Peace
Corps for Colombia I, the first contingent to that country. There
was great idealism in signing on for these adventures. There was
commitment among those who joined Volunteers in Service to
America, VISTA, the domestic twin of the Peace Corps. And
there was commitment in the Vietnam War protest. Godfrey
Hodgson depicts these movements in *America in Our Time,* a
history that has earned wide respect.

But there is a movement which Mr. Hodgson explores hardly
at all. Three million young Americans went to Vietnam, about
three hundred thousand men a year for ten years. They trained
for war and went to war. The twenty-hour flight to Vietnam
covered twelve thousand miles. They came back. Now that is a
movement, a real rally.

Among the welter of chance and motive that brought each
of us to the war zone, there was at least this common thread:
we were honoring a commitment we made to serve as a member
of the United States armed forces. In fact, we did so by oath,
using the old-fashioned words, "to support and defend the Constitution of the United States against all enemies foreign and domestic." The Constitution says the Armed Forces are paid at the
initiative of Congress and are commanded by the president. It
says you and I elect the Congress and the president.

This is what happened. We kept our promise, as we had
made it. The orders said Vietnam. We were trained. We went.
No fighting force ever sent to war was better equipped or trained.
But America makes a promise, too. She promises to keep us in
her heart, whether we live or die. She reneged on that promise.
We soldiers were prepared for the war zone. We were not prepared for our return to America. We were locked out of her heart.
It was a tragic abandonment. We were confounded by a taboo
against talking about dead soldiers and our time at war. The most
searing part of our lives was deemed not to have happened. The
country's cultural energy poured instead into the needs of blacks,
of women, of less developed counties and countries, and into
defining and fulfilling the terms for ending the Vietnam War.

The Vietnam veteran was the nigger of the 1970s. You
create a nigger by depriving a person of part of his or her per-
sonhood. Ignoring that person or inflicting traumatic hurts is the

traditional way to treat a nigger. In this metaphorical sense, woman was the nigger of the 1960s. The black was the nigger of the 1950s. As the hurt dissipates, and ignoring turns into recognition, your time as a nigger begins to end.

Scenes in the journey I took reveal something about this experience of commitments and broken promises.

My dad, John Wheeler, went to West Point, marrying Janet Conly, a West Texas ranch girl, during World War II. While holding me, a newborn baby, in the hospital in Laredo, Texas, she received an MIA telegram on Dad, who was caught in the Battle of the Bulge. He made it back. My brother Bob was born. We had a strong home, even though we moved to twelve new homes and schools in twelve years.

From 1962, when I graduated from Hampton High School, in Hampton, Virginia, until I boarded the airplane for Vietnam at Travis Air Force Base, California, in 1969, I was at West Point, an Army guided missile unit, the Pentagon, and Harvard Business School.

I did not apply to Harvard College. I had visited, and the place seemed disorganized (I was only seventeen). I was granted admission to Yale and also a National Merit Scholarship and presidential and congressional appointments to West Point. I declined Yale, on the theory that the education was more practical at West Point. We are, after all, the Sputnik generation, and science was big in 1962. I wanted to know the solid and fixed, the scientific and engineered, side of life. I have to keep reminding myself that at seventeen years of age our instincts and choices may be sound but our conscious reasons are likely to be invisibly connected to deeper truth and motives.

## COMMITMENT
In fact, what West Point asked of us and gave to us was anything but solid and fixed, scientific and engineered. The animation of all great institutions is a spirit of people and place that is palpable. (With luck, I would have discovered this wherever I went.) The great commitments West Point exacts make it a prism for looking at commitment during the 1960s. West Point also by law draws its cadets proportionally throughout America, so it has a representative quality.

West Point works on intimacy, attachment, and bonding among classmates. Through intimacy, attachment, and bonding we taught each other important lessons. The community hardship of the military life made us rely on each other and trust each other as friends. The important things we learned included the powers of, and means of, animating a body of people. We were the United States Corps of Cadets. "Corps" means "living body." The beginning of our education was the partial dying we underwent in Beast Barracks and plebe year, where discipline and rote made us vulnerable and open to new learning. Inspiring and leading a group requires great sensitivity to other people. It is profoundly artistic in nature. It should not surprise that it can take considerable effort to awaken this sensitivity in young cadets, and that the rigor of cadet life is one technique for accomplishing this. It is like becoming a ballet choreographer—over time, in between the disciplined lines of music and dance movement, you begin to read how to marry dancer and music to create your own piece. But you need to hear the music and you must know the dancers. These qualities define West Point. To a great extent I think they define the spirit of the significant movements of the 1960s.

But there was a difference. The visible foundation of our learning at West Point was our common commitment to country, made at the public ceremony when we were sworn in. The invisible part contained the idea that there are things worth dying for. This means that, for each of us, we might give our life at the call of another person, ultimately the president.

In Beast Barracks that summer we cadets were grouped in squads of nine. The squad leader was a third-year cadet selected because of his ability for ushering new cadets into the life of the Academy. One afternoon, into my room bursts Tom Hayes, my classmate from down the hall. He is worried. We never had spoken before, but we had already been through a lot together. (The games of plebe year require us to constantly forego a sense of self.)

"Can I try on your eyeglasses? Your new cadet-issue ones. Mine haven't come in yet."

"Here." I took mine off, handing them over. The problem was that rifle training started next day. Case-hardened plastic glasses were needed; rifle recoil shattered conventional lenses. My three pair had arrived from supply. His had not. So we shared.

Our paths crossed every day for four years. Same Russian class. Same math class. We recited at the blackboard every day in math. The twelve of us in a class worked the same problems, side by side at the boards. Four or five of us would be called on at random to describe our solutions. There was a tradition at West Point that if you were called on, and if you saw and understood an error on *your* board, you could redeem yourself by properly reciting on a *classmate's* correct board. Tommy invoked it one day in plebe math.

"Sir, I will use Mr. Wheeler's board." Is the tradition real?

"Very well, Mr. Hayes."

We were graded every day in every class. A computer list posted weekly in the sally ports showed our daily grades. We both maxed. West Point cared more about what we knew when we left that class than when we came in, in spite of the fearsome system of daily recitation. And West Point cared most that we learned to read other people and rely upon them.

Much later, in the spring of 1966, I was in a jam. I thought I loved engineering, but I had bitten off too much. On top of the normal course load I was taking a double overload, nuclear engineering and soil mechanics. I was drowning. The problem was civil engineering. Tom and I were in an honors course where a joint project was a major course requirement. We were designing a ski slope for West Point. I never admitted my problem with the course. I was embarrassed at my weakness. But Tom knew. He carried the project on his back, incorporating some of my ideas, preserving our integrity as joint partners. He was spread thin himself, as a senior cadet captain. In the middle of the night in March, he came into my room, leaving behind my copy of our full solution to the design project. I awoke to find it.

Around the edges and between the lines of vignettes like this I think there is visible the idea of bonding among individuals and of an institution that teaches by means of the relationships it fosters.

Men who express this idea well are authors Lucian Truscott and James Webb. Webb's novel *A Sense of Honor* tells of life at Annapolis during the Vietnam War battle of Tet in 1968.

At one point he describes the graduates of the Academy as siblings of the same womb. (Webb joined the Marines on graduating from Annapolis in 1968.) Truscott, who graduated from West Point in 1969 then later resigned in protest of the Vietnam War, sets his novel *Dress Gray* at West Point during the late 1960s. At one point his protagonist realizes the responsibility of conducting a squad of new cadets through Beast:

> War was indeed the reason the Military Academy existed, and by extension, its purpose was to teach young men to kill. But there was a corollary to the academy's mission, unmentioned by West Point officialdom. You had to be willing to die, not for duty, honor, or country but for your own men.
>
> That was leadership, the thing West Point had to offer. And there was its secret. The system counted subliminally but necessarily on human imponderables.

One imponderable is the validity of a word given. The system counted on promises made and kept, and on knowing that a promise made was a promise kept.

We kept John Kennedy's promise. On Saturday morning, November 23, 1963, it was raining at West Point. When it rains, cadets cheer because parade is canceled. At breakfast we were told that at midmorning the Corps would assemble in parade in dress uniform under arms, meaning rifle with parade gear. Assembled in the rain, we heard the general order formally publishing the news of the death of John Kennedy. It was ritual, almost liturgy. We recognized the subliminal order "Keep his promise."

John Kennedy was buried that Monday. I saw the funeral on television in the quarters of Professor Roger Nye of the Department of Social Sciences. Colonel Nye had called me in for an oral examination, a kind of tutorial, in order to authorize me to pass out from the upcoming second-year history course and instead take political philosophy, a special elective taught by Captain Dale Vesser, a young Rhodes Scholar from the West Point class of 1954. I studied all summer for the tutorial with

Colonel Nye. He chose as the topic the causes of World War II.
I answered that the major root causes traced like a trunk through
the vindictive Treaty of Versailles, a badly made peace. We
watched John Kennedy lowered into his grave. The colonel put
me into political philosophy. Tommy Hayes was in the class,
too.

Just as we would be surprised by the apparent and firm re-
jection on our return from Vietnam, we were surprised as cadets
by West Point's reputation between 1962 and 1969. West Point
became very unfashionable among our peers. Even worse, Truscott depicts this in a scene in which Vassar women come to picket
West Point. I banged my knee up parachuting once, ending up
in a bed at the West Point hospital. A plaque by my bed com-
memorated the fact that Marty Maher spent his last days in the
room. Actor Tyrone Power played Marty Maher in the movie
about West Point *The Long Gray Line*. It was a 1950s movie.
Maureen O'Hara played Mrs. Maher. Didn't everyone see it?
Maher was an Irishman freshly come to America at the turn of
the century. He worked his way up in the Athletic Department
at West Point to become its director, Master of the Sword. He
taught or counseled Pershing, MacArthur, Patton, Eisenhower,
Wainwright, Davison, Westmoreland, three generations of West
Pointers. The movie depicts the life of the spirit at West Point.
The story is true. How did West Point become so unfashiona-
ble?

By grace, it happened that a woman set in motion events
for me that shielded me from the worst of West Point's travail.

She was Virginia Stuart, at the time a dancer in the New
York City Ballet. George Balanchine, director of the company,
had plucked her from the ranks of the Boston Ballet. She was
eighteen; I was twenty. For years to come, Leonard Mulhern,
house manager for the theater, would slip me into the press box
as a "reviewer" when I came to him before a performance.

So that our relationship could continue, I elected to join a
Nike air defense guided missile unit in New York City for my
first year after West Point. Cadets can choose these first assignments, in order of class standing. I stood high. Tom Hayes had
helped assure my class standing. The class standing also carried
with it the right to pick schedules and attend graduate school.

Ginny was from Boston. I went to Harvard Business School after the year with air defense in New York City.

I steered upon our relationship. But for her, I would probably have stationed myself in Vietnam earlier. She changed my life. So at a time when fashion was cycling against West Point, I was not hurt personally. I immersed myself in the popular ballet company.

My relationship with the company also showed me women and men working as equals. The women in the company were professionals, equal with the men in pay and output. I acquired a new insight into women and men as partners.

There was also the lesson of sensitivity in woman-man communication. Ballet is tension, and woman-man is the central tension. A natural part of this is sexual tension. Sexual tension is high at West Point. It is almost electric. It is tangible in the language and imagery. West Point is strengthened by able women cadets, but it seems that the place is finally masculine in mission. Sexual life for cadets is like the penultimate note in a song, permanently awaiting the resolving chord of man meeting woman.

The Securities and Exchange Commission, where I have worked, is an example of balanced partnership among women and men. Women and men equally share leadership posts throughout the agency. The SEC is small, with a tradition of integrity, excellence, and merit promotion (thanks to such early chairmen as William O. Douglas and James Landis). In fact, if among government agencies there is a counterpart to the Marine Corps, it is the United States Securities and Exchange Commission. This tradition, combined with the societal boost to women in the 1960s and 1970s, has made the SEC unique among other businesses and agencies.

Life in the company and Mr. Balanchine's choreography also awakened me to another theme—the imagery of dance as an expression of our common life together. Ginny was in the Corps de Ballet. I was in the United States Corps of Cadets. Two "living bodies."

Better than the human behavior courses at Harvard Business School, or leadership courses at West Point, Balanchine showed me how much more than their individual selves a group of people working together could be. The message is crystalline; a perfect example in fact is the ballet *Jewels*. C. S. Lewis uses the same imagery in expressing the spiritual nature of life: "And now, what does it all matter? It matters more than anything else in the world. The whole dance, or drama, or pattern . . . is to be played out in each one of us: or (putting it the other way round) each one of us has got to enter that pattern, take his place in that dance." When I think of parades at West Point, I think of the ballet corps in *Firebird*.

Once the Bolshoi Ballet presented *Spartacus* on the stage of the Metropolitan Opera building at Lincoln Center, right next to the New York State Theater, where the New York City Ballet presented Balanchine's *Don Quixote*. The protagonists in both ballets give their lives. The difference is this: in *Spartacus,* a modern ballet, the crucifixion and death of Spartacus, as he looks upon his wife and infant son from the cross, is the last word. Very Soviet. But in Balanchine's *Don Quixote* the last word is the apotheosis, when the saints march in file to honor the risen Don. The entire company is in the scene. It is electrifying. Truly American.

An opponent in those ballets is death. I think the same opponent altered the way we view the commitments young Americans made in the 1960s.

## DEATH
The headline appeared in *Newsweek* for June 5, 1967, one year after graduation. Page 25. I happened to be flipping through the magazine in my room at the missile battery. The headline was "Home Is the Soldier." I read this:

> A chill breeze swept in off the Hudson River, pewter gray in the patchy afternoon light, and rustled in the dogwood on the plains of West Point high above. Down Washington Road, a cadet band, all in black, played "Lead, Kindly Light," and then there was only the drear cadence of the muffled drums. They moved in slow procession to the cemetery: the band, the honor guard from C-2 Company, the colors, the family, the

flag-draped coffin. It was another spring, another Memorial Day was at hand, and Second Lt. Frank Rybicki Jr. was home from the war.

Frank Rybicki's career as a cadet had not been the Point's most distinguished: he was graduated, only last June, as the 212th in a class of 579. Nor was his death its most glorious: he had spent most of his scant three and a half months in Vietnam chafing for combat, and he had not really tasted it when he was accidentally felled, by his own rifle, while struggling through a jungle swamp half a world from home. And so, on 9 May 1967, he became an abstraction, an integer in the unending statistics of an unending war. He was the second to die in West Point's class of '66, the 101st Academy graduate, one of 10,000 Americans lost in what has now become the fifth costliest war in U.S. history.

Frank Rybicki, like most men of 23, had little to leave in worldly goods or formal biography.

*Memory:* . . . there is the guitar that came home from Vietnam, and a well-thumbed copy of John Kennedy's *Profiles in Courage*. There is the marker now in the West Point cemetery, one on a lengthening gray line of 41 of the Vietnam dead.

"Everybody else was worried to death our plebe year," says Second Lt. Terry G. Stull, a Georgian who was Rybicki's best buddy at the Point and, later, in Vietnam. "But not Frank—he didn't let things bother him. When I met him, I talked to him an hour and I felt I'd known him all my life. He might have blown a test worse than you had, and he'd still be cheering you up. He had a smile for everybody." He had a song for everybody, too. "Frankie started a sing-out wherever he went," his father recalls. "Whenever he saw anybody with their head low, he'd grab the guitar and cheer 'em up."

*Volunteer:* Yet he kept a solemnity of purpose about him. He revered John F. Kennedy; he read a book about PT-109 while still a teenager, built a little Kennedy library around it, bought a desk blotter with the famous "ask not" quote so he could always see it. What could he do for his country? He chose a military career, hoped someday to be assigned to Latin America because he knew it so well. But the country's first order of business, in 1966, was Vietnam, and Rybicki volunteered for infantry duty there.

On 10 January 1967, he and Stull shipped out together. "Gettin' on the boat," says Stull, "he was the funniest thing you ever saw in your life, comin' up the gangplank with two duffel bags, two 'AWOL' bags, his rifle—and his guitar." While Stull went off into the Mekong Delta and was wounded in the leg, Rybicki put in a restless tour running a Ninth Infantry platoon assigned to security duty around the base camp. His men liked his easy, deferential ways; he had scarcely joined the unit when his platoon sergeant dropped in on Alpha Company's topkick and paid Rybicki that rarest of NCO's compliments: "Looks like I lucked out and got a good lieutenant." But Rybicki hankered for action.

*Stuck:* His marching orders came after his buddy Stull's own platoon was decimated in a six-hour battle with two Viet Cong companies. "We're coming down to help you out," Rybicki exulted over the phone. " 'Bout time we worked together again." They never got the chance. Moving out on a five-day search-and-destroy mission, Alpha Company knifed into the Rung Sat special zone—a steaming mangrove swamp southeast of Saigon that had once been a VC sanctuary. The first day out, the march bogged down in calf-deep water and ankle-deep mud. Stuck fast, Rybicki thrust his rifle, stock first, toward one of his men for help. The man tugged. The rifle went off. And Frank Rybicki fell dying in the mud.

Terry Stull and Frank Rybicki flew home together, the quick and the dead, for one last day at the Point.

At Holy Trinity Chapel, Father Edwin O'Brien celebrated the mysteries of youth and death at Calvary, and the Glee Club sang: *"They are here in ghostly assemblage/The men of the Corps long dead/And our hearts are standing attention/While we wait for their passing tread. . . ."* And then the slow pilgrimage to graveside, Frank Sr. mashing a handkerchief, mother Cecilia staring blankly into the grass, sister Annette's dark eyes flashing out of a frame of white lace, 10-year-old brother James trailing, tiny and frail.

They sat at the edge of the grave. Thrushes sang; the grass shimmered in the broken sunlight; there were the ritual words, the three rifle volleys, the last lingering notes of "Taps." The honor guard lifted the flag from the coffin and folded it, and Terry Stull handed it to Mrs. Rybicki. A breeze scented with lilac crossed the Hudson plains. Frank Rybicki was home from the war.

The page went on:

CEREMONIES:
THE JOHN F. KENNEDY

The giant new carrier, *John F. Kennedy,* loomed high over the dry dock in Newport News, Va., dwarfing the speaker's stand at its bow as it would have dwarfed the little PT boat that almost a quarter of a century ago gave young Lt. John F. Kennedy his first opportunity for national service and sacrifice.

It was launching day for the 80,000-ton warship, and on the eve of what would have been the late President's 50th birthday, his daughter Caroline, 9, was sponsor and chief champagne bottle-breaker. Wearing an aqua and white cotton dress, a white hair ribbon and ankle socks, she and her brother, John Jr., followed Jacqueline Kennedy onto the speaker's stand. There they joined Senators Robert and Edward Kennedy and their wives, several admirals and a number

of family friends. Mrs. Kennedy, wearing a simple
A-line white cotton coat dress, quickly smoothed
John's down-flowing mop of hair. . . .

Frank. There was a war on. That article is what moved the fact
from my brain to my gut. Only sixteen years later did I notice
the poetry of the juxtaposition of the Rybicki and Kennedy articles in that issue of *Newsweek*. The wider dying began for me
then too. I bought into the taboo that said we do not discuss the
dead men. I do not think I even told Ginny about Frank. The
taboo was a mutual comfort. I was in a daze. I shifted into automatic. Slowly over the next three years we drifted apart as we
wondered about marriage and our two fiercely demanding careers. We gave a lot to each other. We brought happiness to each
other, but our happiness in the end would be with another person. The beginning of the end was the news I carried around
quietly, inside.

Cadet lectures were usually held in South Auditorium in
Thayer Hall. I recall the whole class seated there. One of every
twenty from '66 gave his life in Vietnam. Two more in twenty
bled from wounds. The odds were one in seven of getting shot.
The story was the same for the classes of '63, '64, '65, '67,
'68, and '69. The war fell across the back of the graduating
classes of the decade. It was like the story of my dad's class,
January, '43, which graduated a semester early to enter the war.
Or Korea for the classes of '51 and '52. Fighting the war was
where the implicit assumption became an explicit question—are
there things worth dying for? What an ugly question. So many
of us said yes when we were young. The average American
trooper in World War II was a draftee, twenty-six years old. The
average American trooper in Vietnam was a volunteer, *not* a
draftee, nineteen years old.

In *The Long Gray Line*, Marty Maher keeps his West Point
yearbooks out, putting a ribbon at the page of each fallen graduate. I did that at Harvard with my yearbook. I showed it to a
girl I was dating. She was uninterested.

My feet were up on the desk the night of April 22, 1968.
I was disoriented. Harvard undergraduates were protesting the

war in rallies. Martin Luther King had been shot and killed on
April 4. Blacks just stopped attending class. On television, it
seemed many cities were on fire. The North Koreans were getting pushy about airspace and seaspace, as though picking a fight.
The phone rang. It was my West Point classmate Art Mosley,
also at the B-School.

"Tommy Hayes was killed in action in Vietnam five days
ago. A bunch of guys are flying up to his funeral at West Point
tomorrow. They wanted me to call you. I've got my car ready."

My roommate Bob Paulson was a friend and an Army officer himself. But he was away on an interviewing trip. There
was no one to talk to. I just left. I met Art, and we drove down.
Nobody asked where I was going.

*"When evening shadows fall . . ." The last verse of old
no. 367, Tommy. At West Point we sang it together. Most significantly to me now, you were chairman of the cadet honor
committee. This is what happened the last day of your life. I
asked your father. You led an infantry platoon. On April 17,
1968, there was enemy activity far out in your area of operations. The size of the enemy force was unclear and, it turned
out, underestimated. Your platoon went by helicopter to the area
of contact. You were embroiled in a firefight. You saved your
wounded men by dragging them back across a rice paddy. This
marked you as the target of choice. You were killed by enemy
automatic weapons fire.*

There was honest service in Tom's life. No country ever
has enough men like him. West Point's motto is "duty, honor,
country." It is a commitment to public service. Because we must
entrust power with those who serve, Americans rightly expect
the highest integrity in their public servants. This integrity is the
object of West Point's honor code—presided over by Tom eighteen years ago.

I think the war created a void into which Tom was cast for
fifteen years, with little or no acknowledgment of honest service
rendered. Not until dedication of the Vietnam Veterans Memorial on November 13, 1982, did his sentence begin to end.

One reason for this attitude probably is that the American
public, when it dwelled on the war at all, chose to visit a large
measure of the sins of the war on its military servants. But cer-

tainly the onus of the policy decisions on Vietnam should not touch Americans who made no policy, but served there.

In Tom's life, and in his death, and in the lives and the deaths of other soldiers I knew, there lay in Vietnam service both a full realization of the tragedy of the war and a fulfillment of allegiance to duty, honor, and country—a country, in this case, unable to set its compass, yet relentlessly committing its soldiers to fight.

A large portion of those Vietnam servicemen still find little acceptance in discussing their experiences and little affirmation of sacrifice in their service. There is much in their lives to heal and much to affirm.

To date, West Point and the Army's senior officer schools have not been able to succeed fully in seeking out and confronting the truths of Vietnam. For example, at the staff school at Fort Leavenworth, vigorous examination of Vietnam policy and strategy, while invited by school officials, is difficult to achieve in the classroom. The same is true at West Point, where the faculty is made up of many of the Army's best young officers.

Yet for our country as a whole to learn from the Vietnam War, the Army has to succeed in the task, because the Army played the central role in carrying out Vietnam policy.

The individuals at these institutions do recognize the importance of these issues, and Vietnam is a subject of study. The difficulties of the faculty and students are no mystery: we find it hard to examine and learn from personal tragedy. One requisite for the learning process is time. Acceptance is also essential, as is affirmation of the good in and the worth of a person's life. Soldiers are no exception.

Learning from Vietnam will proceed, if at all, only when our country can fully acknowledge the integrity of service and the embodiment of cherished values represented in the soldiers sent to Vietnam. Full reconciliation with our veterans requires this acknowledgment perhaps as much as it needs a just resolution of veteran claims to educational, medical, and employment assistance.

*Tommy, your name is on panel 50 on the east wall of the memorial on the Mall, the wall pointed toward the Washington Monument. Line 29, right next to men you died trying to save.*

*Your men who lived, and the rest of us who made it back alive,*
*will keep giving just like you did, until we die.*

It rained. Cadets in dress gray marched to the funeral. Tom's
old company. There were a lot of West Point soldiers there. When
I returned to Harvard, no one asked where I had been.

The funeral was for me the beginning of the National Vietnam Veterans Memorial.

Other deaths followed. Robert Kennedy. The invasion of
Czechoslovakia. Doesn't Czechoslovakia mean there are things
worth dying for? Or Czechoslovakia and Poland together? Part
of my summer work was an analysis for the secretary of defense
of U.S. biological warfare capability. Did we need the stuff?
They brought in Doctor Matthew Meselson from Harvard to
confer over my work. Our results were forwarded to the White
House, leading to the November, 1969 announcement by the
president that the United States renounces all use of biological
weapons. War, plague, and death. The red, black, and pale horses
of the apocalypse. Or are they right who say the black horse is
famine? And who rides the white horse?

## GO-GO

There was so much death and we were so young that this is what
I think began to happen. With a perfectly natural response, a lot
of young affluent Americans said no to the idea that there are
things worth dying for. Causes worth living for were OK; causes
worth dying for were not. The same young people said yes to
the causes and callings which seemed to assert that there are things
worth living for: civil rights, women's liberation, free speech,
preserving the environment, ending the war by pulling out. The
legal profession offers a clue to this attitude. Professor Owen
Fiss at Yale Law School brought it to my attention. Increasingly
in the 1960s the great civil rights victories were *court injunc-*
*tions.* In court you do fight, *but you don't die.* Owen told me
about ''all those young lawyers from Cravath. They'd summer
down there in the South, chewing fat with the black leaders on
the porch, swattin' flies. They'd plan the injunction.''

A sentiment that began to grow in the 1960s was that, if a
promise had some dying in it, it could be broken. However, there
is no promise without some dying in it.

Something more was happening. Men grew long hair. They started "sharing" an idea instead of "telling" it. Some men looked like women, and vice versa, and Americans were doing a double take. The culture became a *bit* more feminine. But for a big country, a bit is a lot.

Since femininity and the principle of things worth living for were both ascendant, I suspect they are connected. Doesn't woman especially represent the principle that there are things worth living for?

Surely Vietnam veterans were men; and surely America veered away from us. Seven million men wore the uniform. But all thirty million men of our generation, save war protesters, were then very, very silent and, save for Vietnam veterans, still are. We still do not know what manliness is. Maybe the masculine principle *is* that there are things worth dying for. This is scary to say, because for some people the principle has a corollary, that there can be causes worth killing for. But it is the principle, not the possible corollary, that is larger and comes first. Like manliness and womanliness, it can be ineffable anyway. What matters more is that we began to act as if we did not care what masculinity really is or what there is to affirm in it.

As a soldier I was well equipped to be *in* Vietnam. To go and perform was my commitment. I could keep the promise. Here was the irony. Our peers disconnected from us before we even flew overseas. In that sense, it is no wonder there was no feeling of acceptance upon our return. In a large sense, there was no home when we left. Whether we came back alive or dead, there was a grave waiting for our heartfelt inner self, in the attitudes of Americans we grew up with.

The turbulence of spring, 1968, caused great anxiety over the draft among my B-School classmates. They did not want to be drafted into the armed forces. A quarter of a century earlier, the attitude at the B-School was vastly different, according to David Halberstam in *The Best and the Brightest,* writing about Robert Lovett and the American World War II planners:

> Together they decided that in order to harness American industry for the great war effort, they needed first and foremost a giant statistical brain to tell them who

they were, what was needed, and where. They asked Harvard Business School, the most logical place, to train the officers they needed for statistical control. This brain trust would send the right men and the right supplies to the right places, and would make sure that when crews arrived at a base there were enough instructors. It was a symbolic step in America's going from a relatively sleepy country toward becoming a superpower (a step which the acceleration in air power and air industry would finalize). We were already so big that our problem primarily concerned control as well as careful and accurate projection of just how powerful we were.

Robert McNamara was one of those young brains.

In 1968, the B-School reacted differently. An extraordinary summer semester was held, so that all students who wished could attend, then graduate a semester early the following January, thereby graduating before being drafted. Eighty men graduated early. The practical result was that many such graduates were placed in key jobs or got married, facilitating their continued exemption from the draft.

My other summer work was financial planning for Kidder Peabody & Company, the investment bank on Wall Street. Wall Street pros call the late sixties the go-go years, after the big dance diversion of the mid-sixties. Jerry Tsai made his name and fortune as a portfolio manager with the go-go technique of quick in-and-out trading, moving huge blocks of stock around daily or even hourly. Jimmy Ling was equally creative and energetic in inventing new combinations of stocks and bonds to finance his company, LTV, in Texas. Professor Colyer Crum at the B-School taught me all this in Investment Management. He was a popular teacher. He had us read *The Money Game* by "Adam Smith" (George Goodman). He also took care that we read *The Great Crash* (by John Kenneth Galbraith, about the causes of the 1930s depression). Colyer knew I was a soldier; each professor had our biographies. But Colyer did not tell me that his brother, Robert, had been killed in action in Vietnam. The taboo was so strong.

Thirteen years later I would call Colyer and tell him his brother's name is at panel 7 east, line 100.

It was also in Manhattan in the summer of 1968 that the women gathered midtown and burned their bras, as seen in that memorable photograph. Sexual tension had become street theater. On television, I watched the rioting outside the Democratic National Convention in Chicago.

The B-School resumed in the fall. Eighty students were now a semester ahead. Everything was go-go: their upbeat talk about the Street, their job offers. There was a kaleidoscope of fire in my mind's eye. Fire in the streets. Fire in the Lake. Light My Fire. The Fire Next Time. Stravinsky's and Balanchine's *Firebird*. The lesson of small-unit tactics, "to make emplaced weapons effective you must have clear fields of fire."

*Mail time at Harvard. Exams were postponed or canceled, so students could demonstrate against the war. Harvard Square had been "trashed" by protesting students. The broken windows of the bank there were boarded up. I opened the envelope.*
HQDA
*That's headquarters, Department of the Army*
WHEELER, JOHN P. III, OF 108030
*That's me.*
RPT NLT 29 JUN 69
*That's soon.*
90TH REPL BN LONG BINH RVN
*That's Vietnam.*
*Going was easy. You caught the jet at Travis Air Force Base outside San Francisco. The jets ran like taxis between Vietnam and California. I left Harvard early, in May. I took my exam by mail. Two friends asked how I felt. I said I was afraid. I went to Travis. I was on automatic. Dad met me there. He flew from the east coast. He was a Vietnam veteran. We had lunch in San Francisco. "I love you, Old Man."*
*"I love you, Jackson."*
*He left. I went to the flight line. There was the airliner I was assigned to, fueling up. Next down the line was a big four-engine jet, an Air Force C-141 with its ramp down. Beside it*

were hundreds of aluminum boxes. I looked at them for a long time. They were coffins. I went to the movie at the post theater. Goodbye Columbus. Ali McGraw slips nude into the swimming pool. She goes on to Harvard. There is the sad ending. Man and woman are separate. I got on the plane. One hundred and twenty men. Officers in tan. Troopers in fatigues. Over twelve of us would die or bleed, one a month, on average, until we went home in exactly 365 days. The in-flight movie was Charley, about a retarded man temporarily returned to his senses. Who was Charley? The one in Vietnam? On which side? We stopped for fuel in Hawaii, in the middle of the night. I got out. I felt lonely. I tried to see palm trees and the beach. It was beautiful. I got aboard. I listened to Dvorak's Slavonic Dances on the earphone system. Why didn't Mr. Balanchine choreograph to them? I did not think he had. Charley had a sad ending—woman and man separated, his love locked inside himself, by a hurt he did not even know he had. Sunlight showed an F-4 Phantom painted in camouflage out of the window. This was the war. Bien Hoa Airfield. I was at home and ready to work. The doors swung open. The humidity sucked air from our lungs. An air policeman came in.

"Exit and form up. We will march. If fired upon, we will double-time. Do not disperse."

War.

# CHAPTER TWO

*My memories of the last war haunted
my dreams for years. Military service,
to be plain, includes the threat of
every* temporal *evil; pain and death
which is what we fear from sickness:
isolation from those we love which is
what we fear from exile: toil under
arbitrary masters, injustice, humiliation,
which is what we fear from slavery: hunger, thirst, and exposure which is what
we fear from poverty. I'm not a pacifist.
If it's got to be, it's got to be.*

C. S. Lewis
*Letters*

*And do not bring us to the test.*

The Lord's Prayer
*New English Bible*

# THE
# WAR ZONE

We were at Bien Hoa Airfield, near Saigon. Almost all Americans assigned to Vietnam came in through Bien Hoa, Ton Son Nhut in Saigon, or Cam Ranh, up further north on the coast.

The one hundred twenty of us marched across the field in a big square formation. There was a blazing tropical sun. Air Force fighters and troop transports took off and landed constantly. There was the distant sound of high explosive detonations, either fighter strikes or artillery fire. The barbed-wire perimeter of the airfield was hundreds of meters distant, with armed watchposts. The familiar tadpole-shaped UH-1 ("Huey") helicopters were everywhere. We were led to a large, prefab metal shed to await transport to the 90th Replacement Battalion at nearby Long Binh, processing point for Army arrivals to Bien Hoa.

In my pocket was a letter from Art Mosley, who had graduated in June, 1968, from Harvard Business School. He was assigned to the headquarters of the 1st Logistical Command at Long Binh. 1st Log was the supply and transportation arm of the U.S. Army in Vietnam. He had told his boss about me. They would try to have me assigned to their shop. "Call me from Bien Hoa," Art wrote. In the metal shed, I called the number he had given me.

Art answered. "It didn't work, Jack. There's some kind of hold on your records. I don't know where you're going. Call me if you hear something. I'm coming to see you at the 90th."

You do not control your life. None of us knew where we were going, except for about twenty-five men, who were segmented and immediately diverted to an infantry division.

The air policemen loaded us onto Army buses. We had no weapons, no flak vests, no equipment. Just one personal bag each. Drivers and armed guards boarded with us. We drove for about thirty minutes on an asphalt highway to Long Binh. The place was huge, larger than a mid-size American town, surrounded by barbed wire and tall watchtowers. It was spotted with groups of small wooden barracks-style buildings and seemed to stretch for miles. At one corner was the 90th Replacement Battalion. You waited at the 90th until you were assigned; then you shipped out. Typically, you went back to Bien Hoa and rode a C-130 troop-carrier airplane to the headquarters of your new unit. You could end up anywhere in the bottom half of South Vietnam, the part below Cam Ranh. The typical wait was a few days, as the staff of the 90th screened your records against the requisitions sent in from the units in the field. Officers were in one barracks area, enlisted men in another. I picked out a cot and checked the mosquito netting. Looked fine. There was an in-briefing. It was a lecture and film on malaria and booby traps. Take a malaria pill once a week. Assume that anything may be booby-trapped. The briefer pointed toward the sandbagged bunkers next to our wooden shelter. "In case of incoming rockets or mortars, go to the bunker and await an all-clear." The briefing was over.

There was a small PX, an Army general store, at the 90th. Younger troopers had already swarmed to it and bought portable Sony and Toshiba radios. You could hear them listening to rock 'n' roll music on the Armed Forces Network, AFN. "Detroit City" was one song; the refrain is, "I wanna go home." The portable radios and televisions were ubiquitous in Vietnam.

Art appeared. We caught up on our lives. Seeing a friend was important. It eased my anxiety as the uncertainty about the future gnawed at me.

It was dark. American artillery harassment and interdiction ("H&I") began. These were outgoing shots at predesignated potential enemy targets, designed to keep enemy soldiers who were moving at night off-balance. I lay in my bunk. Toward midnight a deep undulating shock wave of sound moved through us, making man and wood tremble. The thunder would not stop. It was a B-52 bomb strike, over ten miles away. I envisioned the target zone. It would be nothing but fire and shock wave, for a mile-long corridor. The enemy would not hear the first bomb until it struck, dropped from six miles up. Where was I going? Wait. See what shape is given to your life.

What is war like? Most war literature, and almost all literature on the Vietnam War, tells battle stories, dwelling on the life and thoughts of men during a fixed time while searching for or engaged with the enemy. In general, though, for Americans the Vietnam war zone existed for sixteen years as a vast community placed in Southeast Asia. For the Navy, a code word for Vietnam was "Yankee Station," the name of a Navy rally point off the Vietnamese coast. The American war zone was a kind of country in a country, or rather a country itself. Many people serving in Vietnam could spend their whole tour seeing little or nothing of South Vietnam or the South Vietnamese, except for the soil and vegetation itself, cleaning or laundry ladies, and distant farmers. Long Binh was such a place, created whole and separate by the U.S. Army. The Cam Ranh Bay complex was another. The war zone was defined by place, by attitudes, and by its mission. It had continuity over time, and during its existence three million Americans moved into and out of it, most on a one-year tour. The mission was to carry on the war against the Viet Cong and the North Vietnamese regular forces.

War is the establishment, maintenance, and use of people organized to fight. War takes place over a reach of time and distance, requiring the control and combination of valuable material resources. The battle descriptions and personal experiences found in war literature occur in this context.

West Point teaches small-unit leadership and tactics, but it builds up to imparting this larger picture of war. Anyone wishing to understand or control war needs this larger picture. Peace advocates need it. Antinuclear advocates need it. One cannot understand or control war without it. It is not a mystical or esoteric study. There are dumb mistakes to avoid. Leadership and intuition are important, but so are discipline, wealth, organization, and political will.

Douglas MacArthur made a very moving farewell speech at West Point in 1962. It was reprinted and widely covered by the media. Gregory Peck gives the speech in his portrayal of the general in the 1970s movie *MacArthur*. It includes the line "But always ringing in our ear are the words of Plato, that wisest of philosophers, 'Only the dead have seen the end of war.' " The speech was not baleful or pessimistic; it was an uplifting inquiry into the meaning of duty, honor, and country. But the reminder turned out to be apt. War will play a part in American life in the 1980s and 1990s, and in the next century, whether by financial involvement, efforts at deterrence, or commitment of our own forces.

Here is a key. Probably, the most important thing in studying war is good maps to accompany the text. The map picture unlocks insights into the political, economic, and tactical motivations of participants. Societal and strategic constraints and imperatives become clearer. Cadets at West Point in the 1960s virtually memorized two key texts on war, both written by a team led by Brigadier General Vincent Esposito. They are worth reading: *A Military History and Atlas of the Napoleonic Wars,* and *The West Point Atlas of American Wars.* For example, they are worth the special attention of Americans concerned about the possibilities of conflict in Central America, Europe, the horn of Africa, or the Mideast. You see much of why and how countries project force at great distances. You see, in detail, the wounds in Russian life caused by Napoleon's invasion and by battle on the Eastern Front in World War II. The War Next Time. The Next War. To prevent it or to win it, one thing to do is study the War Last Time. Napoleon anticipated modern war, and Lee, Grant, and Lincoln midwifed it. The texts show this, and they explain the context of life in the Vietnam war zone: a long-lived fighting subculture of our country, maintained at great remove from home. Something like the Gulag Archipelago described by Solzhenitsyn, it was a separate culture that specially shaped the lives of those who lived within it. William Jayne, a Marine who was wounded in the siege of Khe Sanh, wrote in *The Wounded Generation* that returning veterans had so changed during their tour and America had so changed, that the Vietnam veteran was an "immigrant from the combat zone."

Looking back, the seeds of a lot of truths about life in Vietnam were evident after only one day in that country. One obvious fact was our geographical remoteness from home. Twelve thousand miles is as far away as you can get. Go any further, and you are closer. In the study of war, the first diagnostic question about two opposing forces is "where are their lines of communication?" This is the LOC, the complex of message, supply transport, and evacuation paths that underpin the forces. America was carrying on a major war at maximum LOC, an umbilical cord that extended all the way across the world, in theory exposed at every point, and maintained for the better part of two decades. One effect of remoteness was, of course, cost. At one point I was told that one day's flow in the total supply pipeline had a value of over a hundred million dollars.

Another effect was the sense of bonding among the soldiers. We were all in the same remote place. Naturally, you look to each other for support. The younger you are, the more likely the friendships and habit of mutual help are to last through later years. Our average age was nineteen. When my dad's tank company was hit by the Germans in the Battle of the Bulge on December 16, 1944, he was twenty-six, the average age of our forces in World War II.

Our sense of remoteness was accentuated by the Sonys and Toshibas. There were actually men in defensive bunkers at night who watched *Laugh-In* on battery- and generator-powered TV's. Music from home made you homesick. Images of the big rally at Woodstock made you feel out of it. Images of the war protest made you feel estranged. Images of girls back home made you think of love and sex. These kinds of things always happen in war. But in Vietnam technology made the pain of remoteness especially intense. It heightened our reliance upon each other.

The music had great effect, I think. At the B-School the organizational-behavior professors put on a special showing of the movie about a World War II bomber squadron, *Twelve O'Clock High*. The movie showed the dynamics of mutual support, friendship, and also discipline in a fighting force, and the relationship among the groups who command, who manage logistics, and who do battle. The pilots often sang a song in their ready room, "Don't Sit Under the Apple Tree with Anyone Else But Me." It was an American hit song during World War II. The lyrics were about fidelity, support of the soldier, and waiting ". . . until you come marching home." The song stands in my memory as typical of World War II attitudes. The Americans back home seem to be saying to the members of the fighting forces, "We believe in what you are doing, and you can take comfort in our love for you."

By contrast, what stands out in my memory for the Vietnam generation is another lyric, sung by Country Joe McDonald:

> And it's one, two, three
>   what're-we-fightin'-for?
> Don't ask me, I don't give a damn,
>   Next stop is Viet-Nam . . .

The song was sung in the movie *Woodstock*. It was a big hit. I think the lyric, married with its rock beat, is an integral memory of at least every member of any American high school or college class of the 1960s. In the lyric, America seemed to be saying to the soldier, "We cannot say we believe in what you are doing, but there is some comfort for you in resigned cynicism." All the songs of the sixties were part of our life in the war zone. There were troops who listened to Country Joe in the bush and in the bunkers. Such songs accentuated our feeling of remoteness and our sense of reliance on each other. To an extent much greater than in any prior American war, we felt that we might be all we had, just each other. In America, to love us and support us was increasingly to be furtive or contrary to fashion, especially among our peers. Of course, our parents, brothers, sisters, friends, and family loved us. But love was not society's message to us. Country Joe's message was more accurately society's message to us. It made our life in Vietnam harder. It tended to bond us together.

This bonding and habit of mutual help were both reinforced and made technically possible by our ability to talk with each other. By historical comparison communications in-country were superb. As geographically isolated as individual platoons could be, the radio and helicopter communication was constant and reliable. The ability to call in supporting air strikes and artillery fire was so pervasive and efficient that we took it for granted. It represented a breakthrough in logistics. The reliability of in-country mail and air transport were also breakthroughs. In Vietnam the United States enjoyed unchallenged possession of the skies, making such a communications and transport net possible. The constant traffic in helicopters at Long Binh showed this support, as did the flight line of C-130's at

Bien Hoa. I was to spend as much time in a helicopter during my year in Vietnam as I would in my 1966 Chevelle during the next twelve months at home.

An obvious thought occurred to me that first night at Long Binh. I noted the date, June 29, 1969. *In 365 days I would go home,* unless I was hit and evacuated first. The Army made and kept the promise for all of us, all through the war: *365 to the day.* The Marines went one notch deeper, adding another month: *395 days.* Unlike our dads in World War II, we knew the day of homecoming. That fixed our attention. We all counted days. Under thirty days you were "short." At a week you were real short. "He's so short he needs a ladder to get in his tent." Or, ". . . so short he sleeps in his helmet." My favorite: "Man, you're so short you can walk under the white stripes in the middle of the road." This sequence of countdown was something we all shared. It intensified the similarity of our experience in-country. It was augmented by the promise made and kept of a week's rest-and-relaxation leave ("R and R") usually at the six months mark and often where we chose: Hawaii, Hong Kong, Japan, Australia, or Singapore. The poignancy of return to the war zone from R and R added to our commonality of experience. To various degrees, Navy and Air Force people shared these same kinds of experiences, though altered by such factors as different durations for sea duty and for rotations of air crews of bombers and other aircraft. The experience was also shared by the thousands of American civilians in Vietnam, including State Department, Red Cross, Agency for International Development, and senior headquarters secretarial staff recruited for one year or longer tours in-country.

Also, by 1969 those of us going in could sense what awaited when we got home, because we had already seen it at work: "One-on-one and in intimate terms we do not discuss the war, your experiences, or the dead men. This makes the near term less uncomfortable for you and less uncomfortable for us." This taboo would last for ten years after the war, showing material signs of thaw only at the dedication of the Vietnam Veterans Memorial on the Mall in Washington in November of 1982, at a parade and reunion which Vietnam Veterans put on for themselves and attended largely by themselves in front of a country in which most people still search for words to say to us. Generally, the war could only be discussed in anger and in open forums and in newspaper articles, and in terms governed by television film crews, reporters, and producers. This all tended to keep at bay the war we felt inside of us, those who came back alive. There was to be no intimacy in discussing the war. This is in part true of all wars. Like the other aspects of the war, it is especially true of Vietnam. The long term of isolation of the veteran in us gave us even more in common.

In a kind of horrible divorce, America separated herself from us. For years we coped alone, or with help from our war buddies. I think America did, for a while, break its emotional commitment to us, but in turn many of us were slowly and luckily able to strengthen the emotional commitments that remained.

The three million of us who served in the war zone are a sizable cohort in the American population. The cohort is young, with an intense, similar, lengthy shared experience. One strength of this huge chunk of American people is the sense of unity among themselves created by their experiences.

These are not the only reasons for special analysis of the cohort. It is a partially overlooked cohort, in that its strengths and successes have hardly been examined. The focus of study to date, and properly so, has been the individual and collective wounds of the veterans. Yet there is the question of whether the common experiences of this cohort have made them stronger. Folk wisdom says this is often true in cases of shared hardship. It is an important issue. It is part of the larger portrait of how the interconnected events of the Vietnam war years shape America now.

The proper place to start examining the portrait is to look at the way life in Vietnam shaped us while we were there. Just like in *Twelve O'Clock High,* there were three major subcultures at work. The logistics, medical, and supply subculture was second largest. I call it the *M\*A\*S\*H* subculture, because the movie and TV series *M\*A\*S\*H,* although about a hospital and ostensibly set in the Korean War, in fact describe the cauldron of improbable experience that made up the lives of so many of us who formed the infrastructure for combat in Vietnam. The scripts were written, after all, during the height of the Vietnam War. About a fourth of us, or seven hundred thousand, were in this *M\*A\*S\*H* subculture.

Second is the command subculture. Battle was carried out by captains and lower ranks—captains and lieutenants are termed in the Army "company-grade" officers, meaning that they commanded at company level. Captains were company commanders and lieutenants were platoon leaders (platoon commanders in the Marines). Command in the sense of directing the overall battle rested with "field grade" officers, that is majors and above— right on up through four-star generals. America vilified the command culture in Vietnam. In the early 1980s it is still popular among many to think, "Well, the troopers and company officers were just trying to survive. That's OK. The culpable ones were the commanders." Out in the open, this view is so simplistic that it properly becomes suspect. The popular view of Vietnam commanders is not easy to square with a study of the evidence. Relatively few men made up this culture, the battalion, brigade, division, corps, and MACV commanders and their staffs for the war period. Perhaps twenty thousand. Most unit commanders were on senior command staff for six months and then unit commanders for six months. Generals were usually assigned to their commands for multi-year tours.

The battle subculture, the third subculture, is the one fixed in the popular mind, save for the vivid scenes in *M\*A\*S\*H*. At this level, the bullets flew. Its inhabitants were the troopers and young officers. Their story is told in books like *A Rumor of War; The 13th Valley; Fields of Fire; Nam; Everything We Had; Born on the Fourth of July; The Killing Zone;* and *If I Die in a Combat Zone.* It is poignantly expressed in *Going After Cacciato.* Overall, there are some surprising and unacknowledged themes in the life of the Vietnam battlefield. About three-fourths of us were in the battlefield subculture—2.3 million. After six months, many officers rotated out of this subculture into the *M\*A\*S\*H* subculture.

These three subcultures fit together, and the personal side of the first two has been hardly explored at all. Taken together the three subcultures shape the lives of three million vital and young American men, and America, right now. And they will shape us in the future.

## M*A*S*H: BERTHIER

At the 90th Replacement Battalion on my second morning in-country, a loudspeaker announcement called me to the personnel desk. Headquarters U.S. Army Vietnam, USARV (pronounced "YOU-sar-V"), had called. A driver was coming to pick me up.

"Does this mean I stay at Long Binh?" I asked.

"No, sir," said the clerk. "USARV people go everywhere."

"What do they do?"

"I don't know, sir."

America fought the Vietnam War with three key categories of resources, (1) people (2) helicopters and helicopter parts, and (3) everything else: weapons, food, fuel, water, ammo, and lubricants. USARV managed the flow of these resources. USARV was the overall coordinating staff for Army logistics in Vietnam. It was the main logistics arm of the Military Assistance Command Vietnam, MACV. USARV kept track of the skills, assignment, location, and due date home for each soldier in Vietnam. The war moved on helicopters, including almost all medevac (medical evacuation) from battle. The 1st Aviation Brigade kept them flying, and this meant a steady stream of sensitive and expensive parts. For example, after wear and tear in the air, the rotor hub of the Huey had to be regularly overhauled or replaced. No hub, no Huey. No Huey, no medevac. USARV managed the aviation parts inventory and supply. The 1st Signal Brigade interlinked the war zone better than Westchester County, New York, by wire, radio, and microwave. I could pick up a desk phone and call Jeff Rogers, commander of a remote adviser base south of Phan Rang. From the same desk I could call the Pentagon in Washington. Both calls could be made within minutes. The United States Army Engineer Command, Vietnam ("YOU-sa-Cav") built a major road network in Vietnam. The Medical Command supported and operated most hospitals. The 1st Logistical Command managed the actual delivery of most materiel in-country. USARV was the staff that integrated all this logistics activity and communicated back to the States, through the staffs at Saigon and Hawaii.

I understood what USARV did. It is one reason we had

studied Napoleon's campaigns at West Point. In the introduction of his book on the Napoleonic Wars, General Esposito wrote,

> Napoleon was truly a great captain, one who played a major role in the history and development of the military art. Few, if any, commanders, before or since, fought more wars and battles under more varied conditions of weather, terrain, and climate, and against a greater variety of enemies. . . . His understanding of mass warfare and his success in raising, organizing, and equipping mass armies revolutionized the conduct of war and marked the origin of modern warfare. . . . he brought logistics into being as the necessary teammate of strategy.

*Logistics is the teammate of strategy.* The text repeats the lesson until it is ingrained. The lesson is the commonsense aspect of war that is at the same time so familiar and yet overlooked by laity, generals, and government officials alike. "It is very necessary to attend to detail, and to trace a biscuit from Lisbon into a man's mouth on the frontier, and to provide for its removal from place to place, by land and by water, or no military operations can be carried on," said Arthur Wellesley, First Duke of Wellington, on his campaign in Spain. The point is that the man who beat Napoleon had to remind readers of the lesson. In Vietnam, it was a mighty complicated biscuit. The recipe included things like helicopters, 365-day rotation for each person, refrigeration in a tropical zone, massive needs for water, and prevention of tropical disease. According to Frederick the Great, "Understand that the foundation of an army is the belly. It is necessary to procure nourishment for the soldier wherever you assemble him and wherever you wish to lead him. This is the primary duty of a general." The belly stands for the body, and nourishment stands for health, food, and water.

Years later, in 1981, I was setting up the Vietnam Veterans Leadership Program, VVLP, for President Reagan. The program identifies successful Vietnam-veteran executives around the country and gives them staff support so they can work as volunteers to mobilize their communities to help meet the needs of

Vietnam veterans. The program has been organized to erase the false stereotype of the Vietnam veteran as someone to feel sorry for and to place Vietnam veterans into career-potential—not dead-end—jobs. Government funding lasts until September 30, 1984. But at fifty thousand dollars per city per year, local leaders who wish to continue can do so with only a modest fund-raising effort. The key again is logistics: setting up a structure with resources to enable leaders to work their areas of operations. I received a letter from Wayne Hanby, a Marine-veteran justice of the peace in Delaware who was willing to resign in order to staff the Wilmington VVLP. In the dark hours of the morning of August 10, 1969, he was a corporal stationed at Hill 461 in the upper part of South Vietnam. His men were low on ammo, and no helicopter resupply was available. They were surrounded and subjected to harassing fire. Hanby and his men shepherded their grenades and other ammo through the night. Finally, they interspersed rocks with the grenades, forcing the enemy to pause at the sound. Then they ran out of grenades. Before dawn Hanby was overrun, and two enemy grenades hurled at him had opened his throat and chest, blinded him in his left eye, and severed his right hand. *This was because he ran out of ammo.* At dawn the helicopters flew in and the Air Force shipped him home. He was soon in Philadelphia Naval Hospital.

Logistics is life and death. A principal figure in setting up and overseeing Napoleon's logistics arm was Louis-Alexandre Berthier, his chief of staff. In my mind's eye he sets the paradigm for success due to logistics. Esposito quotes Thiebault: "Quite apart from his specialist training as a topographical engineer, he had knowledge and experience of staff work and furthermore a remarkable grasp of everything to do with war. He had also, above all else, the gift of writing a complete order and transmitting it with utmost speed and clarity. . . ."

At the end of a twelve-thousand-mile LOC, USARV was first business for the American general staffs in Saigon, Hawaii, and Washington. The result was the enormous Army post at Long Binh, hewn from raw land.

In my opinion USARV and the logistics arms of the other services met Berthier's standard. Wayne Hanby's experience is an exception. Lack of resupply, even in an emergency, was un-

common, especially by 1969. More typical was the case Jeff
Rogers reported to me: From a mountain near Phan Rang some
harassing fire had hit a light spotter plane. The word was sent
to Phan Rang airfield. Jets returning with undelivered ordnance
plastered the mountain with it as a standby target of opportunity. The resources were there, and so was Air Force–Army co-
ordination. Marine platoon commander Robert Muller in the book
*The Wounded Generation* reports the tremendous supporting
firepower at the disposal of small-unit leaders. "There's a very
strong sense of power when you can call in jet strikes, artillery
and the battleship *New Jersey.*" In *The 13th Valley,* John Del
Vecchio depicts withering artillery fire accurately directed at an
unsuspecting enemy by troopers isolated in the bush. Air strikes
and artillery were of course delivered by the combat operations
chain of command, but it was the infrastructure of supply, communications, and organization in Vietnam that put these resources into the hands of platoon leaders and even squad leaders. Probably the best evidence of USARV effectiveness was the
surgical and medical evacuation system. Perhaps the most popular public image of Vietnam is that of ground radio, air control, covering fire, and helicopters working instantly and regularly to fly wounded men to a medical staff. The metaphor of
Vietnam logistics as *M\*A\*S\*H* is poetically apt.

When the driver appeared at the 90th Replacement Battalion, I was ready, and I wasn't. I understood USARV. And business school training directly applied to logistics. But I was not
ready for the sedan. I expected a jeep. The driver sought me
out. He was a specialist 5—a technical sergeant.

"Captain Wheeler? Do you have your bag?"

"Right. Where are we going?"

"Headquarters USARV."

"Am I assigned there?"

"Yes, sir. I think so, sir."

"Who do I work for?"

"Lieutenant Colonel Ford."

"Do you know what he does?"

"Computers, sir."

I hadn't thought about computers being *in* Vietnam. He
drove several miles to the center of the Army post, past various

smaller camps. We arrived at a modern set of air-conditioned two-story buildings, set on top of a hill, near a helipad—HQ USARV. I met my boss. Lieutenant Colonel Charles Ford had previously commanded a signal battalion in Alaska. Later he would call me Captain Jack in informal moments, and he once told me that at an airport in the States some war protesters spied his uniform and spit on him. It had happened to many soldiers. It was a bald fact, not quite painful, just blindingly unreal. Colonel Ford was a gentle man with Southern roots. He had graduated from the military college at Virginia Polytechnic Institute. He knew I was young for General Staff but that I had taken computer courses at Harvard. USARV Personnel had flagged my records so that when I arrived in-country I would work for Colonel Ford.

In the course of my first afternoon with Colonel Ford, I learned that all Army resources in Vietnam were listed and managed on computers, in about one hundred forty installations throughout South Vietnam. The Duke of Wellington's biscuit was being traced all right, by computer. My estimate is that in 1969 there was a bigger computer network in South Vietnam than the one run back home by the state of California. The typical machines were IBM, UNIVAC, and NCR. Helicopter parts were specially managed by USARV on a large computer in Saigon. Personnel were managed by a large computer at Long Binh. It was this computer that tracked the end of each soldier's 365-day tour and coordinated with the Air Force for the airliner passage home. The computers had become a critical information tool. There were so many computers that they were themselves a critical management problem: keeping track of their repair, air conditioning, and quality of staffing was rapidly becoming complicated. The tropics are a hostile environment for computers, and repair and training were a constant headache. My job was to help Colonel Ford and the incoming chief of our section, Colonel Duane Emerson, an experienced artilleryman who had taught me math at West Point. I was to travel, troubleshoot, and train officers.

Computer technology has advanced so much since 1969 that the scale of this development may be lost. The year 1969 was relatively early in the computer age. The complicated set of field commands in Vietnam required that many different commanders at levels fairly close to the field be able to draw and order supplies. But the very long supply line of twelve thousand miles made errors extremely costly, since shipment required both time and money. And Vietnam, with disparate terrain and an insurgent enemy, was as confusing a war zone as any in history. Things went wrong and the unexpected would happen: the military texts call it the "fog of war." Computers were needed, and the Army had made creaky 1950s and 1960s computer technology work in the field, including the tricky task accomplished by Army engineers of generating constant supplies of steady electric current to the air conditioners and machines. As Stateside office workers now know, even modest current and temperature fluctuations cause even the 1980s computers in office word processors to hiccup and lose memory.

This was the unexpected, one part of Vietnam no one saw, that I could not have anticipated myself. My own involvement in this work is an illustration of how our life in Vietnam exposed us to a new point of view of technology and organization, which we brought back to our life in the States. Colonel Ford and Colonel Emerson were wrestling with the idea of how to use computers to manage computers. The Army was automating the repair and operational records of each computer onto punch cards and tape. If this could be done in one standard format, then one computer could keep track of the health and usage of all other machines, pinpointing replacement and repair needs and possible breakdowns before they became critical. The trouble was that the UNIVAC, IBM, and NCR machines all used different computer languages, so that no standardized single report, readable by one machine, was possible. Each installation was trying to prepare the reports manually, on keypunch machines. But human error riddled the reports with mistakes. The consolidated data was useless.

After studying the problem, I saw that every installation either had a UNIVAC machine or was a short helicopter trip from one. With an Army sergeant at the UNIVAC installation at Long Binh I wrote a special editing program in UNIVAC language on a deck of computer punch cards, then made seventy copies of the deck, delivering it to each UNIVAC unit in-country, with instructions that all usage and status reports would be run at a UNIVAC site before forwarding to us. Distributing the decks meant scrounging special transportation. Exposed to Vietnam humidity, the decks quickly turned into glop. One buddy loaned me a jeep that turned out to be "borrowed" from another motor pool. We were admonished for using mongrel transportation. M*A*S*H. But the distribution was complete. The errors disappeared. We produced useful data. In the late sixties, the Army was using computers to manage computers in a war zone. And all key logistic resources were inventoried on computers. This was new in history, and I doubt that even in the 1980s any other armed force in the world could duplicate the logistical feat achieved by the American support in Vietnam.

My unexpected plunge into computer management in the extremes of Vietnam operational conditions forced me to digest the real fact that computers were revolutionizing the way work could be done. I realized it intellectually, but the massiveness, intensity, and tight operating tolerances of the war zone made the perception an integral part of me. Later, in law school, I was to write about the specific ways that computer technology would revolutionize the financial business and the practice of financial law. My perceptions had been honed by war service. The article led to a surprise offer to join the staff of the SEC as an assistant general counsel to work on computer applications to securities regulation.

I think that young men returning from war have always tended to evaluate both technology and societal relationships in a fresh light.

Federal Express, for instance, is the Memphis, Tennessee, company that pioneered nationwide overnight package delivery. Started in the early 1970s it set the pattern now being copied by Purolator, the U.S. Postal Service "Express Mail" service, and others. Frederick W. Smith, a Marine combat officer in Vietnam, founded the company, based on the idea of owning a fleet of jets which all fly to the Memphis hub in the evening hours, exchange packages, and fly out again in the wee hours for door-to-door deliveries the next a.m. This "hub" system is how many Vietnam helicopter and C-130 operations were carried out. Whether by conscious intent or not, Fred Smith superimposed the air grid and delivery system of the Vietnam war zone onto the United States and invented a successful business. *If you have overnight mail and courier in a war zone you can have it in the States.*

And if computers truly revolutionize war zone logistics, it is best to look for similar specific effects in the stateside economy. The increased use of helicopter evacuation for highway accident victims is related to the history of medevacs in Vietnam. There is the success of Vietnam veteran B.T. Collins in reigniting the California Conservation Corps as a state government program to employ and vitalize thousands of disadvantaged youth. B.T.'s secret was the old-fashioned code of personal example, esprit, and discipline.

There are also examples of fresh approaches, brought back home, that rest on personal relationships. I think that Vietnam veterans will always feel especially close-knit with each other, compared to other American war veterans, because we were especially close-knit in Vietnam and shared a common emotional quarantine on our return to America. Such ideas are speculative, but there is evidence. One sign is the success of David Christian in founding the United Vietnam Veterans Organization, and of Bob Muller in founding the Vietnam Veterans of America. Another is the growth of the Vietnam Veterans Leadership Program. The Program was personally authorized by President Reagan on July 16, 1981, on the basis of an operations plan prepared by a group of Vietnam veterans assembled by Thomas W. Pauken, a Vietnam veteran and the newly nominated director of the federal ACTION agency. The group included Tom, writer James Webb, labor department executive Dennis Rhoades, and me. The Program is housed in ACTION, with a lifetime cost of six million dollars—less than the replacement cost of one F-4 Phantom, the close-air-support jet most commonly used by the Air Force, Navy, and Marines in Vietnam. The goal was to coalesce a group of Vietnam-veteran volunteer executives, lawyers, doctors, and businessmen in all fifty cities. Each group would establish their own local VVLP as a charitable corporation, and ACTION would fund the first three years of office costs and a small local staff to be hired by the corporation, to help the volunteers coordinate the work. Each program would lay out and accomplish its own plan to help veterans who needed a leg up into career-potential jobs.

It was ten years after the height of the Vietnam War. Why would anyone care? The planning group's instinct was that these needs of Vietnam veterans had been on ice for ten years and that such an initiative was only just now possible. It was our position that Vietnam veterans felt a strong sense of bonding from the experiences they shared, and we thought volunteers would muster forth. Wayne Hanby's letter to me was an early confirmation that this spirit existed. The Program is in fact a logistical support system to reawaken the sense of fellowship we shared in the war zone and channel it to solve specific problems in the present. The goal has been achieved.

This accomplishment suggests that the conditions of service in Vietnam did shape many of us in a way that makes possible a later public contribution, even after the intervening decade in which all Americans, including the veterans, freeze-dried their feelings from the war years.

This same direction of emotions toward creativity and of reliance on old personal bonding to create something worthwhile is also part of the story of the Vietnam Veterans Memorial Fund. The key, again, is communication, organization, and planning, in the purest logistical sense. Vietnam veteran Jan Scruggs conceived the idea of a national memorial in 1979. Veterans rallied around him to assemble a plan that would put a national memorial on the Mall in three years with private contributions and no government appropriation. It is no accident that most of the Memorial Fund's board of directors are Army logisticians.

This was M*A*S*H, lived in Vietnam and now enacted among us at home. Computers to run computers, on a tropical hilltop. Building a Memorial on the Mall. Fred Smith re-creates the 1st Aviation Brigade right at home in Memphis. A badly wounded Marine becomes a Delaware judge, but takes time off ten years later to make sure everyone gets fully "back from the battlefield." This is the real M*A*S*H, the story I think that the scriptwriters perhaps intuitively perceived. At the end of the M*A*S*H movie, Trapper John and Hawkeye are at the stateside airport, parting. "Finest kind," they say to each other, their code word of friendship. We didn't want the story to end. It did not end. The movie itself went on to become the famous TV series, and in the early 1980s the Trapper John character reappeared in another TV series, named after him, as an older doctor helping his younger staff along. And now there is the new hit TV series, *AfterMASH*. *M\*A\*S\*H* is also about creativity and healing, and so is the Memorial, the Leadership Program, Federal Express, and, I think, any number of new projects under way in America, not as yet apparent, but rooted in the tension, energy, and fellowship of the huge infrastructure of the Vietnam war zone.

At night, Art Mosley and I taught University of Maryland night extension courses in business administration. We enjoyed it, and the men in the big posts in Vietnam filled many such courses all over the war zone. The enrollments showed a strong desire of many men to convert the combination of tension and boredom in the war zone into an investment in their future life in the States.

Classes were held in converted Army trailers, the kind used for temporary command posts. The first-night mimeo handout for faculty and students reminded us IN CASE OF MORTAR OR ROCKET ATTACK EVACUATE TO DITCHES BY SIDE OF CLASSROOM.

Our West Point classmate Doc Crants took our courses, as he honed his successful application to the J.D.-M.B.A. program at Harvard. Bruns Grayson was a twenty-one-year-old maintenance company commander, a husky man with an engaging manner, a new captain who had been through Officer Candidate School. He extended his Vietnam tour for six months to assume the command. His company supported the regiment commanded by General George Patton (Patton's son). The World War II movie *Red Ball Express*, in which Jeff Chandler plays a harried officer forcing supplies and parts through to Patton Senior, gives some flavor of Bruns' life. He had been a Golden Gloves boxer, is a terrific raconteur. He told me about growing up in Alameda, California, during the 1950s and hanging out at Ryder's drive-in. Things got rocky, and finally, kicked out of two schools, Bruns decided to join the Army, because he had left home and was tired of gypsy life. Late into the night, he read Red Cross books that came to his company. Poetry was one of his favorites.

Bruns was taking the night courses in order to strengthen his chances of being accepted to college. He finally graduated from high school. One night after class he asked for advice. Thereby began a tale that Hawkeye and Trapper John would love.

"What are your college board scores?" I said.

"1420."

"Say again?"

"700 in math, 720 in verbal."

"I'd like you to meet some friends of mine."

In a day or so Bruns met Art, Doc, Dick Radez, a West Point and B-School friend, and Larry Foster, who always carried a copy of *Catch-22* in the knee pocket of his fatigues. Somebody suggested Bruns apply to Harvard and Yale. Yale's application materials promptly arrived, and Bruns completed them and sent them on to New Haven. Two months later, Bruns called.

"I can't get the Harvard application. I keep writing; nothing comes."

I envisioned the occupied administration building of months before. Who knows what was going on? Besides, Harvard *had* always seemed disorganized.

"I even called my mom, from the Red Cross phone in Saigon. She called Harvard. Still nothing. The deadline is here."

"Write your own application," I said. I was thinking. *This might work.* "Use the Yale questions, but type it all out on plain bond. Send it to Nathan Pusey." I explained that Mr. Pusey was the president of Harvard. He had seemed like a straight shooter, but a man under fire. "Talk about yourself in the letter to him."

I told Larry, Art, Doc, and Dick about the plan. They would meet with Bruns. I left for leave in Hawaii. Bruns would be stateside when I returned. Nathan Pusey wrote Bruns saying that he regretted the difficulties Bruns had encountered and that his papers had been forwarded to the right quarters.

Bruns was admitted to Yale and Harvard. There was much discussion about where to go. Months later Bruns told me that even before he left Vietnam, Larry Foster had sat down with him and convinced him about Harvard, and so he went.

Long before George Lucas' movie *American Graffiti*, I had encountered a man from a real kind of *American Graffiti*. Mel's is the drive-in in the movie *Graffiti*. Ryder's was the real thing.

What Lucas would portray is real, and Bruns offered proof, in many humorous anecdotes.

Bruns graduated in 1974 as a Rhodes Scholar. He went on to Oxford, the only Vietnam veteran to enter college after war service and go on to earn the scholarship to Oxford. It was a December night in 1973 when his brother told me the news. I danced on the snow-covered street.

One of the appeals of the *M*A*S*H* story is that it symbolizes healing, since the setting is a hospital. It recognizes that people do look for healing and unity even in harsh environments. This healing and unity did arise from Vietnam, as in the group of us who knew Bruns, and the actual hospital and medical units.

The specific medical story of Vietnam affected us significantly. We grew accustomed to the idea that with technology death can be beaten, even in spite of terrible wounds. Wayne Hanby thought he was dying in the foxhole. He wrote, "When I finally came to my senses, the tragic realization struck me: I was minus a hand and an eye. Fighting the spasmodic pain that possessed my body, I lay there bloodied and mangled, almost wishing that one of the enemy would mercifully finish me off and relieve me of the misery I was in; but God's will prevailed. . . ."

Vietnam veterans carried home this fighting notion about new medical technology. Richard Eilert expresses it in his book *For Self and Country,* in a story that includes thirty-seven operations to save his leg. David Huffman, a furniture-mover-turned-Marine and completely blinded by a Vietnam booby trap, went through the Veterans Administration blindness training and became a lawyer in Wilmington, Delaware.

This attitude carries over to family. Joe Zengerle, a West Pointer in the class of 1964 practicing law in Washington, came up to me once and said in a lawyerly way, "The presumption of a normal birth with a smooth and safe delivery is an easily rebuttable presumption." He was referring to the close call when his wife Lynda gave emergency Caesarean birth to Jason after 30 hours of natural childbirth labor, but he was consoling me about Katie Wheeler, born with an improperly formed trachea and diagnosed as a SIDS (Sudden Infant Death Syndrome) baby.

She still needs a tracheotomy, a nighttime electronic monitoring alarm for her breathing, and daily care of a professional nurse. The cost has been five hundred dollars a week for six years.The prognosis is hopeful; Katie is sunny and unimpaired by her passage. I remember seeing her for the first time, in her tiny intensive-care crib at Georgetown Hospital. She struggled to breathe. The doctor said her twin, John, seemed to have a permanent heart defect. Elisa was recovering from the Caesarean birth and did not know the children were in trouble. I felt it was war, and that death would not win. I still feel that way. We searched out Paul Wankowicz, a medical engineer at Massachusetts General Hospital, who fashioned a special monitor alarm for Katie, one that would detect the passage of air through her tracheotomy. Paul served in Vietnam, I learned years later. John's heart appears to have recovered. When the alarm breaks, Elisa and I take turns by her bed, all night long. We will fight death.

Dave Huffman married, and he had children and adopted a daughter. Joe and Lynda have been married nearly twenty years. Elisa and I for ten. I think that this is the more common story of Vietnam veterans, and it reflects in part the knitting together and the reliable infrastructure that underlay the battle life in Vietnam. Life is more than wounds, and people together are more than the same people alone.

Something Paul Wankowicz once said is troubling. It is about the many large base areas that comprised the *M\*A\*S\*H* subculture of the Vietnam war zone. In Vietnam his men had used "borrowed" Agent Orange to clear the vegetation from his base area. It was an informal arrangement with the Air Force, reflecting the common event of life in the war zone, when one unit exchanged items it had in a kind of barter for items needed from a neighboring unit. It happens in every war zone. Vietnam veterans and reporters will all recall how barren the great base areas were, like Cam Ranh, Cu Chi, Bien Hoa, and Long Binh. Bald. Stripped of vegetation. The question is whether in the earlier days of the war hard-pushed personnel "borrowed" Agent Orange or other defoliants for use in clearing the building zone and the fields of fire for the base areas. The dioxin in Agent Orange tends to filter down into soil and to dissolve slowly if at all. *If* this kind of thing happened, then *perhaps* the dioxin was present in the water tables from which military engineers drew supplies for the base areas all through the war. The engineers may not have been anticipating the need to screen dioxins, given the urgent threats of microbial and other disease.

This is tenuous reasoning. But more complex difficulties have arisen, and the stateside questions about Times Beach and Love Canal are a basis for considering possibilities. One import of this hypothesis is that concerns about occasional exposure to Agent Orange, largely by touch (and inhaling) need to be joined by concern about prolonged exposure through ingestion. Also, it was commonly the base area that provided water to troops in the field, through canteens and huge canvas bags. What should we be examined for, if this were a possibility? Are there compounds which can be safely drunk to dissolve dioxin from the body, even after fifteen or more years? I regard Katie Wheeler's childhood difficulties with her trachea in this light.

In 1982, the questions of Agent Orange and dioxins were turned over to the Centers For Disease Control in Atlanta. While investigations about Times Beach and Love Canal are handled by the Environmental Protection Agency, it makes sense that EPA and CDC coordinate their findings. I do not know if CDC and EPA are considering this hypothesis in fashioning their research protocols. I do not feel bitterness in contemplating any of the possible truths in all this. I do worry about Katie. I remember, back in my Pentagon days, how skeptical Matt Meselson was about the use of herbicides. I did not have enough information to come to my own conclusion. I focused on biological weapons and feel that America made the right decision in rejecting use of biologicals.

## COMMAND: LEE

On the subject of Vietnam, I think of Robert E. Lee as the paradigm American commander. Like Washington, faithful to his men. Courageous and honest. Do the American Vietnam commanders meet this standard? No book better expresses the resentment heaped on the Vietnam commanders than C. D. B. Bryan's book *Friendly Fire,* about Michael, the son of Peg and Gene Mullen of Iowa, killed on February 18, 1970, by an American artillery round that had not been set to clear the trees on a mountaintop. En route to a target the round hit the trees and prematurely detonated.

There is a 1950s movie about the Korean War, *Pork Chop Hill*. In it Gregory Peck plays a young infantry lieutenant assigned to attack and take the hill. It was a popular movie, and Peck depicted a sympathetic character. Mike Mullen's brigade commander in Vietnam was Colonel Joseph Clemons, the real-life character depicted by Gregory Peck. Michael's battalion commander was Lieutenant Colonel H. Norman Schwarzkopf, West Point '56, who had volunteered for his second tour in Vietnam. The company commander was Captain Tom Cameron. The Mullens suspected a cover-up about the cause of their son's death. Why were the Mullens so sure of Army wrongdoing?

Mr.Bryan brings his report to a close with a conversation between Peg, Gene, and him:

> Gene had said, "You wanted the story, and you wanted the truth."
>
> "Well, that's what he's getting," Peg then said.
>
> "Now, I'm not going to like the truth if it isn't in my favor—"
>
> "Oh, Gene!" Peg laughed.
>
> "You can understand that," he said, ignoring Peg.
>
> "Yes, but I also understand that the truth is neither in your favor or their favor," I said. "It's somewhere in between."
>
> "The truth is in *their* favor?" Gene asked, beginning to get angry all over again.
>
> "Gene, of course, doesn't want the military ever to look good," Peg said. "We have a very slanted bias. A hatred for the military. And there's nothing that will change that, I suppose."
>
> "I can understand that, too," I said, "but I think it's important for you to know that both Schwarzkopf and Captain Tom Cameron, your son's company commander, were fine officers. Fine men."
>
> "Well, I don't buy it," Gene said. "I don't buy Schwarzkopf, and I don't buy the military."

There is a stereotype about Vietnam that depicts the commanders as generally heartless careerists, aloof from their men. Schwarzkopf explained why he signed up for a second tour:

> But my first and foremost reason, as I have said, was that based upon my experience, that first tour with the Vietnamese Airborne, I felt I definitely had something I could contribute as a battalion commander. I felt I could accomplish the mission with the minimum loss of life—none, if possible, which is what it's all about really. After all, this is what I had been trained for, what the Army kept me around to do and I felt it was my obligation to do so . . . and all right, *yes,* commanding a battalion successfully in Vietnam has enhanced my career. But if I turn around and make a mistake in my next assignment or get a bad efficiency report, my career will suffer just as much as it would have otherwise. The only difference between an officer and anybody else is that that officer has got the responsibility and you get into terrifying situations because you flat have got that responsibility. . . ."

Attitudes toward Army commanders change with the times. The American attitude can be hostile. At West Point in plebe year, we cadets were reminded that there is a certain traditional American ambivalence toward things military in general and toward commanders in particular. The history of forced British and Hessian occupation of colonial homes probably figured in the tradition.

The truth about American command in Vietnam is as difficult to sort out and comprehensively study as any part of the story of the Vietnam war zone. In my opinion the view that six-month command tours were detrimental is too pat. Battalion (and, for that matter, company and platoon) command is draining *especially* when you feel loyal to your troops. American officers were professionally trained, and they knew how to call upon and integrate into their operations the vast resources of the logistical system. There is a heavy burden of proof for those who argue that American commanders in Vietnam were not effective, or somehow fell short.

One measure of the commanders is results. At least by the end of 1969, the Viet Cong had been nullified as a ground force. They were stymied and weakened. A major step in nullification was the military defeat suffered by the VC in Tct '68—the great battle which the American press now regards as having been misreported as a VC victory. President Johnson did not succeed in correcting the misreport. I think he may have felt he lacked the power to credibly correct the report. The burden of fighting shifted from the VC to the North Vietnamese regular forces.

By the end of 1972, the North Vietnamese regular forces were also nullified. The evidence for this view is that the North Vietnamese in fact negotiated and signed a cease-fire. But the result in war is not just what happens in the war zone.

Years later, I discussed this with Richard Armitage, Annapolis '67, a three-tour Vietnam veteran, fluent in Vietnamese, who lived among villagers and who became assistant secretary of defense for International Security Affairs (the same slot held by John McNaughton in the 1960s, under Robert McNamara). I asked him what the North Vietnamese commanders thought of the American fighting men. Armitage said, "They respected us. But they knew we did not have full support at home." These views of events in the war zone are personal, and they rest on the evidence I have seen. Obviously, there is evidence I have not seen, and time and evidence can change judgments. Yet, just as with Agent Orange, the truth is worth knowing, and I think that the best available evidence indicates that the American Vietnam commanders delivered the specified, secured military objective within stringent constraints on freedom of American operation and at the end of a maximally long logistics train.

Even more important, the commanders kept faith with their men. Napoleon said this: "The man who cannot look upon a battlefield dry-eyed will allow many men to be killed uselessly." The American commanders were dry-eyed, but they felt bonded to us soldiers, and I think they bore the pain of doing their job correctly.

General Bruce Palmer knew General Hayes, Tommy's dad. One night at a supper in General Palmer's hootch—quarters—in

Vietnam, Tommy asked to take command of a infantry platoon, switching from his normal engineer assignment. General Palmer acquiesced. Years later he told me about the burden of seeing a friend's son go into battle, and the pain of hearing of his death in action. General Michael S. Davison was a Field Force commander in Vietnam, where his son Michael, West Point '64, served as combat company commander, wounded and cited for valor. Generals' sons were in the battle line, just like Peg and Gene Mullen's son. Army, Navy, and Air Force sons permeated the war zone: Jeff Rogers, James Webb, John Wheeler, Bill Haneke, John McKnight. *There was no favoritism.* But the knowledge mattered. *"These are my sons and my brothers' sons."* In the count of families who bore the risk of bleeding in Vietnam, the commanders' families do not come up short.

In normal course, Colonel Clemons rotated Lieutenant Colonel Schwarzkopf's battalion to a deadlier area of operations. C. D. B. Bryan writes:

> A portion of Bravo Company had been patrolling and suddenly one man and then another detonated mines. The company commander, a young captain, and the platoon leader, a young lieutenant, were both badly wounded. A medical evacuation helicopter was called for, and Lieutenant Colonel Schwarzkopf and his artillery liaison officer, Captain Bob Trabbert, immediately flew in their command helicopter to Bravo Company's area and landed. In order to save time, Schwarzkopf turned his helicopter over to be used for med-evac. After he helped load the wounded on board, he and Trabbert stayed behind as the helicopter flew out.

*   *   *   *   *

> "I don't want to die," the kid was whimpering. "You've got to get me out of here."
> "I'll get you out," Schwarzkopf said gently. "Just keep still. You're all right."
> "I'm not! Goddamn you, can't you see my leg?"
> "Take it easy son." Ten feet to go.

Trabbert pulled out his sheath knife and passed it to one of the men. The man took a step toward the tree and triggered another mine. "Oh, my GOD!" Schwarzkopf cried, horrified. Trabbert had taken the full force of the explosion. One of his legs was blown off, an arm broken backward so that the white bone of the elbow socket showed, and a great hole was gouged in his head. He would survive, but the other three men were killed instantly. They lay where they had been flung. No one moved. Only the young private, pinned beneath Schwarzkopf, was twisting about to get a better look. "Are they all dead, sir?"

The commanders help in the present. General Westmoreland and General Davison, superintendent and commandant of cadets for much of the West Point tour of the class of 1966, were instrumental in building the Vietnam Veterans Memorial, as advisors and fund raisers. General Davison proposed the compromise sculpture that led to ground-breaking for the Memorial; he is father of the Vietnam Veteran statue on the Mall. Brigadier General George Price repeatedly testified in Washington in support of the Memorial. General John Vessey, chairman of the Joint Chiefs of Staff and a battalion commander in Vietnam, joined the National Sponsoring Committee of the Memorial. He has publicly urged caution against again sending American combat troops when there is insufficient home front support.

The summer 1983 *Wilson Quarterly* reports that Army discipline suffered with drug use and assaults on officers only *after* President Nixon's 1969 decision to withdraw. The decision naturally created a morale problem. Who wanted discipline and fighting when it appeared we were quitting?

In 1983, Schwarzkopf was a Major General, the Army commander of the successful Grenada rescue assault. Toward the end of *Friendly Fire,* Peg Mullen says about Lieutenant Colonel Schwarzkopf:

I guess that I really don't know how I feel about him. I'd learned to hate him after hearing the boys talk. But he told us he was hated because he insisted on discipline, on taking the proper precautions. And I couldn't help thinking, if only Michael had had his flak jacket on that night, he wouldn't have died. . . . Schwarzkopf, you know, repeatedly told us what a fine man Michael was.

## BATTLEFIELD: LEVY

Did our troopers and company-grade officers fail our country in Vietnam?

Walter Neville Levy gave his life retrieving his wounded men in battle. The action is recounted by his friend and fellow Marine platoon commander Phil Caputo in a passage that has been recited at least twice in ceremonies in the White House and at countless ceremonies across the country. When parents send a son into battle, one of their heartfelt questions is "Who will care for him?" Caputo responded:

> So much was lost with you, so much talent and intelligence and decency. You were the first from our class of 1964 to die. There were others, but you were the first and more: you embodied the best that was in us. You were a part of us, and a part of us died with you, the small part that was still young, that had not yet grown cynical, grown bitter and old with death. Your courage was an example to us, and whatever the rights or wrongs of the war, nothing can diminish the rightness of what you tried to do. Yours was the greater love. You died for the man you tried to save, and you died *pro patria*. It was not altogether sweet and fitting your death, but I'm sure you died believing it was *pro patria*. You were faithful. Your country is not. As I write this, eleven years after your death, the country for which you died wishes to forget the war in which you died. Its very name is a curse. There are no monuments to its heroes, no statues in small-town squares and city parks, no plaques, nor public wreaths, nor memorials. For plaques and wreaths and memorials are reminders, and they would make it harder for your country to sink into the amnesia for

which it longs. It wishes to forget and it has forgotten. But there are a few of us who do remember because of the small things that made us love you—your gestures, the words you spoke, and the way you looked. We loved you for what you were and what you stood for.

*Walter Neville Levy, there is a Memorial. Your name is at east panel no. 2, line 87, twenty-five thousand names from Thomas Jay Hayes IV. Phil Caputo helped us build it.*

The kinship among men who served in the battle line in Vietnam is the most evident of the lasting effects of the war. It is signaled in every book by Vietnam veterans on the war. In *Fields of Fire*, Robert E. Lee Hodges, Jr., gives his life in saving his men. In *The 13th Valley*, the black company commander Rufus Brooks gives his life saving his men. The books depict efficient units who wrote their story in red on enemy breasts. But at the test, when nothing else availed, unit leaders and troopers covered their men and buddies with their own lives. This theme is stirring and spiritual in nature. The theme does not vindicate war, but it suggests that war is more than a simple equation of good and evil. At the end of *The 13th Valley*, author John Del Vecchio expresses this in an evocative last supper scene among Brooks and twelve of his soldiers.

A telling exercise is to leaf through a listing of the Medal of Honor citations for the Vietnam War. Every six or seventh citation seems to be for a soldier who threw his body on a grenade to save his buddies: Donald E. Ballard, Rodney Maxwell Davis, Emilio A. De La Garza, Jr., Daniel Fernandez, and Hector Santiago-Colon:

### SANTIAGO-COLON, HECTOR

*Rank and organization:* Specialist Fourth Class, U.S. Army, Company B, 5th Battalion, 7th Cavalry, 1st Cavalry Division (Airmobile). *Place and date:* Quang Tri Province, Republic of Vietnam, 28 June 1968.

*Entered service at:* New York, N.Y. *Born:* 20 December 1942, Salinas, Puerto Rico. *Citation:* For conspicuous gallantry and intrepidity in action at the risk of his life above and beyond the call of duty. Sp4c. Santiago-Colon distinguished himself at the cost of his life while serving as a gunner in the mortar platoon of Company B. . . . From the wooded area around his position heavy enemy automatic weapons and small-arms fire suddenly broke out, but extreme darkness rendered difficult the precise location and identification of the hostile force. . . . Due to the heavy volume of enemy fire and exploding grenades around them, a North Vietnamese soldier was able to crawl, undetected, to their position. Suddenly, the enemy soldier lobbed a handgrenade into Sp4c. Santiago-Colon's foxhole. Realizing that there was no time to throw the grenade out of his position, Sp4c. Santiago-Colon retrieved the grenade, tucked it into his stomach and, turning away from his comrades, absorbed the full impact of the blast. . . .

I think of the translation of the Lord's Prayer that includes the petition, "And do not bring us to the test." This was the test: in battle, when nothing else avails, we would know the right thing to do.

The bonds among these men are expressed in living fellowship, just as much as in dying. Washington, D.C. Doctor Ralph Wadeson was a battalion surgeon with the Marines in Korea. He told me that Marines in the freezing battle line would spontaneously begin to sing the Marine Hymn together, in a low steady voice. Bill Jayne told me the same thing happened in Vietnam in the siege at Khe Sanh.

The memory of sacrifice and fellowship both expresses and strengthens the bonds among Vietnam veterans. The bonds reach across social and political lines. These bonds are not the only ones in the lives of the men who came back alive or necessarily the most important, and they do not convert Vietnam veterans into automata with duplicate views. But the bonds help diminish antagonism and faction among the Vietnam veterans. This is a lasting effect of life in the Vietnam war zone, crystallized by experiences remembered in the war zone.

A story illustrates this. In 1981, I was looking for a possible volunteer to incorporate and chair the Baltimore Vietnam Veterans Leadership Program. I was searching the biographies of the Martindale-Hubbell lawyers' directory for Maryland. My theory was that the perfect chairman would be a young partner in a law firm who had served in Vietnam. Rank as a partner would indicate an ability to reach key people in Baltimore and get things done. Vietnam service would indicate a willingness at least to consider the task. My eyes fell on a name in the firm of Miles & Stockbridge: Treanor, Mark C. At the end of the bio was "U.S.M.C. 1968–73." I looked up his school—Annapolis, 1968. *An Annapolis Marine.* I called him. He listened while I explained the leadership program. The attorney/litigator in him emerged. He asked for facts and figures. I said, "We're bringing everyone back from the battlefield. We each know someone killed saving others in Vietnam. By his death that man said the life of each soldier is of infinite value, so whatever we do is worth the cost of our time. It's like a promise to keep."

Mark accepted the job. His program excels.

*I went on leave to Hawaii in April, 1970. I did feel lonely, but I had wanted time to think. I was interested in what was going on in America, as much as one could tell in Hawaii. It was a beautiful place, the place I had peered at from the airport during the midnight stopover months—years—before. I spent the week hanging out at the University of Hawaii campus. It was the week of Earth Day, April 22. The day was beautiful. I went to the big outside rally with all the speakers. A speech was made about the car being buried alive somewhere in the States. There were beads and long hair and the constant presumption that the war was bad, evil and not to be intimately discussed. I felt alone. I was alone. I did not understand.*

# CHAPTER THREE

*The political impact of the Vietnam
era on women, like the economic impact,
can only be understood in terms of
a continuum that includes the civil
rights movement of the early 1960's, the
antiwar movements of the late 60s and
the feminist movement of the 70's.
Many men, including some perceptive
historians and political analysts,
still do not realize that politically
conscious feminism emerged from both
the civil rights and antiwar efforts.*

Susan Jacoby
*The Wounded Generation*

# AMERICA

I wonder what the Air Force B-52 pilot thought when told his navigator was Certain. Bob Certain later told me he had spent his life dodging the idea of becoming an Episcopal priest. Actually our slang in Vietnam for "chaplain" was "sky pilot." So this all fits together. One dodge led to another, so in December, 1972, he was perched in the navigator's roost of a B-52 eight miles over Hanoi. He had brought the plane twelve thousand miles, first to Guam then to the IP; initial point for bomb run, over Hanoi. His perch was that same complex electronic core of the plane manned by the black lieutenant in the movie *Dr. Strangelove*. The right place, but a bad time. Surface-to-air missiles (SAM, but not our Uncle), antiaircraft artillery, and fighters defended Hanoi. SAM shrapnel punctured the aircraft. They were crashing. Bob pulled the ejector. The explosive drove his seat at bullet speed straight down, out of the plane's underside and into the North Vietnamese night sky. The chute opened. He landed. No broken bones. He hid in a ditch. A search party with dogs captured him. He was freed in March, 1973, with our other POW'S. He says the missile hit and the high-altitude ejection got his attention. He is now rector of Trinity Episcopal Church, Yazoo City, Mississippi.

Wartime experiences spur within all of us a fresh look at things. The epitome is the experience of POW's, because their separation from our old life is so sharp and extensive. They are usually able to see our country with new eyes. In the January, 1983, *Anglican Theological Review*, Bob wrote about America and Americans,

> The human personality can be likened to a large mobile; one part out of kilter throws the whole thing off

balance; and you have to fix the right part to restore
the balance of the whole. The part that is causing the
out-of-balance condition is not always obvious, especially when it is in the subconscious. Many would
say that the United States is currently exhibiting an
out-of-balance condition, that something isn't quite
right in our corporate "psyche". . . . It may be that
the process of open forum on a small, though public,
scale will effect catharsis on a large scale.

Bob's image of a mobile is a reminder that the events of the
1960s are interconnected. Using another metaphor, if the various commitments we each of us make are the bone of our culture, then the backbone is connected to the hip bone, and the
hip bone is connected to the leg . . .

We committed ourselves to many causes in the sixties,
creating a whole new tension of relationships and ideas, and when
one part moved, everything shifted. We called these commitments movements: civil rights, women's, war protest, and environmental. A spiritual wind stirred the mobile. The wind was
youthful idealism, the natural product of our comfortable up-
bringing and the great hopes of our parents.

Or, muscle is moving these new bones. The muscle was
the machines that facilitated communication: computers, cars,
presses, mimeograph, Xerox, TV, radio, phone, and jets. The
civil rights volunteers went into battle *in buses,* the Freedom
Buses. In its 1983 50th Anniversary retrospective on America,
*Esquire* published an article on campus unrest in the sixties, "The
Leaflet Wars" ("If you wanted to hold a meeting or start a revolution, first you had to find a mimeograph machine."). At West
Point, cadets are told, "Wirepower is firepower."

It was confusing enough to be *in* America, but to fresh eyes
the picture was dazzling and disorienting. No wonder I felt un-
settled in Hawaii. It is no accident that ballet and symphony
progress in "movements." The word connotes the same kind of
thing that was happening in America. Different movements connected by a theme of idealism. In fact the poetry of the time was
the music that suffused the whole culture. From Provincetown
to Nha Trang the music and lyrics were everywhere in our lives,

without limit: classical music, opera, and ballet boomed along-
side rock and country. The Saratoga Performing Arts Center,
where I worked with the New York City Ballet and the Philadelphia Orchestra, was born and prospered then. *The Graduate*
and, later, *American Graffiti* reflect this. They are marriages of
song and act. Just like our national life, they are a kind of dance.

The decade was a creative watershed. Americans sense this.
*The New Yorker* of August 1, 1983, ran a note from "a young
friend" born in 1960:

> What looms as so novel and attractive about the Six-
> ties, to one used only to the lowercase seventies and
> early eighties, is that a number of people appear to
> have been thinking about and asking fundamental
> questions in that period—asking them insistently, and
> as if the answers mattered. . . . My time has been a
> limp time. Even the music. . . . Because upheavals
> like the Sixties', with the corresponding opportunities
> for real change, happen rarely in America, my gen-
> eration may not get a chance at providing lasting an-
> swers. And if the change came to us, there is no rea-
> son to imagine we'd do any better than our older
> brothers and sisiters did. But the chance to make his-
> tory is better than reflecting on it, and there are times
> when I wish that I'd been born ten years older.

By tradition, West Point plebes did not go home for Christmas.
My dad flew out to visit at Christmas, 1962. My brother Bob
had just gone to prep school in the East. So I asked, "Is Mom
lonely now?"

"Lonely is not a problem. We're going to have a baby in
the spring." The telegram announcing Janet Marie's birth was
delivered to me at noon-meal formation on March 28, 1963.

For my own sister seventeen years younger, I add to *The
New Yorker*'s "young friend" note: *"Young friend, the creativity and tension are intact, intensified and matured by ten hard
years of rumination. Our generation is just now using its energy
to create new solutions and healthy relationships. There are
glimpses in a company called Federal Express, and in the Viet-*

*nam Veterans Memorial, and in the movies* Star Wars *and* E.T. *by geniuses George Lucas and Steven Spielberg. Your generation has a chance at providing lasting answers, in work together with us.''*

Wine is better when it matures. What casked us up was the Vietnam War. Irving Howe realized this effect of the war; he wrote in the September 19, 1982, Sunday *New York Times Magazine:* ''. . . the Vietnam War soon eclipsed everything else in American life.'' Howe is not optimistic. He writes of the ''spillage of idealism,'' but ends by describing a visible ''margin of hope.'' Writing from points of view outside the generation, the tendency is to be pessimistic, because the pain and destroyed dreams are overwhelming. What is not so evident in the early 1980s is the feeling of strength, maturity, and available wisdom beginning to be evident among the generation. I think that this energy will begin to surge, and soon, and in graceful, tempered ways. We have been through a lot, but that experience empowers us. There is more than just a margin of hope here. It is positive good news.

The Vietnam War and the relationship of each of us to it does appear to be the backbone of change, but only the backbone. It is only one of interconnected parts. Lance Morrow of *Time* magazine told me the war is ''the central drama of the formation of a generation.''

A number of writers and thinkers have viewed the war in this context. James Michener wrote in a letter to me, ''I first came upon the Vietnam phenomenon while doing work on my book on Kent State, where I met some of the veterans, heard their stories, sympathized with their confusions. I knew then that a story of tragic dimension was under way.'' In classical tragedy, a gradually revealed flaw in character is the seed of destruction. In comedy, strength of character might provide the seed for a surprising redemption. That is why Dante found a title in *The Divine Comedy* and Saroyan in *The Human Comedy*. I wonder if, as he comes to know our generation, Mr. Michener would see this hope in us too?

James Rosenau of the University of Southern California has for several years conducted systematic studies ''to comprehend the profound changes that have swept through the American polity and the political culture on which it rests in recent years.'' He reports that ''the position-on-the-war variable . . . was more closely correlated . . . than was any other variable . . . : neither occupation, ideology, age, sex, party preference, military service, nor level of political interest was as good a predictor of a respondent's belief system as was the position-on-the-war variable.''

The civil rights movement is a second great limb of the sixties culture. Columnist David Broder writes in *Changing of the Guard* about us who came of age during the Vietnam War years, ''The shaping experiences for this next generation of American leaders were the civil-rights struggle and the war in Vietnam—or more precisely, the effort to end the war in Vietnam.'' Harrison Salisbury says in his *Without Fear or Favor,* ''Vietnam at home not in Asia; the consequences of *Brown v. The Board of Education* . . . have changed the . . . institutions and, supremely, the balance of forces within the American Establishment.''

Creativity and tension in a culture usually imply a great deal of accompanying anger. Anger is a thread running through the events of the sixties. Rage names the sixties as much as any other name. In *The Wounded Generation* James Webb says, ''In my opinion, this is the most creative society politically that has ever existed. We are a multicultured society, living side by side in a state of continuous abrasion. On any moral issue, we are going to be at each other's throats, and that's beautiful, because it's creative, as long as we can sort of hold the outer fabric together.'' The abrasion in the sixties was killing. My wife, Elisa, became a strong civil rights worker in South Carolina in 1964. She told me that by 1968, ''the anger everywhere burned me out.''

America then was both a process and a place. It was made up of movements, poets, machines, and I think most importantly the souls scarred and nourished by movement, poet, and machine.

## MOVEMENTS
The movements of the sixties matter because of what they accomplished but perhaps even more because of how they shaped

those of us who participated in them and those of us who followed them in the media. Because we were so young at the time, the basic attitudes formed by these movements among members of the Vietnam generation are likely to endure and govern our attitudes throughout our lives.

In rough terms the chronological sequence in our own lives was civil rights participation and the birth of the Peace Corps, emergence of war protest, emergence of a powerful women's movement, creation of VISTA, and an invigorated environmental movement followed by a proliferation of other important and newly energized movements, notably those focusing on world and domestic hunger and the rights of specific groups including American Indians, Hispanics, and homosexuals.

Alan Brinkley, himself in the generation, teaches a course at Harvard University called "The American Century," covering 1945 to the present. We discussed these movements. He agrees that interconnections among them exist, but he points out that the Vietnam War and civil rights activism developed in a strikingly parallel manner and gradually intertwined, starting in 1954 (Geneva Agreement and the *Brown* v. *Board* antisegregation case), and including 1963 (Diem assassination and Saigon coup; "I have a dream" by Martin Luther King), and 1968 (Tet '68; King, by now an antiwar activist, is assassinated). One of the common threads in the early 1960s through United States civil rights policy, policy in Vietnam, and the birth of the Peace Corps was idealism and a belief in the manageability of great events.

The first stirrings of that idealism begin with freedom riders in the South in 1961. Many of these riders formed a core of activists who created the West Coast free speech movement, centered at the University of California at Berkeley, and which was in turn a core group for the antiwar protest. Tom Hayden actually made these stops in his own personal journey, and Sam Brown has noted the same connections. The role of women received special notice. Lucian Truscott wrote for the *Village Voice* in New York City. He reports the gradual coalescing of many movement activists from among the women in the antiwar protest. Writer Susan Jacoby notes the same trend. The energy and results of work in civil rights and war protest encouraged these women. As the two movements intertwined, some saw differences. Mary King, an early feminist and civil rights activist who became deputy director of ACTION, told me ''the antiwar movement was less antiwar than a don't-draft-me movement. Self was not so important in the civil rights movement; rather, community was important.''

The lasting memories and attitudes from these experiences run very deep. Given their depth and the relative youth and size of our generation, it seems most likely that the effect of the experiences and attitudes is only just beginning to be felt in our country.

There are over eighty thousand returned Peace Corp volunteers, most now in their thirties and forties. David Broder quotes Dick Celeste, a 1963 Peace Corps staffer who was named director of the organization in 1979 by President Carter: ''The experience of having been a part of that is widely shared. And it's a very strong network. It's like Yale Skull and Bones used to be in the Foreign Service, but instead of there being fifteen people a year, this is a network that produces thousands.''

With the distance of time, other trends and common themes are discernible. One has to do with respect and self-esteem. Professors Harold Lasswell and Myres McDougal taught me at Yale Law School that one of the most important governing features of a society is the spoken and unspoken rules with which groups and individuals accord respect to other groups and individuals. To accord respect in the view of these two teachers means to ''bestow recognition for merit in performance in the common interest and to *preclude the arbitrary discrimination irrelevant to merit* which breeds psychopathic personalities with predispositions to violence.'' Surely, in my own mind, the power of the civil rights movement in the early 1960s was the perceived wrong in the diminished respect and self-respect felt by the black American. Eldridge Cleaver's book *Soul on Ice* expressed this outrage. Women felt the same hurt. And the men who returned from Vietnam were expressing it. The stereotypes, barriers to communication, and diminished respect are equally imposing in all three situations.

There seems to be another interconnection having to do with respect. According respect in a way that precludes the arbitrary discrimination irrelevant to merit is a fundamentally democratic and American idea. It is an objective of the kind of freedom John Kennedy spoke of in his inaugural address. Respect among individuals was in this sense one animation of the Peace Corps and VISTA and also of the formative steps in Vietnam policy, as augmented by John Kennedy in 1961–63.

Anger is another common theme. It applied to blacks and Vietnam veterans. And it applies to women: robbing a person of respect is to take away some of her humanity—it is to depersonalize her, to make her appear to herself as an object. In his book *Guilt, Anger and God,* C. Fitzsimmons Allison identifies anger rooted in disesteem as a key to human motivation. Disesteem is diminished self-respect in the sense of judging oneself in an irrelevantly harsh way, often in a way learned from others: "I look in the mirror and do not like what I see—a walking lie, a hypocrite. . . . Disesteem is fundamental to the whole category of human discontents. If self-esteem is strong enough, anger will be more appropriately handled and the self-damaging aspects of human difficulties will be obviated."

Anger is America's Vietnam-era story. Why so much anger? Is the energy and strength that produced it still intact? W. Taylor Stevenson, professor at the Episcopal Church's Seabury-Western Seminary in Evanston, Illinois, brings into the discussion a somewhat scary word: "defilement." There is something in this. Discrimination, exclusion, and broken expectations can make a person feel dirty. Stevenson uses as an example the act of students in raising the Viet Cong or North Vietnamese flags at antiwar rallies. In the *Anglican Theological Review,* he looks first at the scene in *Fields of Fire* by James Webb, where at book's end Goodrich, a young Marine amputee, returns to finish college at Harvard in 1970. He is wheedled by antiwar activists into speaking at an antiwar rally. At the rally he watches as the American flag is hauled down and replaced by a red and blue flag with a gold star in the center. In his mind's eye he sees his comrades who gave their lives in Vietnam. He says to those present at the rally:

IT'S TIME THE KILLING ENDED. I'D LIKE TO
SEE THE WAR END. SOON. ISN'T THAT WHY
YOU CAME HERE? TO TRY AND END IT? THEN

WHY ARE YOU PLAYING THESE GODDAMN
*GAMES?* LOOK AT YOURSELVES. AND THE
FLAG. JESUS CHRIST, HO CHI MINH IS GONNA
WIN. HOW MANY OF YOU ARE GOING TO GET
HURT IN VIETNAM? I DIDN'T SEE ANY OF YOU
IN VIETNAM. I SAW DUDES, MAN. DUDES.
AND TRUCK DRIVERS AND COAL MINERS AND
FARMERS. I DIDN'T SEE YOU. WHERE WERE
YOU? FLUNKING YOUR DRAFT PHYSICALS?
WHAT DO YOU CARE IF IT ENDS? YOU WON'T
GET HURT.

Stevenson cites Paul Ricoeur to the effect that "Dread of the
impure [that which defiles] and rites of purification are the background of all our feelings and all of our behavior relating to
fault." In regard to fault or evil, this dread is "our oldest memory." Stevenson writes:

The examples could be multiplied; we all have our
own. As far as those who actively opposed the war,
however, nothing expresses so clearly and dramati-
cally the rage about Vietnam than the occasional use
of the flag of North Vietnam in antiwar rallies. On
the surface this was taken by participants and observers to be an expression of support for North Vietnam.
It was no such thing. The demonstrators neither cared
about nor even knew anything about North Vietnam.
The point of using the flag was otherwise: It was and
was meant to be an obscenity. It achieved its purpose
very well, as James Webb shows us so well in his
famous scene in *Fields of Fire* depicting the antiwar
rally at Harvard. It is not helpful to interpret the use
of that flag moralistically. Webb doesn't. (He drives
away from the rally with his car smeared with spray
paint.) The use of the flag was a way of saying: We
are the defiled ones. We carry the symbols of defilement. We wish to defile others (make them recognize
their own defilement?). Rage. The "support" of the
flag of North Vietnam and Ho Chi Minh disappeared

about the time the last American helicopter pulled away
from the American embassy in Saigon. They no longer
served the purpose of expressing "our oldest memory."

There is a photograph of Jane Fonda in Hanoi during the Vietnam War, astride a North Vietnamese antiaircraft gun aiming
skyward. The same skies from which Bob Certain fell. The picture is many things, but it is in some sense an expression of defilement. It is hard to find a Vietnam veteran who has not seen
that photograph or heard of it. Jane. Pointing the gun at Tarzan?
This is the woman who posed for Roger Vadim in the glossy
pages of *Playboy* in August of 1966. In the eighties, she celebrates the female body in her bestselling exercise workout book.
And she celebrates the woman's body as womb in her other
bestselling workout book for expectant mothers. Several years
ago, she married Tom Hayden. What will they do with all their
money? Are they still angry? What is their agenda? There is great
sexual tension in the images she forms. In succession she has
employed the powerful symbols of sexual partner, gunner, self-
confident woman, and mother-to-be.

One theme reflected through this succession of symbols is
a feminization of the culture. Jane Fonda's journey is just a sign
of this. In popular culture, war is a largely masculine experience. If the Vietnam War represented a defilement, then in some
sense the fashionability of being a man, and of expressing oneself as a man was eclipsed. Men grew long hair. Some became
"flower children." The language reflected a recoil from the verb
"to tell." Instead one would prefer "to share" an idea. We shrank
from the exercise of power and strength, which in the culture of
our childhood was largely associated with masculinity. The effect is noticeable. David Broder writes that in 1980,

> What was . . . disquieting . . . was the sense I oc-
> casionally had that some of these young people might
> be as uncomfortable giving orders as most of them
> are in taking them. It may be just a stylistic trick, a
> part of their characteristic "cool," but many of them
> felt called upon to deny that their love of politics had

anything to do with the pursuit of power for power's
sake. There is no harm, I suppose, in their striking
such an attitude, as long as they know it is a pose.
For leadership *is* the exercise of power, and leadership is what the country will demand of this generation.

Along with underlying themes of creativity, anger, and a certain
feminization of culture, the movements of the sixties converged
in ways that further entangled the lives of those of us in the war
zone. When long after the war, North Vietnamese commanders
told Richard Armitage that they had kept their eye fixed on political developments back stateside, they expressed a truth which
most GI's sensed in the sixties. "Somehow, the irresolution back
home is jeopardizing me while I'm here." The mechanisms would
be indirect, but wouldn't they tell in some American deaths? There
is the possibility that all things considered, the protest at home
saved lives. Who knows? One thing that matters to a trooper in
war is *his* life *in the next fifteen minutes.* One mechanism of these
deaths was the rigorous controls on American troopers on engagement, pursuit, and free-fire. The rules were implemented and
enforced by use of the complex and effective communications
and data processing network created by the logistical commands
in Vietnam.

The occasional breaches of these rules made sensational
news, sensational because they were exceptional. South Vietnamese lives were saved. But so were lives of the enemy, who
were allowed to escape, return, and kill. Philip Caputo speaks
of defensive fires that could not be made, for these reasons. So
his men were hit. My West Point classmate Sam Bartholomew
would watch the enemy withdraw safely into Cambodia, to be
resupplied off the Ho Chi Minh Trail. One reason for these tight
constraints was certainly the great political vigilance back home.

Another indirect mechanism of our deaths was the but-
tressing of will among North Vietnamese leaders, due to the evident and growing protest at home. Could the Peace Accord have
been signed before 1973, given the American military victory at
Tet '68, if North Vietnamese leaders had found more consensus
for the war stateside? The great movements finally focused in

1968 to dissolve the ability, or will, or both, of the president to successfully correct the misreports in the media that Tet '68 had been a North Vietnamese and Viet Cong military victory. This was unimagined Friendly Fire. Many war protesters felt, and still feel, that they supported the Americans in the field, that they were saving our lives.

Taylor Stevenson is optimistic that the cleansing of these remembered hurts will begin and proceed among our generation. I share his optimism and think that one starting place is sorting out these persisting themes of cause and effect among the movements of the sixties.

Two other common effects of the movements were the adoption of a global and systematic frame of reference for considering national issues, and strengthening the drive to do work that helped others. The global and systematic view is embodied in the environmental movement, and was fed by the photographs from astronauts of our blue-white-tan marbled globe suspended in space. The view infused the thinking of all of us. The urge to help others led to new energy for those concerned with world hunger, Indian and Hispanic rights, gay rights, handicapped rights, and other causes. In fact, Common Cause was born, created by John Gardner and energized by the felt desire to serve, especially among the Vietnam Generation. In law schools young men and women learned how to use the litigating forum to implement social change. At Yale I learned that platoons of young lawyers from Wall Street were at the disposal of Martin Luther King and his successors. Their coordinators were our teachers, including Burke Marshall.

The image I have of these movements is that most of us in the generation were climbing different slopes of a great mountain. Our work had to do with fulfilling commitments and honoring our idealism. Our goals had been shaped by respect and esteem. The work was dangerous. People got hurt or were killed. It was exhausting. Then Vietnam eclipsed everything for a while. The anger of many burned many of us out. No wonder we grew tired. Collectively, we have arrived on a common plateau, together again, intact, mature and experienced. What happens next is in our own hands. We can look around to see where we have been. We can look and decide what future we might choose.

## POETS

The pace and vigor of the movements of the sixties can be remembered or understood only if you hear the music and lyrics
of that decade. What is so striking is the diversity of the growth
of the arts, the way we integrated words, music, and symbols
from the arts into our lives, and the great pleasure so many of
us in the generation find in revisiting the music of the time. We
still find fun and even nourishment in listening to those songs.
The Beach Boys have *always* been in concert.

The Beatles, Janis Joplin, Simon and Garfunkel, Phil Ochs,
Bob Dylan, the Beach Boys, Peter, Paul and Mary, the Kings-
ton Trio, Bobby Darin, the Big Bopper, Elvis, Bill Haley.
American Bandstand. We *invented* rock 'n' roll, country and folk
groups. We *are* rock 'n' roll, country and folk groups. In Vietnam, the American M-16 rifle had a switch for two firing modes,
semiautomatic and automatic. Automatic made the weapon a
machine gun; the GI's called automatic "rock 'n' roll."

"In the clearing stands a boxer and a fighter by his trade."
"The Boxer," Simon and Garfunkel. I hear that song and I think
of Bruns Grayson, the Golden Gloves boxer, knocking at the
door of Harvard. When I received my orders to Vietnam, I was
listening to Simon and Garfunkel's "Seven O'Clock News" on
the cassette player, where a news report of Vietnam War events
and domestic discord is dubbed over the lyrics of "Silent Night."
The war books by Vietnam veterans tell us which songs they
remember.

We learn about each other by telling which songs we love
best. "Punky's Dilemma" is the Simon and Garfunkel song with
the lilting reference to our various movements:

> Wish I was an English muffin,
> 'Bout to make the most out of a toaster. . . .
> I prefer boysenberry more than any ordinary jam.
> I'm a Citizens for Boysenberry Jam fan. . . .

I remember visiting my brother Bob at Yale during his senior
year in spring, 1969. He awaited a draft notice and did not know
where he would be in the fall. A year later, after months of suspended uncertainty, the draft lottery would begin, and his num-

ber would exempt him. The night I visited him he was listening to Janis Joplin's: "Take another little piece of my heart . . ."

This diversity of artistic growth and expression is probably most important as an indicator of our future.

Bob Dylan, Eldridge Cleaver, Betty Friedan, and Germaine Greer articulated our feelings. They were poets to us. Because of the wizardry of TV and mass media, the poet could hold up the mirror to life instantly in (as the computer experts say) "real time."

Poetry incorporates society's myths. The force of the developments in the sixties is expressed by Lance Morrow. He addressed a group of women and men assembled by the Vietnam Veterans Memorial Fund, to discuss reconciliation in the wake of the war. Like Taylor Stevenson, he dwelled on our oldest memory:

> It seems to me what's always important at any given time in the history of the country is its operating myths and what its idea is of itself and what it's doing. Particularly what the young people think they are about. It seems to me that for much of American history, we had a very highly pluralistic and diverse country tending toward one central idea of what it was up to. What happened in the sixties was that the operating myths split apart. You no longer knew what the operative myth was. And so, what was the country up to, what was I as a man up to, what was it all about? The sixties were a terrific mythmaking time, a highly theatrical period.

It is in our generation's hands to establish what myths we have created and altered.

## MACHINES

Technology during the sixties had as much influence on us as the movements or music. There was a rush of development and creativity in the machinery we used.

On July 20, 1969, in Vietnam, I listened on a portable radio to the live broadcast of Neil Armstrong's commentary as he descended the ladder of the lunar module to step onto the moon. It was daylight, early afternoon in Vietnam. I distinctly remember my feelings. *What if something goes wrong? They are so far away.* Then I felt pride in America. *Armstrong is like Columbus.* I also felt united with, yet remote from, my country. *It's night in America; Vietnam is twelve hours away from home.* I wonder if troopers in the bush felt they were on their own moon.

Earthrise from the 1969 lunar base is one of the famous pictures that enabled us to see the world as an interconnected entity. As well, computers made us *feel* interconnected. The cliché of the computer as an instrument of impersonal treatment (the mass-mailed form letter) is false. Computers in complex automated switching centers enable Americans to Touch-Tone–dial anyone at anytime in the United States. The 1980s telephone ad "Reach out and touch someone" rests on the computer technology implemented in the 1960s.

Computers make it possible for us to be treated as individuals even in our roles as members of large groups. On many campuses, financial aid records are put on computers. Scholarships and loans are administered with a clearer view of how the needs and abilities of each student fit into the overall campus profile of needs and abilities. The Army used computers in the same way. The detailed, *daily* tracking of the whereabouts and due date home of each trooper even in a war zone was a humanizing effect of computers.

Computers give immense power to our culture, but the power needs balanced application. The collapse of the go-go years on Wall Street was a scary lesson, one that the young bankers, lawyers, money managers, and Wall Streeters of the sixties will never forget. Several brokerages went bankrupt because the fast growth of trading orders, aided by computers and new communications technology, outstripped the capacity of the computer support in the "back offices," where the paperwork is done after a trade. Insurmountable paperwork backlogs developed.

Computers can speed up life, and either increase our margin for error or decrease it. It depends on how we balance our ability to process the data and the data that results from our decisions.

Jet planes also had a unifying effect, and accelerated the

pace of business. Peter, Paul and Mary (''I'm leavin' on a jet plane. . . .'') and Gordon Lightfoot (''This old airport's got me down. . . .'') focused on the separations caused by leaving, but people have always left. The jet also made trips short in time, speeding returns. In Vietnam we called our homebound jets ''Freedom Birds.'' The revolution in business communication because of the jet was thorough. One key to the success of Fred Smith's Federal Express company is the use of the company's own fleet of jets, all flying at night, when passenger travel is light and the airport and air traffic control systems can more easily accommodate the traffic of Federal Express and its competitors. In a poetic sense, at sundown the American airnet transforms and becomes the full embodiment of the power of air communication that we glimpsed in Vietnam.

Medical technology accelerated in the same Vietnam war years. Lifesaving machines began to proliferate during the period. Heart-lung machines became more available. Organ transplants were no longer rare. We saw successive revelations of how the intertwined modules of DNA work as the genetic code for building up the human body.

Some of the advances in medical technology seemed scary. There is a radical effect of this knowledge upon those of us who came of age in the sixties. Quietly, implicitly we understood what was coming: the human body *as machine* became a contemporary concept. A baby could be conceived without a father present. The baby could develop without a mother present. In a sense, penis and testicle, vagina and womb were machines replaceable by alternate technologies. In the absurd and extreme, a society could at some point subcontract all baby creation to a huge corporation or administrative organization. In fact, the genetic structure of the child could be selected. By 1969, this was already evident in research on some forms of animal life.

The surprise is that this radical technology has a humanizing message. The technology of our bodies has always been integral to our lives together, but only part of our lives together. More important is that we face each other and *choose* to have relationships with each other. The real issue is commitment. The technology of our bodies is one strong way to enter and build relationships. But bonding is paramount.

In the sixties, we glimpsed this reality. Our new knowl-edge about the machinery of life stripped things bare. We do not *have* to bond for procreation. Woman and man do not *have* to love. We realized, subconsciously, something that has always been true, that bonding, child rearing, family, and love are mat-ters of choice.

## SOULS

For choosing among the different futures before us, what mat-ters most is how our history influenced us. If we each under-stand how our past shapes us, we can govern how our past shapes us. Collectively as a generation if we understand how our past shapes us, then together we can govern how our past shapes us. We can select among our possible futures, with better hope of achieving the life we want.

I think that the beginning for each of us is to crystallize our memory of how those events of the sixties made us feel and act. This is an individual undertaking.

Journals of antiwar protesters recount the heat of protest, as do stories by civil rights and women's movement marchers. But these reflect only a portion of the human beings among us then. Twenty million men in the generation faced the draft in uncertainty, eventually not to go into uniform. My brother was one of them. The uncertainty of the draft in 1966–69 was hell. It was almost like a possible death sentence. For some of the men who did not go into the military there is now a feeling of having missed something, of not having been present for the acute suffering and testing. For the men who used direct and indirect means to deliberately avoid the draft, the acts of youth take on new significance. What example is shown to sons? To daugh-ters? To voters? Nonveteran writers like Sam Brown, Michael Blumenthal, Christopher Buckley, and James Fallows have be-gun to put their thoughts about all this into print. Little is said by men who were among the seven million to wear the uniform, but did not go into the war zone. Yet military service of any kind is a significant shaping experience. The relative silence on these topics shows how sensitive they are. The fact that these writers are now surfacing is a sign.

Amid the welter of confusion and change in the sixties, I

think great hurts were overlooked. In the preoccupations of the movements, the loneliness and separation caused by the war—any war—were not widely felt. This kind of pain was unfashionable, for instance, the pain suffered by women in love with men who were serving in Vietnam. These women, their parents and in-laws felt terribly alone. Peg and Gene Mullen were exceptions in expressing their agony. It must have been hell for over seventeen million wives, lovers, children, parents, in-laws, brothers, and sisters of the three million of us who went into the war zone.

Lynda Siegel Zengerle graduated from Smith College in 1966. In Washington, she met and married Joe, who went to Vietnam, into the teeth of Tet '68. She and Joe now practice law in Washington as partners in major law firms. Their children, two sons, Jason and Tucker, are ten and five. Lynda Zengerle:

> When Joe was in Vietnam and I was working here in Washington, I was an economist with the Arms Control and Disarmament Agency, so we were really on opposite sides of the effort. I was trying to stop the war and he was in Vietnam, not necessarily because he wanted to be, but because he had to be. I was a woman alone in Washington. I had no friends or family here when I came. I just sort of met people while I was here. I was often invited to cocktail parties and dinner parties where people would come and say, "Well, where is your husband?" Back in the sixties that's how you were identified. I would answer, "He's in Vietnam." Talk about a conversation killer! I was left alone so quickly. I would look around and, all of a sudden, nobody would be talking to me. They didn't want to know about it, they didn't want to hear about it. I was a pariah, and it was not just Joe that was an outcast—I was outcast. There was nobody that I could talk to in 1968 except other Army wives, and I was not living on a military base. I was not affiliated in any way. I was not one to put on white gloves and hats to go to teas; I just didn't have any of those con-

nections. I was really isolated. That was the whole
beginning of my realization of what was done to me.

When Joe came back, one of the first things I said
to him was that *he was not the only one out there who
was being touched by all of this.* As worried as I was
about him, I was angry about the way people were
treating me just because my husband was over there.
And these people were all young professionals, these
were not kids on college campuses.

At the future site of the Vietnam Veterans Memorial on the Mall
in Washington a ceremony was held on Memorial Day, 1980.
There was a large crowd. We asked those who wanted to, to
step before a microphone and speak the name of a loved one
killed in Vietnam. The line was long. I saw one woman, slender
and strong, come forward with two little girls. One of the girls
uttered her father's name.

Months later Bob Doubek, the Memorial Fund project director, told me about several widows who had volunteered to
help with administrative tasks. I phoned a volunteer on the list,
Donna Seay. She said she remembered me. She was the mother
with the two little girls. Her husband who was killed in action
was Air Force fighter pilot Bob Swenck. My phone call was on
Good Friday, 1981.

Later, Donna Seay spoke at the Memorial Fund's seminar
on women, men, and reconciliation:

I'd like to make a statement, and this is going to be
my last statement. I really appreciate your letting me
participate in this. I've been able to communicate with
a generation that I've never communicated with before, and listened to a lot of your ideas, now that
you're grown up. You were children, you know, when
I was watching all this on television and disliking every
one of you for doing what you were doing. I appreciate the guys of the Vietnam Memorial Fund letting
me have the opportunity to put Major Robert B.
Swenck's name on a memorial. And I'm really sincere when I say this, this is my last statement. After

the memorial I'm going to start rebuilding my life, because I'm going down on the other side of the hill now. Up until a few years ago, I was going uphill like you are. Now I'm going over to the other side.

And Lance Morrow said in the same conversation,

It seems to me that after the Civil War, after World War I especially, less so after World War II, but after the Civil War, guys came home deeply, profoundly disillusioned, deeply, profoundly alienated. After World War I even more so. You had a whole literature of tremendous alienation: Robert Graves, e. e. cummings, just tremendous psychic pain and alienation, and terrific battlefield horror in both wars. Is Vietnam any different, and if so, how? How is it different? How is it different in its effect upon the people who fought it?

The answers to Lance's questions lay in the length of the Vietnam War, the longest in our history, in the vast size and shared events of our generation, and in the flood of change *in America* during the very period of the war. This concatenation is unique in power and in history. It molded and divided a generation under fierce pressure. The pressure was the pressure of a creative revolution of movements, poetry, and machines—politics, the arts, and technology. What is also different, in fact unique in history, is that in the 1980s we have begun to recognize these influences while we are still young, and flexible enough to heal our wounds.

*One night in late 1969, Jeff Rogers and I were walking through Long Binh, Vietnam. He spoke of his wife, Susie, an energetic and attractive Army spouse, daughter of a career Army officer. Jeff pointed at the constellation Orion and said, "I see that every night from our perimeter down below Phan Rang. Orion moves a little as the seasons change. When it has moved over there to the east, I'll be home. I'll see Susie." He did not say what we both thought: would Jeff live so long? There had already been the day he led the troops up the mountain. They were pinned down by rifle fire from the next adjacent peak. Jeff's troopers froze. They had to move or die. He went up past the point man and led by example, bullets striking the rocks around him.*

*Later, in the spring of 1970 Jeff stayed in my hootch on his last night before catching the jet home. It was Saturday. We had a drink. We went back to my room. "Here, you take the cot," I said. He was still in his fatigues and boots, saving his tan uniform and shoes for the flight. "No. The floor. Just like the bush. It's fine. Really." We talked late into the night. My eyes opened. Dawn. I looked down. Fatigues and boots on the floor, as if Jeff had flowed out of them. The tans and shoes were gone. He was gone.*

# CHAPTER FOUR

*Walking through the ruins of these cities, thinking
of their own country, they have become prophets,
and their message is not very different from the
message of the ancient Hebrew prophets.*

Paul Tillich, on American soldiers in
World War II: *Shaking of the Foundations*

*At the site of the Memorial, on Memorial Day,
May 26, 1980, a ceremony was held in which people
were invited to join a line and speak in turn the
name of a man who was killed in Vietnam—a brother,
a father, a friend, a husband. There was an eleven-
year-old boy who spoke his father's name. There was
a mother, thirty-five or so, with two little girls; one
of the girls uttered her father's name. And there was
a weeping woman, in uniform, who spoke her husband's name. Then an old soldier came up and spoke
the name of a battalion commander felled in Vietnam.*

*The pain, the reality, and the brokenness were
there for all to see. And the barriers to learning
and the need for reconciliation were there for all
to see as well. The important thing was to hear
the power of a name, while sensing the pain. But
in fact this country has not wept yet over this
war's dead. We still deny them. We fought, angry
and divided. As yet, we have not wept over, nor
said to the war's dead . . . goodbye.*

Vietnam Veterans Memorial Fund
Design Competition Booklet

# COMING HOME

To us the most important reception on coming home from Vietnam was the reception by our peers. They had been the generation we grew up with. The cues and attitudes we picked up from them would naturally continue to overshadow support our parents gave us and whatever formal statements of thanks or recognition we received from the armed forces.

The wonderful thing to me is that for the overwhelming number of guys who came back from Vietnam, there were, in time, women who loved them making a vast difference in their lives. For Jeff and Joe, there are Susie and Lynda. Phil Caputo said about his wife, Jill,

> I was shortly out of the Marines. I remember we were in a restaurant and I was looking at everybody, and I knew what was going on over there, and in fact I had recently heard of one who had gotten killed. And I was watching everybody eating dinner and they were all well dressed and everything, and she said, "What's the matter?" And I said, "Let's get out of here. In about two minutes I'm going to get up and start busting heads." And I think that . . . that the reason I married the girl I did was because she was the only person I could be around that I didn't feel like breaking her jaw.

Bobby Muller, brutally wounded and a paraplegic, said about Virginia, "Were it not for the fact that I met the woman who is my wife, I'd be dead today, I am convinced. . . . My wife literally has saved my life through finding the love that we've developed in our relationship and the ability to temper what's in me and give it a practical and effective application." Dean Phillips recovered from being wounded as a long-range-recon team member. He says, "If I've adjusted at all, it's been because of my wife. She just passed the Virginia Bar. Now she's a lawyer. I met her when she was an emergency-room nurse. She took care of me pretty well, I guess. If there's stability in my life, it's mainly because of Carla."

This was also true in my life. Elisa and I met at a picnic in 1972. From our first conversation, I dwelled only lightly on Vietnam. Like me, she did not know how *much* it had meant to me. On the eve of our tenth wedding anniversary, Elisa said, "I knew you were in Vietnam, but I did not know what a difference it made."

The returning veteran would not recognize how formative his year had been. America signaled, through every one-on-one conversation we had, that we were not to discuss the war, it was so painful. So for us who came back, I think we tended to keep to ourselves the fresh perspective, creativity, energy, and idealism that accompanied our war experience. We tended to keep our sense of loss and grief inside of us, too. To others, including those who love us, and especially to those outside our generation, what has been mostly visible for ten years are the wounds, which while real are only part of the truth. Things like amputation stumps, Seeing Eye dogs, rash behavior by severely disturbed Vietnam veterans, guys who still live in jungle fatigues and get angry when they perceive the massive (but not cruelly deliberate) investment that individual Americans have made in devaluing our experiences in Vietnam, or in criticizing our choices and motives during that time. Many of our peers who did not wear the uniform treated our homecoming with silence.

But the creativity is there nonetheless, in the young computer entrepreneurs in California's "Silicon Valley," Apple Computer, and the movies brought out by George Lucas, Steven Spielberg, and Sherry Lansing, the writing of John Del Vecchio, Philip Caputo, Tim O'Brien, and James Webb, and the instinct of humor in Jim Henson's "Muppets," Cathy Guisewhite's "Cathy," Garry Trudeau's "Doonesbury," and Lynn Johnston's "For Better or for Worse."

"It's alright, Ma, I'm only bleeding," Bob Dylan's lyric.

The wound looks bad, but the interior is what matters. Phil said he felt anger but "I don't know why." This is all natural, I think. Ten years is not a surprisingly long time for intense emotions to simmer in each of us. One reason for the silence and the delayed recognition is that each of us in the generation lost something in the sixties, while we were young. Many Vietnam veterans gave up a great deal. Kris Kristofferson, a former Army helicopter pilot, put this into the lyric of "Me and Bobby McGee": "Freedom's just another word for nothing left to lose." In Vietnam we shared a common joke: if things went wrong, and somebody up the chain of command was upset, we said to each other, "What're they gonna do, *send us to Vietnam?*" No one could touch us. We'd done been touched. In 1983, on her television show *Frontline,* Jessica Savitch showed a documentary film of the events in Washington, D.C., during the 1982 National Salute to Vietnam Veterans. In the myriad images, there is a fleeting vignette: a guy about thirty-five years old saunters up to another guy in a hotel lobby, cocks his head, salutes, and says "One more Marine reporting in, sir. I spent my time in hell." Hell is being or feeling separated from others. Vietnam was some hell, but we troops had each other. Back in America the real hell began because we were atomized, split up and disbanded. Feeling or being separated from others is a kind of wound. But along with the pain it can make you stronger and provide a fresh perspective. It is a kind of blessing. The French word for "to wound" is *blesser.*

Acceptance is one thing, understanding is another. Why were some like Phil Caputo so angry, while others in our generation were so resolute in their silence? These core questions affect the intimacy in relationships. Couples in which a partner is a Vietnam veteran need to sort out the hidden effects of the Vietnam experience, including the strengthening effects, so that intimate acceptance can be married with intimate understanding. I think Vietnam-era choices also affect couples in which the man avoided the draft or shrugged off involvement in the great movements of the sixties. The effects are probably most obvious where there are children to teach. In large part, the core questions underlie differences among the generation that subtly but firmly divide us from each other, and even from parts of ourselves.

The shock for a lot of us coming home was the gradual realization over the first few hours, then days, that there was a social taboo against our experience.

**FIRST DAY**

On July 1, 1970, I shed my fatigues, put on the tan uniform, and boarded the jet. The Army did not tell me my next assignment, except that it was to be in Washington, D.C. At twenty-five, I was an old man on the plane, maybe the oldest. There were few officers. I was a captain. I might have been ranking man both by age and grade. Some months earlier, a Huey had picked me up to fly me to a site outside Long Binh. It was a Sunday morning. I was reflective. The next oldest man on board was the aircraft commander, a warrant officer about twenty years old. The copilot looked younger. The two helicopter door gunners were eighteen or nineteen. I was in a war machine piloted by a guy younger than my own kid brother. This was all right, since in a Huey, reflexes really helped. Looking forward out of the Huey, with the big Plexiglas screen and all the dials, is like looking at a video game. In fact, with the exquisitely tight and complex constraints placed on the Army, the whole war took on aspects of a video game: engage here, do not engage there; fire here, and you are punished; but miss the enemy there and he will kill you; assume these people to be neutral civilians, but assume those to be daytime friends and nighttime foes. Reflexes helped.

That chopper flight marked the day I became a stick-in-the-mud. Parachuting and flying, I say with a smile, lost their romance. It's not that I don't believe in Bernoulli's principle (a fluid, like air, generates lift in flow over an airfoil, like a helicopter blade or a wing). It's just that you're so *vulnerable* up there. "But, Jackson," my dad always says, "I fly all the time, and I've never been left stuck up there. You *always* come back down. . . . Hey, do you want to live forever?" He called Army aviation, TWA—Teeny-Weeny Airlines. He earned his laughter in airborne reconnaissance while running strikes against the Ho Chi Minh Trail. "Gemmun," the old sergeant said in a West Point summer, "they's a thousand ways to dah. One of 'em is Mr. Charles [the enemy]. The rest is because you are dumb. Your brains are off. You are slow and sloppy.'' Reflexes. The closest that I know death came to me, reflexes wouldn't have helped. A rocket blew the medical unit at USARV to smithereens. It could just as well have been my hootch. Bruns came home to his hootch one night to count thirty shrapnel holes all through the cots, walls and lockers. A big black puff mushroomed under my helicopter one afternoon. We rollercoasted up and down. I looked at the starry smoke trails. The only cause for the explosion I can piece together is that an in-flight American artillery round prematurely detonated under us.

At 4:30 a.m., I stepped onto the dark field at Travis Air Force Base. I peered out, but could not see the C-141's and the caskets. Everything I had was in the kit bag in my hand. Bruns was up at 4 a.m. to meet me, just like he'd written. We had some coffee, waiting for my clearance to go on leave. He was painting his parents' house in Alameda. At dawn, we drove past San Francisco, the Golden Gate, and Marin County to his home.

My main feeling was that I wanted to belong again. I wanted to fit in with America, which in my imagination and over the radio and on television in Vietnam had seemed to pull away like a ship. The mass rock gathering at Woodstock in August, 1969, epitomized the evidence that my country was changing. Confirmation lay in the conflagration of protest over the attacks on the North Vietnamese communication line in Cambodia.

I was tired. Bruns arranged for me to sleep at his sister and brother-in-law's home. At his sister's he put on some new records. Although I was dropping from exhaustion, Bruns filled me in on how Jimi Hendrix's lyrics recounted the changes in our country; I couldn't hear. I was going to sleep, with the new sunshine just breaking into the living room window. I remembered how in Long Binh we had all hustled over to Bruns' hootch when his sister sent him the new Beatles album, *Abbey Road*. ''Maxwell's Silver Hammer'': now *that* was a song that spoke to troops in-country (''Clang, clang, Maxwell's silver hammer came down upon his head . . .'').

Bruns returned. It was late afternoon. ''Mom has a supper for us. She really wants to meet you.''

At her kitchen table, Helen Grayson served Bruns and me

a fresh roasted tom turkey, with potatoes and gravy and stuffing and rolls, and wine.

(In Mrs. Grayson's eyes and expressions, I saw Bruns' eyes and expressions. When Bruns married Penny, I went over to Helen during the reception and whispered, "Now relax; I think Bruns is going to turn out *just fine.*" She laughed and hugged my arm, because she understood; she and Bruns and many friends and I had passed through the narrow gate of Vietnam, in a defeat of death, and found new life.)

This fellowship with a Vietnam veteran was my first bond to home. If there are three million of us, then this kind of story was repeated over two million times. In America, we were travelers in a strange land, finding and helping each other as we could.

At the Radisson hotel in Wilmington, Delaware, in July of 1981, I sat at another table in the same sense of fellowship. I had driven up to meet Wayne Hanby and David Huffman for lunch. They were considering working for the Vietnam Veterans Leadership Program. This was the beginning, the first guys willing to think about joining. We would attempt to defeat the false stereotypes of Vietnam veterans and mobilize the civic leaders of the community to open career-potential jobs to Vietnam veterans on a nationwide scale. This was staggering optimism, given who we were. We were three men, three brains, three good eyes, and five hands. Six feet. David had finished law school and was in a law firm. Wayne was a judge.

When I called Wayne, the answering machine clicked on: "It's the last inning . . . Hanby's softball team is losing two to one . . . bases are loaded . . . two outs . . . Wayne swings . . . it's a hard shot . . . shortstop picks up the ball, throws to first. Wayne is out!"

At lunch he explained that he had always loved and played baseball. He managed a local team. The tape was for his young daughters, who liked surprise tapes. His hand was curled around his right eye, the one with some vision. It funneled the light so he could make out some of my features. It was guys blinded in battle who rushed in first to help with the Leadership Program.

The joke around town was that as an equal-opportunity initiative VVLP wanted to bring in some *sighted* guys, but the directors Bill Jayne, Ed Timperlake, and Wheeler were so ugly the sighted veterans all stayed away. I think that Wayne and David responded to the fellowship that has been the key of the Program. David left his firm and Wayne resigned the bench to organize programs in Delaware and Washington. Blinded Marines. They gave me confidence. Unanticipated strength and support is one sign that things are developing under good providence. The New Testament nigger was the man from Samaria. Why not the man from Vietnam? Wayne and David were signing on. They were helping *me* sign on. We became fishers of men. Jesus included fellowship and leadership in his teaching. He said, "Follow me, and I will make you fishers of men." That is one view of leadership taught in the military and at West Point: you will become a fisher of men. The motto on the statue of the Army infantryman at Fort Benning is "Follow Me!"

A fourth man was present, in a way, at the lunch—the president of the United States. A few days before, Tom Pauken had forwarded to him our one-page decision memorandum on VVLP. That night, President Reagan looked over our memo recommending the three-year program, and ending with three options:

—— APPROVE    —— DISAPPROVE    —— HOLD

The memo was returned with initials in the "approve" blank: RR. I think the president must have smiled at these guys approaching him with this six-million-dollar domestic-spending initiative, right in the midst of his budget-reduction effort. I believe he recognized that the VVLP rested on fellowship and that the money was the least part of the program.

## FIRST WEEK
Bruns and I went to see the movie *Woodstock*. I felt odd in civilian clothes. The movie was kaleidoscopic, showing hundreds of thousands of people my age at a days-long rock 'n' roll picnic, with big-name singers from all over America. The film and sound work were brilliant. The unmistakable theme was celebration of freedom, personal and sexual.

From the first day, I realized that I did not fit easily back into America. During the first week I began to feel isolated and strange. In part, because of the natural inability to instantly assimilate and store away my war zone attitudes and experiences. My Uncle Sam could move my body back at jet speed, but my spirit listed where it would, taking a slower trip home.

Shock and lag. In the sixties the term "culture shock" described the disorientation we feel when we travel quickly from one culture to another. It was one preoccupation of the Peace Corps: how to prepare the volunteers for entry into a radically different culture and then, after the tour, *how to bring them back smoothly,* so that the volunteers' experiences and attitudes learned in one culture could be combined gracefully and in an enriching way, with the volunteers' reentry. It was tricky. It was a process that took time. Alvin Toffler expanded the idea in his book *Future Shock,* with the thesis that by the sixties the pace of societal change was outdistancing the American in America. The culture was changing so fast that we each experienced our own culture shock without leaving town.

Besides obvious differences, one key difference between the war zone culture and the stateside culture was the underlying role of commitments and promises. In Vietnam a common thread, rarely spoken of, was that the presence of each of us included the aspect of keeping a promise, even though it was unpleasant and hard to keep. In America in the sixties the fashion ran somewhat against the discipline of commitment. Institutions became suspect, as did the old-fashioned promises to the ideals embodied in institutions. Marriage is in a sense an institution. Sexual fidelity and the permanence of marriage both took a beating in the sixties. At Harvard Business School, we learned that in the first five years after graduation, many graduates switched companies three times in the quest for more responsibility and a higher salary. "Seasoning" in the job was not the custom.

There was simultaneously an emphasis in the popular culture on self-fulfillment, on pleasing oneself, using self-fulfillment as one important standard for making choices, including moral choices. This probably had some effect in accelerating the sexual revolution and the broad, open resistance to the draft. By contrast, in the war zone there was somewhat more emphasis on group fulfillment, on the sense of identifying oneself as part of a small group of peers or friends. Often this identification took the form of valor, as troopers like Donald Ballard or Hector Santiago-Colon or officers like Tommy Hayes and Walter Levy threw themselves in harm's way for the men they served with. This attitude infused the whole American war zone culture, in ways which demonstrated a strong sense of interdependence. Logistics *is* the recognition and management of interdependence. Probably the best example of this awareness was air support. In the tropical midnight bush a battalion could call in a B-52 strike in urgent situations. Naval, Marine, and Air Force fighter pilots were on call always to come make the mountains shake and the earth burn, where the enemy hid. In turn, air base perimeters were kept secure from attack by riflemen. This sense of interdependence was possible due to the disparate technologies: riflemen sweating in the jungle; pilots moving fast in flying machines. *We are in this fight together and we protect each other.*

Another key difference lay in intimacy. In Vietnam for almost all of us there was at least one friend to confide in. He knew you were afraid, and why. In America, the Vietnam veteran typically was instantly separated from war buddies and sent home. In a way, the men we shared our war zone life with were a part of our family. Reestablishing this intimacy with others became difficult because of the societal taboo on recounting our personal experiences in Vietnam. Again, this taboo was natural and understandable in that it held at bay the painful reality of war, but it also held at bay for many Vietnam veterans a new intimacy founded on mutual understanding. Fortunately, there was intimacy to be found with the women who *accepted* us, even if *understanding* would have to be long delayed.

This culture shock was felt even by career military people who accepted new military assignments in America. Donna said when Bob Swenck "came back from Vietnam, he was not Bob anymore. For years I have tried to understand why he had the compulsion to go back. He didn't have to go back. And then I realized that he had to be part of the team. What he saw in the States he could not relate to. . . . He was asked once to speak before . . . his old high school graduating class, but not to wear his uniform."

Clothes are important. Having been in Vietnam, the B-school, and West Point, I did not have much of a casual wardrobe. Jeans, open shirts, and flashy cloth belts were the craze. What Bruns did in taking me to see *Woodstock* was to serve up what, in his best judgment, was a description of America as it related to men our age. I noticed the clothes, the attitudes, the available sex. The music picked you up and made you move. I wanted to be part of it but felt like a hick in Paris.

On screen Jimi Hendrix played the "Star-Spangled Banner" on his electric guitar. I took it as a patriotic act, done in protest. It was interesting to hear which songs the entertainers chose. John Sebastian sang to a newborn baby. Joan Baez sang "Amazing Grace." After Thanksgiving supper with Bruns, her song is my signal memory of my first week back in America.

The lyric bottoms on Christian faith. Stephen Neil, missionary bishop of Tinnevelly in India, wrote that grace is "forgiveness and enabling power." Grace is one of the great building blocks of faith. "I once was blind but now I see," she sang. It makes me think now of Hanby, Huffman and Szumowski. "I once was lost . . . ." Rick Eilert in Ward Three South, his leg at risk with thirty-five operations to go. The lore among Vietnam veterans is that journalist Colonel William Corson, United States Marine Corps, retired, discovered Rick and the story of Three South and vowed not to die until Rick's story was published.

The next day Bruns drove me to the airport. I flew to Los Angeles to meet Han Swyter, B-School '65 and my boss for the Pentagon biological warfare analysis. Han had become a real estate developer, working for a company owned by the recently bankrupt Penn Central, the greatest American bankruptcy. New, harsh lessons for B-Schoolers. This was the collapse of the go-go era. Woodstock and Penn Central: America was in a tumble dryer on a long cycle. We had exchanged letters all through my year in Vietnam. We flew together to Dulles Airport in Washington, D.C. Han was starting his own company in Washington. I invested. I put five thousand dollars into Han's new company and the rest, in years to come, in Elisa's engagement ring and wedding band, and tuition at Yale Law School. It was a way of carrying new life out of the war zone.

Mom, Dad, Janet Marie and Bob met me at the airport. I introduced them to Han, who then slipped away. Like when she first looked me over on December 14, 1944, Mom checked for toes, fingers, ears, and eyes. I think that for mothers their son's homecoming is like another birth. I was glad to be home. The next day Bob drove me down to hip Georgetown. He supervised my purchase of (a) a woven earth-tone yellow and red fabric belt with a ring buckle, (b) handcrafted leather sandals with leather loops for the big toe, and (c) Levi jeans. Schooled at Yale during the season of Bobby Seale, Black Panthers, the first class of Yale women, and the cool Kingman Brewster, Bob helped me pass into the culture so that at least I did not *look* strange.

## FIRST YEAR

I could list names from memory for an hour: David Huffman, Larry Pressler, David Szumowski, Chuck Robb, Tom Ridge, Tom Pauken, Sam Bartholomew, Bobby Muller, Dean Phillips, James Webb, Chuck O'Brien, Terry O'Donnell, Mark Treanor, Sandy Mayo, and John Morrison—all went to law school. Referring to Officer Candidate School, Peter Braestrup told me *"law school was OCS for you Vietnam veterans."* ORDERS: DEPART RVN REPORT LAW SCHOOL. Or business school. Ed Miller, running Island Courier, a Caribbean Federal Express; Townsend Clarke, West Point's all-American linebacker now at Eaton; Bill Murdy now at Morgan Stanley; Bob Carpenter, running Integrated Genetics, a genetic biological engineering company; Rick Sonstelie, at Puget Sound Power & Light. Or into medicine. Or writing. Or the National Football League, like Roger Staubach, Annapolis '65, Dallas Cowboy and Navy Vietnam veteran. He wears a Superbowl Championship ring, just like Rocky Bleier, Pittsburgh Steelers, wounded in action in Vietnam en route to the Superbowl.

I met Charles and Lynda Robb at a Georgetown party in late 1970 or early '71. I met Chuck again in 1982 when as governor of Virginia and a former Marine combat company commander from Vietnam he spoke at groundbreaking of the Vietnam Veterans Memorial. He used no notes, and looking directly at the crowd, he told about the bleeding men he had held in his arms. The power of his remarks may have surprised even Chuck.

Like a mama St. Bernard the memory of the war zone grabs us by the scruff of the neck, yanking us from where we thought we were. As we walked off the speaker's platform, Chuck asked, "Where now?" Our shovels were set in a line of shovels across twenty yards of muddy ground. Each of one hundred and twenty of us would simultaneously turn the earth, in a line that traced the two arms of the Memorial. I could not resist the truth, with a laugh: "Over there, Marine. Through the mud. Like the old days."

Given the America we saw with fresh eyes, it is my opinion that most veterans turned inward for a while. Consequently, their creative energy has only recently become visible. For a lot of us, this inward focus meant that we quietly planned graduate schooling, started businesses without fanfare, and invested emotionally in marriages and rearing children. For others it meant learning to use our bodies again. For others, this inward focus meant a poorly understood isolation and a succession of hassles in finding work. In any case, we found ourselves set on a course of shaping our own life pretty much alone after the very unsettling experience of Vietnam. In retrospect, the armed forces could have eased in some limited way or at least illuminated the journey for us with a four- or five-day "decompression" and counseling session en route home from Vietnam. Yet realistically, no one back in the late sixties and early seventies visualized the gulf. Plus, the focus of the trooper was HOME. Who could have concentrated on anything else during a days-long decompression course? A follow-up a year later could have helped, but again, who recognized the depth of the problem? And at that point most of the veterans were out of uniform and spread all over the country. But in future wars, the country should consider how to cope with decompression. The fortuitous decompression that occurred on troop ships after World War I and II does not automatically apply in jet planes.

Still, like our fathers after World War II, we brought back from our war zone experience tremendous creativity and capacity for service. But unlike our fathers, we put down new roots and nurtured them in isolation with wife, family, or lover, without public support. Nevertheless, for the majority of us the important resources were at hand: the women who accepted us, GI

Bill educational benefits, training for amputees and blinded men, and monthly disability payments for those disabled, retired, or discharged due to various handicaps. The major difference between us and our fathers was the popular attitude of our peers. We represented in the sixties and seventies a painfully unfashionable and burdensome side of life. We were a reproach to affluent parents whose sons avoided wartime service, for whatever reason. We were a reproach to men who dodged the draft, for whatever reason. In *The Four Georges,* Thackeray writes, "Bravery never goes out of fashion." We numbered among us demonstrably brave men in a society where that truth made people nervous. Allan Bakke applied to medical school in California, but was turned down, ostensibly for age. He was a Marine veteran of Vietnam. Two members on the admissions board were reported to have felt strongly against admitting him because he had been a Marine. When Dean Phillips applied to graduate school, Dean said one admissions professor did not want any Vietnam veterans accepted.

The first year home marked the beginning of our journey. At its end, over a decade later, our situation was changing. In fact, politicians our age would try to trade on our experience by joining the reserves in the 1980s or by letting the fact that they wore the uniform stateside be interpreted as a tour of duty in Vietnam. Nevertheless, society is not particularly interested in *who we are.* The first thing we should do is walk off the treadmill of our Vietnam experience. Bravery gives men authority in any culture. *It was so hard to embrace us that instead some Americans embraced surrogates who also displayed commitment and bravery: the Viet Cong and the North Vietnamese Regular soldier.* No wonder that in those lonely first years a lot of veterans were despondent. America for the returning Vietnam veteran was a furnace in which hellish fires of separation from others and from self burned a lot of us up. Yet if the heat is higher, the steel that is extruded is stronger.

At a party in Washington in July, 1970, a woman asked where I worked. I said I was not sure what my assignment would be. I was just back from Vietnam.

"Oh, is it like on the television news?"

## GRIEF

In the mornings, John Wheeler, six years old, gets dressed with me. We shine shoes, listen to the radio, brush our teeth, talk. We shared a shovel at groundbreaking of the Vietnam Veterans Memorial. He wore his yellow Tonka-toy hard hat. Six months later, one spring morning he introduced a new subject to our talks.

"I wouldn't want to be in a war." His face was serious. He was looking out the window.

"Why?" I asked.

"Because, it's so painful."

The hard journey we took deepened the sense of compassion among the Vietnam veterans I know. Marcia Landau, a war protester in the sixties, handles media relations for the VVLP in Washington. She noted that many veterans told her about the plight of children they had seen in Vietnam. She mentioned that one common quality among the men who worked in the Program was compassion, "an identity with how women or poor people can feel." She gave as an example Paul W. "Buddy" Bucha, a volunteer in the New York VVLP. West Point '65, he found himself in Vietnam as an infantry company commander with his men, surrounded and cut off. He held them together for a day and night, crawling alone to rescue a group of isolated wounded. He told them to feign death and wait until the morning when he could crawl out to them and lead them to safety. His company held, inflicting over eighty enemy casualties. For his action he earned the Medal of Honor. Marcia is right. Because of their own experiences Vietnam veterans are attuned to the great hurts of discrimination and spiritual and material hunger in our country.

For the past decade, Vietnam veterans had to repress the part of their identity formed in Vietnam, in the sense that we were not to articulate that part of our life or to affirm it as a strengthening part of our life experience. It was the last thing we surrendered, after giving up the public esteem of our peers, two or more years of our lives, parts of our bodies, and our former starting place on the career ladder of civilian economic success. When the popular press described us, the Iron Law of Image turned us into people to feel sorry for, people to help. As in Tet '68 the popular image was based on true but partial, incomplete analysis. The Big Story in 1968 was that Charles had been annihilated. It was as if *no one wanted the truth*. In 1978, the partial but true picture of Vietnam veterans was of men in urgent need of help. The Big Story was the countless, individual ways they were invigorating society.

An unexpected source of help came from the gentle hands of the old men from the World War II and Korean War generations. An example is judicial clerkships, the plum jobs for law school graduates, where you learn the inner workings of the courts. By the late seventies, I could not help but wonder at the flood of Vietnam veterans moving through law schools and into the chambers of federal judges, the custodians and important final arbiters of American legal values. The Vietnam veterans did well in law school, but I think that their flow into chambers was so broad and fast in the 1970s that their success must be partially linked with the judicial perception of the value of the veteran. Joe Zengerle clerked for the Chief Justice. Joe clerked first for Circuit Judge Carl McGowan. Rhesa ("Rees") Barksdale, West Point '66 and number one at Ole Miss law school, wounded and cited for valor in Vietnam, was brought in by Justice Byron White. Circuit Judge Edward Tamm brought in Bob Kimmitt; Circuit Judge Roger Robb brought in Nicholas Glakas; District Judge Oliver Gasch brought in Joe Cornelison. And Circuit Judge George MacKinnon brought in John Wheeler. John Shad, a Navy assault control officer during the Kamikaze attacks in the Okinawa landings and Harvard MBA '49, would later as chairman of the Securities and Exchange Commission bring me back from the VVLP to serve as his special counsel.

Justice Oliver Wendell Holmes, Jr., said that "if we would be worthy of the past, we must find new fields for action or thought, and make for ourselves new careers." He had been wounded three times in the Civil War. His father, Oliver Sr. *(The Autocrat of the Breakfast-Table),* wrote a famous article in the *Atlantic Monthly* during the war about searching the dreaded trains and camps for his son, not knowing if he would find a body or a wounded boy. The junior Holmes came home to applause and welcoming arms, although, as James Fallows wrote, "The contemporaries of Oliver Wendell Holmes felt permanent discomfort that Holmes, virtually alone among his peers, had volunteered to fight in the Civil War.'' Vietnam veterans came home to apply themselves with imagination and energy to new fields of thought and action, but without the popular welcome accorded the soldier back from war. Our welcome has been delayed, but like Holmes, we are earning it.

The process of introspection and of finding new work was painful for Vietnam veterans. It was painful for me. At the end of my year in the Pentagon, I knew I was not cut out to be a career soldier. It was a secure career, and the Army had been my home for twenty-six years.

I asked to be permitted to resign. In 1971, the Vietnam War was winding down and the Army had thousands more captains than it needed. On the day I left the Army, I made that trip to Virginia Seminary. Then Dick Cavanagh, a B-School friend, called asking if I would like to work for Amtrak, the new passenger rail company. As a consultant at McKinsey & Company, Dick was helping form Amtrak. David Watts, the new vice president of planning, needed a senior planner. Amtrak was one consequence of the Penn Central collapse. I met David. I told him I lived at the seminary. Might I take two hours of course work at the seminary, provided the railroad work got done? ''Sure,'' he said.

I needed the job.

At the Seminary, I learned to take seriously the old-fashioned words like grace, call, sin, and the Resurrection. They expressed truths which able writers had done their best to describe. But my own question of call remained murky. I was fairly certain I should go on to Yale. I was not called to be a priest.

Priests affirm a promise of love and healing that does work inside the constraints of space and time in this world. They are a special witness, but only one kind of witness. It is not that priests are not directly involved in the world. Christians and Jews and Moslems believe that God acts in history. That is direct enough. I was not an ordained priest, as clearly as I could see things. In 1972, I applied to Yale Law School and was admitted. All I knew for sure was that I was not through learning.

The pain in these decisions was goodbye upon goodbye without realizing what was being given up. I turned my back on my Vietnam experience. No one at the Pentagon, Seminary or Amtrak asked me about Vietnam. I assumed, innocently, that the wartime service and leaving the Army affected my interior life not at all. Well, it did, but I did not realize it until 1975, after law school. Then I grieved over friends killed in battle and over a part of my life spent at a task assumed by society to be despicable, but which was not despicable. I had felt that I let Tommy Hayes down, for not seeking battle command as he did. My friends who had been killed and my service were parts of my life which I did not even pause to think about on a conscious level. If I recall correctly, I was the only Vietnam veteran in Yale Law School my three years there. I was never asked about Vietnam, and that was comfortable for me. I never brought up the subject. A statistically based survey finding runs through the book about Vietnam veterans *Strangers at Home,* concluding at one point, "With the war experience suppressed, the emotional catharsis of homecoming was nullified." The Vietnam veteran was not permitted to grieve. America did not let herself grieve.

Close experience with the building of the Southeast Asia Memorial at West Point and the National Vietnam Veterans Memorial has shown me the need to recognize the value of grief with respect to national assimilation of the impact of the war. A classmate asked in 1977 if the Southeast Asia Memorial "hadn't died of its own weight." The comment showed the denial and anger of suspended grief. I think that some of the anger in the controversy over the design of the Vietnam Veterans Memorial included a long-delayed expression of grief over broken expectations, over dead and crippled friends.

One sign of suspended grief is the continued wearing of jungle fatigues by some Vietnam veterans. Occasional wearing of a hat or other small items is a sign of pride, like the tactical service issue watchband made of olive-drab nylon. Living in jungle fatigues is something else. In part, for some men, living in the new America which negated the values embraced by the veteran, was harder than staying in fatigues and staying, somewhere in their hearts, in Vietnam.

Physicians teach that dashed expectations set in motion recognizable phases of grief: denial, anger, a search for knowledge, and a resolution. If the process is left to chance, and not confronted openly, then the involved individual or group—or even nation—is suspended too long at the initial stages of denial and then anger.

The phases overlap, with anger interrupting denial, and glimmers of resolution showing as angry outbursts lead to a temporary calm where knowledge grows. All this is evident in the events of the last twenty years concerning the Vietnam War.

Denial was the name of the social attitude toward Vietnam veterans, from the 1960s virtually to the dedication on November 13, 1982 of the Vietnam Veterans Memorial. The Disabled American Veterans launched a Forgotten Warrior Project to address the problem with counseling centers. Denial that the Vietnam warrior was back home was part of the denial that there had been a war. In fact, for years many government officials insisted on the euphemism "Vietnam conflict." The Vietnam Veterans Memorial and the emerging self-awareness of Vietnam veterans are signs that a prolonged denial phase may be winding down.

By beginning to discuss their experiences and to put their thoughts into print, it is the Vietnam veterans who have started the national labor of bringing knowledge to bear on how the events of the war years, in Vietnam and at home, shaped America's last twenty years and will affect the next twenty years. Some former antiwar protesters and nonveterans like Sam Brown, Christopher Buckley, and James Fallows have contributed to this literature, creating a kind of dialogue which needs to develop nationwide, if our residual anger is to energize the development of useful knowledge. Necessary subjects include how future national leaders will be influenced by the individual choices they made during the 1960s regarding military service and civil disobedience.

Looking back on my years in the Pentagon, Virginia Seminary, and Yale, it seems plain that some practical measures help this process. A basic starting point is to sort out exactly what expectations we each had back in, say, 1964, that we feel were eventually dissipated by national events. Grief is, finally, individual, so we each need to clarify what we feel we lost. After identifying what we feel we have lost, we can then discuss our experiences to determine if these feelings are justified.

My courses at Yale were hard because I was still unsure about where I was headed, or why I felt so estranged. On an Allegheny flight back from Washington to New Haven one winter weekend, I met fellow law school student Jan Schneider. With mention of Vietnam, I admitted I felt disoriented at the law school. Alone. Unsure of where I was going. She became a friend and changed my life by suggesting I see Professor McDougal.

Two days later, I knocked.

"Come!"

I opened the office door. Surrounded by bookshelves seven feet tall, Myres Smith McDougal sat at his desk. He was writing. For over thirty years he had taught at Yale, becoming preeminent as an international lawyer and writer on jurisprudence. His former students were spread throughout the world. His face was rounded, with a smile. He held a large magnifying glass and wore an eyeshade, both tools to fight a persistent erosion of his eyesight. I gave him the outlines of my life and then blurted out, "I don't know if I should stay here."

He asked what I'd like to work on, if I stayed. Financial law and computers, I answered. He suggested I take a course with him and do a paper in the area. That was the beginning. He drew me out as a writer and scholar. Then he taught me law by teaching me the questions that jurisprudence has to address. He let me channel my pent-up energy by probing first securities law and then the complex of policy and law and treaties that affect world hunger. Typically a law school education progresses in the reverse manner, with broader papers and generalized jurisprudence coming at the end. Mac took me through law school backwards because it would work for me, and I needed his help.

The old pro fished me out of the water. He taught me a lawyer's skills, and the skills were critical as I worked with the teams that set the strategy for walking the Memorial and then the VVLP through Washington politics and bureaucracies. And he enabled me to find "new fields for action or thought" in financial law and world hunger. The Episcopal Church funded me to attend the 1974 World Food Conference in Rome and a subsequent fact-finding trip to European capitals. I was brought in as a special counsel in the White House to help set up the President's Commission on World Hunger. My Yale article on securities led to the call to join the Securities and Exchange Commission.

The new was evolving in my life. My real problem was my past. Unlike Holmes, I could affirm it only in later years, after embarking on a new career. The past was always the obstacle.

## SAYING GOODBYE

There is a process of saying goodbye that I began experiencing in the late 1970s. Peer acceptance of me as a young soldier was never to be. It had been a surprising hurt, and I was unprepared for it. The early 1970s could not be changed. There was some health simply in realizing it.

The killed men could not be resurrected. There was some health in remembering them and telling their story. The truth about American soldiers in the war zone had been beyond the power of the American press to comprehend under the deadline demands of the sixties and seventies. The true picture would emerge later. The instant trip home from Vietnam had set us up to be steamrollered by the frenzied outer surface of American culture. I cannot go back to Tet of 1968 and say, "But wait, but wait, there is a different story here." I cannot go back to 1971 and change my image according to the popular American youth culture: "Your whole story is your wounds and hurts and broken relationships, and on that basis you can be one of us now. We always knew what was happening in Vietnam and understood so *we will teach you*." Few Vietnam veterans bought it.

The importance of exposing the past and saying goodbye is evident at the Vietnam Veterans Memorial. According to the Park Service, it now ranks with the Lincoln Memorial and the Air and Space Museum as one of the three most visited sites in Washington. Morning light one day revealed a pair of jungle boots, side by side, resting heels first against the walls. Who left them there? Who had worn them? Goodbye. Like a child's first shoes, cast in memory if not cast in bronze.

The daily flow at the Memorial is 3,000 to 12,000 people.

Photos of young soldiers and sometimes letters to them are left on the walls. Often a flower is inserted between panels, near a name. This will go on for years, because saying goodbye, like depicting the truth, is a process. It takes time. It is not instantaneous, even when we want it to be.

When I expressed this, Lance Morrow said:

> I keep thinking, just sort of idly, about the Civil War and what the Civil War meant in spiritual terms in the United States. And, you know, we've only barely assimilated the Civil War. What the South has done over the last fifteen years or so, ten years, is finally to process the spiritual meaning of that war better probably, than has the North. I think what happens in the late twentieth century is that there's something unnatural in the spiritual process, or development, of dealing with these things. It's a perfect sort of artificial agitation. These things are compacted, they're rushed, they're hurried up and away. They're not dealt with adequately in spiritual, cultural terms. I deal every day with journalists, and I know how their minds work. Their metabolisms are constantly consuming things . . . at an unnatural rate.

> They'll say "We've done that." Okay, Watergate's over, whoosh, it's gone. But it may not be. There are things that are simply not digested. And they're not digested because television, magazines, and so on run them by us at an unnaturally rapid speed, and then announce to us that, "We have assimilated that" when the fact is we have not. And so you have to go back to them again and again. And I have a feeling that these things are going to keep coming around in our spiritual rolodex constantly until we somehow deal with them and resolve them.

Visitors to the Memorial are drawn to the names. They touch the names, running their fingers over the letters. To an observer, there is evident satisfaction and a kind of healing in it. Pictures of this touching have often appeared in the media. The pictures convey healing.

More important than what I said goodbye to are the memories I am keeping. At the Memorial, people say goodbye to what they need to say goodbye to and keep what they need to keep.

I keep the names of the killed men I knew. Our name is a sacred part of us. Naming is a ceremony with great power. During baptism, parents are instructed, "Name this child." Pronouncing the name, the priest says, "You are marked as Christ's own forever." *You will not be lost. St. Paul said so: no one and no thing will separate you from the love of God, or God's power of healing. Not height, not depth, not destruction of the body, not hell. No one, no thing. Ever. It is a promise.* At the Memorial Fund we printed the alphabetical list of names on the Memorial. It was an unexpected best seller. We had to reprint. In the war zone, we were able to locate every soldier every day because of computer technology. Because of helicopters and medical technology by 1983 there was still *no unknown American soldier of the Vietnam War.* And we have every name on one memorial in Washington.

All his life, Justice Holmes referred to the killed men from his wartime experience. The men, and what they stood for, to him, were like talismans. In his 1884 Memorial Day address, he said it poetically, in a kind of song:

> There is one who on this day is always present to my mind. He entered the army at nineteen, a second lieutenant. In the Wilderness, already at the head of his regiment, he fell, using the moment that was left him of life to give all of his little fortune to his soldiers. . . . His few surviving companions will never forget the awful spectacle of his advance alone with his company in the streets of Fredricksburg. In less than sixty seconds he would become the focus of a hidden and annihilating fire from a semicircle of houses. . . .
> He was little more than a boy, but the grizzled corps commanders knew and admired him; and for us, who not only admired, but loved, his death seemed to end a portion of our life also.

This is a song about Vietnam, too. It is a Vietnam veterans song. It is any war veteran's song.

No one gives up the memories of the wildly improbable humor. It is a sign of health when the veteran tells you a funny story. Larry Brinker flew those big four-jet C-141's between the States and Vietnam. He was empty for a flight home.

"Sir, can we ship some seals back with you?" The special parachuting Navy frogmen are called seals—for sea, air, land.

"Oh, sure." He saw them at flight time. They weren't seals, they were *seals*. From some biological test, some research, some something. Barking on the runway at the airfield. Flap, flap. Arf. Onto the plane. *They poured water into the rear deck to create a pool for the seals.* They fly toward America. *The pool in the back of the plane freezes, and the seals start frolicking around on their tummies like otters.* Flap, Flap; arf, arf. Everyone gets home fine. True story.

The names and the laughter are the most important things I keep, that any Vietnam veteran keeps. Find them in one of us, and you become intimate with us.

I keep my admiration for the men who were with me over there. All of us do. There was special admiration for the strangers who appeared suddenly, and into whose hands you placed your life. Often it was a pilot and aircrew.

Here is something that wives, lovers, and family do not generally know about Vietnam veterans. There is for almost every Vietnam veteran the memory of the sound of helicopter rotor blades. That sound anywhere brings the mama St. Bernard that wrests our memory back to Vietnam. The rotors hit a certain pitch as the machine passes low. If you are with a Vietnam veteran when a helicopter passes, watch him. Ask him about it.

Whup . . . whup . . . whup . . .

*I heard it.*

WhupWhupWhupWHUPWHUPWHUP

*Louder.*

WHUPWHUPWHUPWHUPWHUP

*The noise passes through me. In memory I climb in under the rotors. I climb out. It is the Vietnam sound. Primal sound, like a mother's heartbeat as I formed in the womb. That sound is associated with fear or relief or rescue.*

WHUPWHUPWHUPWHUPWHUPwhup . . . whup . . .
*I never forget.*

I keep my bush hat, with the black camouflage captain's bars and airborne wings, and "Jack" sewn on the back. Straight *M\*A\*S\*H*. I got it in-country. If it is rainy, I wear it to the hardware store or whatever errand I'm on. I am proud of it. The old boot camp singsong chant pops into mind at the oddest times. It happens to many Vietnam veterans. (The verses are myriad. Two: "I want to be an Airborne Ranger/Live my life in constant danger; I don't know but I've been told/Navy wings are made of gold.")

The phonetic alphabet. It is a source of the odd poetry of military names, like Checkpoint Charlie, War Zone Delta, map grid coordinates Whiskey Zulu, Yankee Station, Echo Company, Bravo fire team, alter status to Romeo Echo Delta, the wounded man Delta Alpha Victor India Sierra. We use it for clear spelling over the radio, to avoid garbled messages, to make our fire orders clear and accurate. Most of us still remember it. Language is the structure of memory. The alphabet is a key to feeling at home in the many books by Vietnam veterans about tactical operations in-country. The letters are like the genetic building blocks of a special poetry. What are the phonetic letters of your initials? How about a rescue Huey with the unit designator painted on the tail boom "PW"? Or a bachelor fighter pilot down south with the squadron designator "DR"?

| | | | |
|---|---|---|---|
| Alpha | Hotel | November | Tango |
| Bravo | India | Oscar | Uniform |
| Charlie | Juliet | Papa | Victor |
| Delta | Kilo | Quebec | Whiskey |
| Echo | Lima | Romeo | X-ray |
| Foxtrot | Mike | Sierra | Yankee |
| Golf | | | Zulu |

We called the enemy Charlie. Mr. Charles. Chuck. Now you know why. The Viet Cong. VC. The phonetic designator for VC is the most painful poetry of all. Angry blacks in Vietnam and the States called whites Chuck. Why did Revlon name its smash perfume of the seventies "Charley"?

*At Yale weeks before talking to Mac, I went in one after-noon to talk with Professor Geoffrey Hazard. He taught litigating procedure. He told us he was a resource for us. I took him literally. I told him I did not know if I should stay in law school, and in his office I suddenly found tears in my eyes without knowing the reason. He said that adulthood came slowly. He was right about me, and that was part of the truth. The part neither of us could anticipate was that adulthood also accelerated at wrenching speed during that first year in America after Vietnam: either define yourself as a person right now or be bent by fashion into a personality that is false. I think each woman and man in our generation was pushed early into this personal battle by the interconnected events of the sixties. We barely realized the battle was upon us.*

# PART II
# NOW

I don't know what the methodology of
reconciliation is or, for that matter,
if there really is such a thing, but
I know what I would like to do. . . .
I would like one day to put my arms
around Elizabeth McAlister or Philip
Berrigan and even Tom Hayden, for that
matter, and literally say that we—all
of us—went through something together.

*Philip Caputo*
The Wounded Generation

William Bundy: "The facts . . ."

Professor Austin Scott:
"The *facts*, Mr. Bundy? Only God knows
the facts! Just tell us the evidence."

*Classroom exchange*
*Harvard Law School*

# CHAPTER FIVE

*I think that, as life is action and passion, it is required of a man that he should share the passion and action of his time at peril of being judged not to have lived.*

Oliver Wendell Holmes, Jr.
Memorial Day, 1884

*Finally, if there is anyone who stands in a position of indifference to all of this, that would be the greatest scandal of all.*

W. Taylor Stevenson
*Anglican Theological Review*
Issue on the Effects on
America of the Vietnam War

# SEPARATIONS: MAN FROM MAN

In the 1980s there is great creativity pulsing within our generation. A sequence of passion, disappointment and success, plus the resolve to carry on with our lives tells the story of so many of us that in aggregate the generation is on its way to making mature, creative contributions to our national life that will dwarf the activism and changes of the last twenty years. An image of the generation as burned out in the denouement of Vietnam is erroneous. On the grand scale, the domestic movements of our early youth were successful and the terrible years in Vietnam brought a harsh but strengthening acceleration of maturity. The perfectly natural result is a period of comparative silence and of tending to the adult work of creating families and careers.

The early evidence supporting this view is the health, size, and education of the generation back in the early sixties. These advantages make for resilience. There is evidence suggestive of this creative strength in the new balance of blacks and women in business and government, thanks to the civil rights and women's movements, and in the emergence of new companies like Federal Express, Apple Computer, and Genentech. World War II service shaped writers Kurt Vonnegut, James Michener, Herman Wouk and Norman Mailer, and similar potential runs among men who served in Vietnam like John Del Vecchio, Philip Caputo, Tim O'Brien, and James Webb. The popular artistry of George Lucas, Steven Spielberg, and Jim Henson provides glimpses of a large creativity and energy stored within the generation.

This perception of emerging creativity is probably accurate. Yet the evidence is only preliminary. The perception balances the one that focuses on the out-of-work black Vietnam veteran or individuals whose political disaffection or drug use, or both, in the sixties or early seventies leave them now outside the economic or political mainstream. People who hurt and must have help are on the surface of every generation, but they do not necessarily tell the spiritual story of the generation. A somewhat similar example is the beatniks of the early and mid-1950s. After World War II and Korea, our parents' generation evolved the "beat" subculture of sweatshirted, somewhat cynical coffeehouse poets. Mort Sahl was one. That same generation went on to put the first humans on the moon, end segregation, conquer polio, and turn world history through companies called IBM and UNIVAC. However, our parents' generation shared a great unity through their common experiences. Reared on the depression and war, they knew there were causes worth dying for and saving for. This made for ease of communication and understanding across the generation.

To be creative as an entity, a generation needs to some extent to be able to communicate within itself, one group to another. Separation among groups makes for tension that can be creative, as in competition among economic and political regions, as in "sunbelt" versus "frostbelt" states, agricultural interests versus industrial, exporters versus importers. Common values, as well as political institutions and political parties, mediate enough mutual acceptance and communication among the groups that differences can be resolved, gross stereotypes can be punctured, and, in general, competition stays relatively creative rather than destructive.

In the generation that came of age during the sixties and seventies there is evidence of separations that could so attenuate communication and acceptance among the generation that their creativity would be stunted for lack of unity.

Sam Brown was a leader of the antiwar movement as national coordinator of the Vietnam Moratorium Committee in 1969–70. In 1974, he was elected state treasurer of Colorado and from 1977 to 1980, he was the director of ACTION, the federal agency that included the Peace Corps and VISTA. He writes in *The Wounded Generation,*

As I travelled to college campuses in the fall of 1980, I frequently ran into people whose trip to the post office to register for the draft was their first act of citizenship and who were appalled when I told them that I favor not only registration but a military raised by equitable conscription and, moreover, that I believe in national service for both men and women. *My feelings toward members of my generation are different. We remain split from within and from the generation before and behind us.* I feel a sense of separateness from those people of my age who *simply responded* to what they regarded as the nation's interest by going to war. I am pained by the personal stories of tragedy of Vietnam veterans. I do not think that they were foolish, stupid or criminals. *Just used.* [italics added]

This illustrates the kind of gaps among us. Sam feels the separateness. He reflects on the sixties and endorses national service. Yet there is some cant in the phrase "simply responded." Condescending. Patronizing. The interior motives and fears attendant to going to Vietnam were anything but simple. His word choice suggests that his was the complex, elegant, and true course. *"Just used"* is an unfortunate phrase. Sam, *nobody used us.* In America going to war has been very largely a matter of individual choice, especially for the middle and upper class. Your own freedom to protest and not to serve is evidence of that. The flights to Canada and President Carter's amnesty for draft evaders are evidence of that freedom. The right to protest is an honored principle. We went to war for all the reasons and chances that influence a man to go. But the average American trooper who gave his life in Vietnam all through those years was not a draftee, though many were draftees. Most volunteered. A common thread among all was an underlying sense of commitment to community and frank willingness to take great personal risk in the name of the community.

*"Used?"* In Vietnam we inflicted suffering and death on an armed enemy which outnumbered us. Read *The 13th Valley*

or Harry Summers' *On Strategy*. Now look at Southeast Asia in 1984. *Who knows the truth?*

Sam Brown then writes,

> The split inherent in any generation between the classes, a split that our society has traditionally been able to keep indistinct, became pronounced and rigid, codified by the Selective Service classification system—1-A, 2-S, 1-Y, 4-F. We all remember, don't we? Anyone who grew up during the war knows who went and who didn't. The poor, less-educated and lower-middle-class men went and those of us who were upper-class and college educated didn't. The fact that many of us didn't because we found it *morally impossible* does not negate the fact that one class of people was used while another remained privileged. *The knowledge that so many men of the upper middle class used the system to beat it only accentuates the divisions between men of my generation.* I am saddened by the cynicism of many people whose prime motivation for being involved in the antiwar movement was merely self-preservation. *Once the heat of the draft had ended, they went on with the business of being stockbrokers or lawyers or whatever else they had hoped for in their lives.* [italics added]

These are serious divisions, with great emotional energy coursing between them. James Fallows dodged the draft by going on a super–crash diet while at Harvard. A journalist, he wrote speeches for President Carter. In *The Wounded Generation* he says:

> There was that indisputable element of sincere opposition. . . . The second element was the way the first part got tainted and polluted by a sense of anti-Americanism and anti-servicemanism. . . . the third significant thing about people of my sort in that time was the convenient fact, rather than the motivating fact,

that the pursuit of these critical opinions you had also
meant not being in combat yourself. . . . I think most
of my college and graduate school friends are not
happy talking about these things because they're afraid
they're going to be yelled at.

At Yale College during the Vietnam War, Christopher Buckley
was jubilant at the news that his doctor's report of a bout of
asthma during childhood sufficed for a 4-F classification. He wrote
speeches for George Bush and is now a journalist. Buckley notes
in the August, 1983, *Esquire* lingering thoughts after dedication
of the Vietnam Veterans Memorial, of people he knows:

> I didn't suffer with them. I didn't watch my buddies
> getting wiped out next to me. And though I'm re-
> lieved, at the same time I feel as though part of my
> reflex action is not complete. . . . I haven't served
> my country. I've never faced life or death. I'm an in-
> complete person. I walk by the Memorial and look at
> the names and think, "There but for the grace of God
> . . ." The dean once told me, "You know, the one
> thing your generation has done is [to have] made
> martyrdom painless. . . ." It's guilt at not having
> participated. At not having done anything. I blew up
> neither physics labs in Ann Arbor nor Vietcong in-
> stallations. I just vacillated in the middle. It's still
> confusing to me. Only in the last few years have I
> tried to straighten it out in terms of my country. And
> now I know I should have gone, if only to bear wit-
> ness.

The divisions among us are probably starker than men like Brown,
Buckley, Fallows, and I earlier perceived them to be. One reason is that the tug of silence is so strong. We keep our feelings
buried. Intuition tells me that these issues should not be buried
until they have been understood and laid to rest in collective
knowledge. The National Salute to Vietnam Veterans in November of 1982 was funded and attended almost solely by World
War II and Korean War veterans, and the Vietnam veterans and

their families. This is largely the same group that paid for the Memorial. The others in our generation, the women and the men, hung back. During that week *The Washington Post* interviewed Sam Brown, who was in Denver. He was "now working in investments." He said the Memorial dedication and the events of the week were "your event." Not *our* event? *Together?*

The strained silence of our generation about all this is a sign of what I believe to be the deeper aspects of these divisions. The divisions have to do with very touchy issues.

Now that many in the generation have children, the divisions are more obvious. What are we teaching our children? Buckley: "Whether it's guilt or malaise, what I do know for certain is that if someday I have a son and he asks me what I did in the Vietnam War, I'll have to tell him that my war experience, unlike that of his grandfather, consisted of a hemorrhoid check."

There is powerful sexual imagery associated with the warrior. Rightly or wrongly, there is political and social authority in having accepted the risks of war. There is political power in being a veteran. Some political analysts find this sentiment among voters: "This man is obviously rational and compassionate. And he is competent. He is not bitter. His life in Vietnam and America have made him stronger. *And long ago he kept his promise to serve. He is a man who keeps his word.*" Able people rise to leadership in any generation, and this will be true of able men who weathered service in Vietnam. It is a healthy reflection of a culture which values merit to any large extent. About ten percent of the men in our generation went to Vietnam. It is possible, and I believe it is likely, that among the three million men who came back, a fair number have leadership ability and will be able to make a contribution to our country.

In the 1980s scriptwriters have begun to depict the Vietnam veteran as strong. In the successful TV series *Magnum P.I.*, Tom Selleck plays Magnum, a Vietnam veteran. He is perceived in the media as a stong and attractive male sexual symbol. The black "Mr. T." on *The A-Team* is a sexually potent symbol of a Robin Hood fighting for justice. In the made-for-TV movie *Rage of Angels* an adviser tells the good-guy protagonist he should run for political office, that he has the credentials, good war record in Vietnam, good record here in the States. Yet how will women in our generation respond should war come again and there is some bleeding to be done, and the war affects their sons? Whether or not young women are called to war, young men will be. Bruce Caputo's 1982 senatorial campaign collapsed when the press reported that he had led people to believe he was an in-country Vietnam veteran when he was not. Gary Hart joined the Reserves. Sam Brown said that to fight in the circumstances of the 1960s was *"morally impossible."* I think we need to know what *is* morally possible. *Is anything worth dying for?* He implies the answer is yes, by embracing a draft and national service. *Well, what, exactly?* And how would that system of sending men to war work, exactly? Who would support them at home?

What things are worth dying for? The Vietnam veteran has become an emotionally, sexually, and politically charged symbol, and now he symbolizes this question. It is a threatening question, and it is urgent. It is not an abstract question. World leaders judge America and also individual American spokespersons, in part, based on an assessment of the answer to this question. The Soviets, for example, care deeply about the answer. Fallows: "But in the long run, a nation cannot sustain a policy whose consequences the public is not willing to bear. If it decides not to pay the price to defend itself, it will be defenseless. That is the risk of democracy."

The answers to these questions by our generation would finally get down to the brass tacks of who goes to fight, and how they are selected. The answer will finally rest on words like commitment and promise. These are old-fashioned words. These words suggest that *not all relationships are fungible.* That is a frightening thought. It is most comfortable in the near term to leave it buried. To a patient, doctors are often fungible. Dr. A, the general practitioner, has the same effect as Dr. B, the general practitioner. In the general lawyer-client relationship another lawyer can usually do as well. The same is true of grocers. Many providers of service are fungible. Not all relationships are fungible. My relationship to my country is most certainly not the same if someone replaces me, for whatever reason, when it comes to fighting. Or to serving in some other capacity. Marriage provides another example. With divorce rates running very high, our generation in effect is treating the marriage relationship as fungible.

Still if we have the will, it is possible for us to identify fundamental divisions among us, assess whether they are unnecessary impediments to intimacy, to relationships, to unity. If we will, we can bridge these divisions.

Separations and bonding are the stuff of life. In our young adulthood the especially strong and distinct political, sexual, military, and social forces of the sixties created sharp and enduring separations. The sequence of events in separation is not mysterious; we have all experienced them. It is the kind of dynamics which separates the man in the generation who did serve in uniform from the man who did not. It particularly separates Vietnam veterans from the men who did not serve. And naturally for many veterans there is a status hierarchy among degrees of exposure to fire, body wounds suffered, and citations for valor. Also, many veterans see officers as distinct from enlisted men. Especially in light of the harshness of the societal attitude and course of personal survival that each Vietnam veteran faced on coming home, the major distinctions among men in the generation are three: not in uniform, in uniform, in Vietnam ("in country").

The treadmill can sometimes be stopped when members of the generation recognize this pattern at work. They can forgive. One asset toward this end is underlying ties such as love, or friendship, or common goals, or common values. Such ties are not as strong across racial or ethnic barriers as across social and political gaps that divide people.

## HURTS

On the eve of July 4, 1980, a group of climbers reached the peak of Mount Rainier. All were handicapped. Most were blind. Their photo at the summit made the front pages across the country. The president brought them to the White House. The first to the summit was Charles L. ("Chuck") O'Brien of Pennsylvania. Chuck led an infantry platoon in the Ninth Infantry Division in Vietnam. Wounds led to amputation of his lower left leg. On the evening the team reached the summit, back in Philadelphia Chuck's wife prematurely went into labor and delivered healthy twins.

Chuck served in the state administration of Governor Richard Thornburgh and is a partner in the Philadelphia law firm of Pepper, Hamilton & Scheetz and chairs the Philadelphia VVLP. In congressional testimony about the need for the VVLP, he stated,

> I discovered I have a natural affinity for Vietnam veterans. They are more disciplined, more generous, and cooperative under pressure. And I just like their company. I've worked in the state government and the private sector and I know that to succeed requires hard work and discipline. These are characteristics of the men who served in Vietnam. *These men have labored under tremendous disadvantages. They've had 2–4 years taken from them. Persons my age who were not in the service are now partners in their firms. This is a fundamental inequity and yet one that can be worked around.* [italics added.]

Chuck testified before a panel of the House Veterans' Affairs Committee, chaired by Pennsylvanian Robert W. Edgar, who is Chuck's age. Edgar is a minister and sixties activist. The gap Chuck spoke of was visible in the very setting of congressman and witness. In the 1970s and 1980s, in both the private and public sectors, formal hiring preferences for veterans came under intense fire. In fact, in November 1977, Joe Zengerle, who was to become an assistant secretary of the Air Force, prepared a white paper distributed in Washington which examined the top-level appointments by President Carter. Figures were hard to gather, but he captured the order of magnitude of results. There are roughly seven hundred top presidential appointments in an administration. About six hundred went to traditional recipients, such as senior supporters and party leaders. About one hundred were given to the following: sixties activists (about fifteen), women (about forty), blacks (about forty), and Vietnam or Vietnam-era veterans (not more than five). The five included Max Cleland, the triple-amputee who headed the Veterans Administration.

In President Carter's administration, Joe found that the chairman of the Civil Service Commission was "urging curtailment of the Congressionally-mandated hiring preference for veterans seeking competitive posts in the Executive branch." He also observed the "old boy/old girl" network of former activists who made a strong push for special attention to blacks and women. "The reason cited by the CSC chairman for opposing the hiring of veterans is that it dilutes the help needed by other groups in getting jobs, notably women."

The law states, "It is the policy of the United States . . . to promote the maximum of employment and job advancement opportunities within the federal government for qualified disabled veterans and veterans of the Vietnam era." The whole idea of recognizing that military service pulled us out of the civilian career mainstream was under frontal attack by our peers within eighteen months of the fall of Saigon. One reason Allan Bakke applied to medical school so late was that he had a military tour as a Marine including service in Vietnam. In the Supreme Court case, the Carter administration wrote a draft legal brief which supported Alan's claim that the Affirmative Action program favoring blacks and women had led to reverse discrimination against him. Joe learned that "many of the appointees from the protest movement made known their opposition." The Supreme Court decided in Bakke's favor, and he became a doctor. Despite the vast media coverage of the case, there was scant mention that Bakke served in Vietnam. Bakke's veteran status might not have been legally relevant to the case, but it was relevant in explaining why Bakke applied so late and with such urgency. Joe noted that it was painful for Vietnam veterans to bring up this matter.

In the midst of the Bakke debate, Joe noted the "victory celebration in New York after the admission to the United Nations of the Socialist Republic of Vietnam, made possible by President Carter's decision not to continue to resist the inevitable by an American veto in the U.N. Security Council. The mood of the victory party was described as 'joyful, but not markedly forgiving' of the United States. In attendance at the party, among others, was Sam Brown, director of ACTION.''

John F. (''Jock'') Nash is chief counsel of the Senate Subcommittee on Criminal Law. Reared comfortably in Hawaii, he volunteered for the Marines and was an infantry platoon commander in Vietnam. He testified during the same hearing with Chuck,

> The first thing many of us discovered when we returned from Vietnam was that we were only a small part of things. Most people had stayed home, gone to school and then gotten jobs. In very real terms we lost five years and they were crucial years. . . . I love this country. I don't feel it owes us anything. But we have some important and valuable skills that came into use during our years of service and in the years since. All Vietnam veterans need is to be recognized. We shouldn't have to continue to sacrifice. As a group we've been on the fringes of doing something relevant with our lives; those five years may or may not make any difference ten years from now, but boy, right now they sure do.

Meanwhile, whites, blacks and women collided with the men back from Vietnam. The white males who graduated from law and business school years earlier were already in the higher altitudes of government and their professions. In one instance, one of them criticized his Vietnam Veteran peers for their ''lack of seasoning,'' especially in ''management.''

The *Wall Street Journal* in 1983 ran a front-page story about Bob Kimmitt, the Vietnam-veteran National Security Council staffer who is a special assistant to the president, and other congressional and executive branch staffers who play in an off-hours rugby league in Washington. One point of the article was that the rough-and-tumble of political life in Washington is like rugby, a nonstop cross between football and soccer, with yelling, screaming, and constant passing of the ball. The hearings in which Chuck and Jock presented their statements were part of the rough-and-tumble over creation of the VVLP and the appointment of Vietnam veteran Tom Pauken to succeed Sam Brown as head of ACTION. At Tom's first appointment hearing, he was excoriated for having been an Army intelligence lieutenant in Vietnam. A primary concern was that since the Peace Corps reported to ACTION, foes of America could enhance their argument that the Peace Corps was composed of spies. This was a plausible concern, and could have been handled a number of ways. Eventually the Peace Corps was made separate from ACTION. But at that hearing and in the events surrounding it, there was something else evident. Young Senate staffers for the hearings, the people Tom's age, were angry. It reminds me of Taylor Stevenson's defilement idea.

There was an aggrieved tone that the staffers and Peace Corps volunteers used in the hearings and their discussion of the hearings with the press. Since the Peace Corps stands for commitment, sacrifice, love, and dedication, their implication was that someone like Tom would be inappropriate as the director of ACTION. *Their argument by implication was that soldiers do not know about commitment, sacrifice, love, dedication. There was absolutely no awareness that self-giving was the essence of life in the war zone.* You could *feel* the disesteem in all this. Reporting in the July, 1981, *Atlantic Monthly,* Jim Fallows wrote, "If asked to choose between Pauken's assertion that the passions generated by his nomination included a considerable element of refighting the last war and the other side's denial that Vietnam was a factor at all, I would find Pauken's the more believable view." It was to get worse.

There are other kinds of hurts. One is the potential hurt feared by men who did not wear the uniform. They are afraid they will be "yelled at" and embarrassed for having avoided service. There is also the sense of loss, of not having been tested, as Christopher Buckley suggests.

Michael Blumenthal wrote the book of poems *Sympathetic Magic* and served as special assistant to Joseph Duffey, chairman of the National Endowment for the Arts. On January 11, 1981, the *New York Times* printed Michael's reflections on dodging the draft during the Vietnam War. He had aggravated a childhood case of asthma by deliberately inhaling canvas dust from the sewing machine tables of a tent factory in upstate New York. He believes that he would not serve in war if it broke out again. Still, reflecting on men who wore the uniform and those who did not, he writes

> To put it bluntly, they have something that we haven't got. It is, to be sure, somewhat vague, but nonetheless real, and can be embraced under several headings: realism, discipline, masculinity (kind of a dirty word these days), resilience, tenacity, resourcefulness. We may have turned out to be better dancers, choreographers, and painters (though not necessarily), but I'm not at all sure that they didn't turn out to be better *men,* in the best sense of the word. . . . Ultimately it may have to do with everything that follows: with having a family, with making commitments, with knowing what it means to sacrifice, with being an adult (another dirty word these days).

Christopher Buckley wrote: "It may be time for those of us who do have misgivings about not having fought to think, out loud, about the consequences of what we did—and didn't do. For those who never left, there is no ceremony and no coming home; if the healing is to be complete, then all the wounds from that war will need healing." The hurts on all sides are expressed in words having to do with authority, power, maturity, sex, manhood, family, children, and commitment. No wonder the subject is one thousand degrees hot.

## ANGER, GUILT, AND DENIAL
In less than eighteen months, Tom Pauken was hauled up before congressional hearings three more times. Each time VVLP was an issue. A quick forward pass in the rugby atmosphere of Washington is a General Accounting Office (GAO) study. GAO is an arm of Congress. Staffers and congressmen launched a full-fledged GAO study of Tom's administration, including

microscopic review of every document and course of action pertinent to VVLP. The GAO study found that Tom, ACTION, and VVLP were sound. I found a certain poetry in coming to the home of Peace Corps and VISTA to find volunteers to help Vietnam veterans. Symbolically these organizations expressed the best in our generation. To others, at least in the early eighties, they seemed to express defilement.

In his reflections, Sam Brown suggests that guilt could be one animation for this behavior. "For some men who opposed the war, the fact that they used the country's repugnance toward it to avoid the draft has left a residual guilt of not facing one's obligations." One way to handle a guilty feeling is to avoid it, or to say that it is someone *else* who should feel guilty.

Fallows concludes his article on the Tom Pauken appointment, "As the children of the baby boom—those of college and military age during Vietnam—move through their thirties and forties, they will be grabbing for bigger brass rings. The misunderstandings and hostilities left over from the 1960s are likely to give that competition a nasty edge." Yet, in the concern over funding and political appointments, there is in all debate a trace of an assumption that respect and power in America are a zero-sum matter, that there is only so much respect and power around. If one person has some, another must have less. But the economic wealth, creativity, and freedom of expression in America have always demonstrated that respect and power are widely available and freely created. *The sixties show it:* new businesses, new public figures, new movements, new laws.

## SILENCE

A key question regarding the idea of separations is the attitude of the twenty million men who did not wear the uniform and the seven million Vietnam-era veterans who were not in-country. In 1980, I organized for the *Washington Post* a symposium on how the Vietnam war divided our generation. A friend, Lee Spencer, saw me after it was printed. A sensitive man who did not serve in the military, educated at Princeton and Yale Law School, he expressed thanks for the symposium but wondered if others would regard the *Post* effort as "much ado about nothing."

Lance Morrow raised the question in the Memorial Fund reconciliation seminar:

> This morning, by coincidence, I was talking to two friends of mine who were trashing University Hall at the time that Jack was across the river at B-School. And I asked one, I said, "Do you have any sense of division from those who went to Vietnam?" And he said, "None whatever." And I said, "What is your feeling now?" And he said, "Well, my feeling was that it was a class war. I never had the slightest animus towards those who went to Vietnam." I don't quite believe that but he said it.

Christopher Buckley reports, "Most people I know who avoided the war by one means or another do not feel the way I do, and I'm in no position to fault their reasons or their justifications. But I do know some others who are still trying to come to terms with all this."

My intuition is that the silence on these matters is so studied and smooth that the measure of feeling is in fact very deep, so deep that some men can honestly say that they are not aware of any feelings on these issues. I agree with Lance; I don't quite believe it.

The silence has another aspect. Given the treatment of the men who came back from Vietnam, one clear societal signal to the seven million others who wore the uniform elsewhere was "America does not celebrate or affirm your service. Put it in the closet." Those guys, too, had missed a chunk of years in the race up the American career ladder. I know Vietnam-era veterans and Vietnam veterans who either glossed over or struck out the reference to military service in their resumes. They did not mention it in their Martindale-Hubbell lawyer's reference entry. I know one Vietnam-veteran bank vice president in Kentucky who said, when told about the VVLP, "I'm sympathetic. But I have succeeded here without people knowing I am a Vietnam veteran, and I do not want to upset things." A vice president of an investment bank in New York City called me about an article

I published, thanked me, and said he was thinking about telling his friends about serving in Vietnam, but that "it will take some time to get ready to do that."

## TIES
The openness to inquiry and the friends whom I have discovered in exploring the themes of this book show fundamental ties among the men in our generation, ties that reach across the divisions. The ties are a basis for hope and reunity. *Washington Post* editorial writer Michael Barone's instinctive recognition of these issues and his approachability about them is an example. David Anderson, who also did not serve in uniform, writes editorials for the *New York Times* and has freely discussed the issues and offered his thoughts on how the issues might be framed. Vic Fischer, a war protester, was the professional pollster who helped me in assembling the women and men for the Memorial Fund's reconciliation seminar. James Fallows, Christopher Buckley, and Alan Brinkley have offered encouragement in launching *The Century Generation,* the monthly report that covers developments and statistics on how the interconnected events of the sixties and seventies are shaping our generation. Jim was instrumental in the success of the *Washington Post* publication and its printing as the book *The Wounded Generation.* Sam Brown's participation in the same book was also generous; there was little fun and reward in grasping the red-hot topic. Michael Blumenthal was generous in talking through these matters after publication of his *New York Times* piece. I called him because of the way he concluded his piece, talking about life, and why we live. He said, " 'Fun' and safety are hardly what we're here for."

Ralph Wadeson, the battle surgeon in the Korean War, sees fundamental health in this. "You are the 'insight generation,' " he told me. "It doesn't promise you will succeed, but you are willing to try to have insight into your lives."

*In my second year at Yale Law School, teacher Jan Deutsch asked what would make me happy at Yale. I said I'd like to be a note and comment editor on the Law Journal. Getting my own*

*writing through the Draconian process of review by a committee
of three from among the pool of published journal editors was
severe. The note and comment editor was the writer's advocate.
I wanted to ease that tension by getting my editees into print.
Deutsch laughed and said, "Have the courage of your conviction." Looking back, I see a repeated theme. The Yale Law
Journal note and comment editor is a Beast Barracks squad
leader. The work is to teach, discipline, and advocate. It is in
a sense a task of leadership. I do not know by what grace the
outgoing Board of Editors voted me in as note and comment editor on the Board for Volume 84, my third-year law school volume. I found out the news one morning. I floated up three flights
of stairs to a pay phone to call Elisa. We were joyous. The new
editor-in-chief was my classmate David A. Martin, whom I
vaguely recalled meeting in my first year. While I was en route
to the library in the afternoon, our eyes met. We asked in uni-
son, "Don't I know you?" I told him how I saw my new job.
He concurred.*

*At the Law Journal banquet in spring of 1975, I wore black
tie and Elisa wore a formal dress. There was a surprise, a par-
ody of Jimmy Dean's coal miner song, "Big John." It was "Big
Jack,"*

> *He called committees for each of his boys,
> And disavowed any fancy ploys.
> He told each editor "I'm warnin' you
> Nobody leaves 'til this Note gets through."
> Big Jack*

*It showed acceptance. It showed I was home. It showed love. It
was my proudest moment at Yale Law School. Mac was there.
Jan Deutsch was there. Elisa was there. And so was David, the
man who pushed us into third gear, the conscientious objector,
the draft counselor in Baltimore during the Vietnam War, at Yale
the first write-in candidate elected to the Common Cause Board
of Directors, law clerk to Justice Powell, professor of law at the
University of Virginia, who listened to me en route to the library. My friend.*

# CHAPTER SIX

*For those of us who knew the pain*
  *of valentines that never came . . .*
*Inventing lovers on the phone, who*
  *called to say, "Come dance with me. . . ."*

Janis Ian
"At Seventeen"

*That . . . the very idea of manhood*
*was rightfully being challenged by the*
*feminist movement has to be factored*
*into any new conceptualization by*
*our culture of what it means to be*
*a man. This is a task that seems to*
*me to be as profound as any we*
*will face in the next ten years.*

Sam Brown
*The Wounded Generation*

# SEPARATIONS: WOMAN FROM MAN

Writing in this area of fundamental personal concern is so subjective and there is still so little statistical and objective literature that inaccuracy is a peril. A producer of CBS *Morning News,* Jeanne Edmunds, wrote to me after we had discussed this idea of separations of woman from man in our generation. She is in her thirties, reared in Virginia and a graduate of the University of Texas.

> I think you should say something about the sexual revolution and how that "grand experiment" didn't work. I don't know if it was fear of the draft or fear of nuclear holocaust, but SOMETHING fostered an "if it feels good, do it" attitude among our generation and the result was a loss of the ability to be truly intimate. I think perhaps this is a lesson that Vietnam veterans learned of necessity that those of us who stayed behind are just learning now. . . . we can talk and talk and communicate ourselves to death but if we can't be truly intimate, and if we don't appreciate the value of truly intimate friendships and love relationships, we will never be happy.

At Yale Law School, I found an environment where women were numerous, and they were peers. They represented a revolution in the law schools and the legal fraternity. The same revolution was occurring in business schools and business. Jan Schneider and Ruth Glushien both gave me shrewd advice about my legal career as well as about getting articles published. Jan gave me the key to getting my first note published. ("Tie it into some

currently pending legislation. That makes it timely and contro-
versial.'') Elisa in her work was in the midst of writing more
books. Holly Kendig and Laura Corwin were fellow officers on
the *Journal*. It was natural for me to work on an equal footing
with women, because (a) the women were competent and (b)
the change fit in as just one of the series of undulations of culture shock on coming back home from my war experience. When
West Point admitted women in 1976, I felt the decision was
overdue. At a stroke the Academy doubled the raw intellectual
caliber accessible to the admissions officers.

I think that women will save our generation's hide. A signal creative force at work among us is that within a decade the
raw intellectual power at work on the problems and opportunities of our time has doubled. Power and respect are *not* zero-
sum qualities in American life; they are being created new among
us now. I realized this at Yale Law School. The committee of
two hundred businesswomen created by Chicago banker Susan
Davis suggests this potential. In the technologically and politically volatile world of the eighties and nineties we need all the
brains, disciplined scholars, and originality we can produce. Why
should the culture tie one hand behind its back?

There is another reason to regard women. My intuition has
been that it is a bit easier for women than for men in our generation to discuss separations, attitudes toward the war, bonding, commitment, masculinity and femininity. Perhaps the capacity is equally present in both sexes, but I doubt it. For men
who did not wear the uniform, these matters are so sensitive that
I think it is naturally easier for women to engage in discussion
of them.

Women can also be more objective, since relatively few go
into uniform. They observed us men as we divided into our various military and nonmilitary labors of the sixties and seventies.
In a general sense, women and women's publications have a potential as a catalyst in verifying and healing divisions that run
among the generation.

However, there have been forces which separate woman
from man, and which draw direct cause and momentum from
the turbulence of the sixties.

## HURTS

To use a space metaphor, in the sixties the women's movement rocketed into orbit. The space shuttle vehicle was the women's movement, as assembled with the technology of organizational techniques learned in the civil rights and the antiwar movements. The energy and structure of the previous stages go back to the nineteenth-century history of women's activism in America. But the energy that boosted women, including Sally Ride, into orbit was the "all bets are off" attitude in the sixties, in which many fundamental assumptions of American life were held up to reexamination. That is why it was so natural for me to study with women partners at Yale Law School. *Everything* was changing, like flipping switches at Mission Control. The Vietnam War, as Irving Howe and others perceived, was the primary catalyst of the upheaval of the sixties. In this sense, *the Vietnam War was the proximate cause of women's equality in America.* This is a redemptive aspect of the war. If the war had been over quickly and been won, the women's protest movement would not have flourished. *The protracted, tangled war formed the great land bridge in the American woman's Exodus.* In the course of negotiating the military successes in Vietnam and of fashioning the political withdrawal at home, the generation doubled its creative reserve. Without the war, partnership among women and men would not have happened when it did.

The price of this success was borne by the people whose names are on the Vietnam Veterans Memorial. It is borne by those who loved them. I think it is borne by all of us.

There is also a somewhat hidden aspect of this cost. Much of the fiery energy of the women's movement came from the idea that the Vietnam War, the institutions of war, and perhaps all institutions were inhumane or stifling, that the war itself was defiling. War was a masculine thing, not a feminine thing. In evaluating my own journey into the war zone, starting with the decision to attend West Point, I consider my commitment as a statement that there are things worth dying for. It is a masculine statement. I think it is *the* masculine statement. This is why war has tended to be viewed as a masculine enterprise. I once asked Marcia Landau, "What is the *distinctly* feminine trait?" She answered, "Nurture." Woman expresses the idea that there are

things worth living for. The movements of the sixties were tied
to the concept that there are things worth living for. The environmental movement. Earth Day. War is bad for children and
other living things. In the sixties, at least, masculinity was a
symbol of preparedness to die, and femininity was a symbol of
preparedness to live. Femininity was ascendant. The war was
dirty and so too was masculinity. It was evident in the fashions
of dress and language of the sixties. In America masculinity went
out of fashion.

In Vietnam masculinity did not go out of fashion. And in
coming home most veterans never let it go, even if we had to
turn inward and remain silent for ten years or longer.

Barbed wire is conventionally used as an obstacle in de-
fending the perimeter around a fighting base. It was first used
on a wide scale in World War I. In wars ever since there have
been men who fell, wounded, slain, voluntarily or involuntarily,
across the barbs, forming a bridge for buddies. It should not be
shocking. It is like the men who threw themselves on the grenades in Vietnam, like Hector Santiago-Colon. There is a certain sense in which the women's movement sped to fulfillment
across the backs of the American men in Vietnam. But for our
presence in battle, their protest would have died. But for the effectiveness of our fires, Hanoi would not have invested in getting good press in America and there would have been no meetings in Hanoi with American media figures. But for our fires
and our dying, there would have been no revolution. No story
for TV. No sense of defilement. No overweening sense of righ-
teousness and anger and unmasculinity.

By its design, the Vietnam Veterans Memorial unites the
Washington Monument and the Lincoln Memorial. It is like a
bridge. I think that it symbolizes a bridge that was necessary for
the true emancipation of American women. In fact, the Memorial was designed by a woman. We did not know the designer
at the selection. When the design was unveiled to the Memorial
Fund board and staff in 1981, no one spoke. I said what I think
is true: "This is a work of genius." I clapped. We all clapped.
Then we found out that the designer was Maya Ying Lin, an
architecture major at Yale College. We felt buoyant at such a
surprise.

We would soon discover that women were colliding with veterans in the competition for jobs. A lot of women were winning. In the early eighties, the media discussed the "gender gap," which denotes the apparent preponderance of disapproval of government policies among American women, as compared to men. The core idea is that in future presidential and other elections there are likely to be more female than male voters.

Part of the price of women's progress has been a new double standard. The double standard operates against men. Under it, America has learned to celebrate both the femininity *and* the professional accomplishments of women. The duplicity is that men are not affirmed in their masculinity, but only in their professional lives. For example, Barbara Thomas has been admired in the press both for being a Securities and Exchange commissioner and for bearing and nurturing a baby at the same time. In the integration of her professional and personal life, she symbolizes the truth that there are things worth living for. Yet, since the 1960s America has not affirmed the maleness in men. In fact, because of the Vietnam War we have denied that there is an essential male quality to affirm. Roger Rosenblatt noted this in his essay in *Time* magazine of July 18, 1983, about the fashionable tendency of American men to fill a mold cast by actor Alan Alda,

> an androgynous ideal, a male hero with certain indispensable facets of his masculinity intact but displaying in great and blatant measure the desirable female attributes of gentleness, forbearance and sensitivity.
> . . . Underlying and supporting this image is the assumption that while women possess a superabundance of qualities that would, if transplanted to men, bring peace and glory to the lesser sex, men do not possess a comparable set of gifts to bestow on their opposites.

When war protesters say, "No more Vietnams!" they mean, "I wish we lived in a world where nothing is worth dying for!" But the witness of a billion souls, from the South China Sea to Cape Cod and to the Gulag is that there *are* things worth dying for. Michael Blumenthal says that being in a war is not the greatest tragedy that can occur in life. Nor is death. Who can blame society for strewing perfume and flowers around these caskets of truth and pretending the truth is not there?

There are also potential hurts that may affect women in our generation. In the July 24, 1983, *Washington Post Book World*, Robin Marantz Henig reviewed Elissa Melamed's *Mirror Mirror: The Terror of Not Being Young*. Henig writes,

> Women past their "prime"—the age of childbearing, usually the twenties and early thirties—are considered useless goods. . . . Why is an older man allowed to be distinguished, charming, debonair, powerful, successful, even lusty, while an older woman is at best "gracious"—or that most neutered of all compliments—"handsome"? Why does an older man retain, and sometimes increase, his sex appeal with age and power, while an older woman, upon turning fifty or 'so, becomes a sexless matron? Why do most men accept their aging with goodwill and equanimity, while most women view the gray hairs and wrinkles as death knells for their self-esteem?

I think that part of the mystery is the relationship among man, death, and willingness to die, on one side, and woman, life, and commitment to things worth living for, on the other. Somewhere inside masculinity is the idea that death is not the worst fate. Is that one reason why Jesus is male? Elsewhere in galactic space is there a culture of life redeemed by God incarnate as female? Or will it be Sally Ride's great-granddaughter who carries the Gospel to them?

Back on earth, in the late eighties and early nineties, another question arises: as the women who are wives in our generation age, which marriage commitments will endure? Which men will keep their promise? Well, which men kept their promise in other fields of societal life? Will that make a difference? How true will be the man who wore the uniform or the man who went to jail rather than fight, compared to other men? Are these questions worth the pain, anger, and misunderstanding they expose? I believe that there is health in discussing these questions. Light on our motives and hurts is more effective than darkness.

## ANGER, GUILT, AND DENIAL

Suzanne and Jim Woolsey are in our generation. Now a partner and management consultant in Coopers & Lybrand, Sue spent a season as an editorial writer for the *Washington Post*. In the late 1970s, Sue served as the associate director of the Office of Management Budget in the Carter administration. She was responsible for the portion of the federal budget that includes health, welfare, and veterans programs. Jim, who is a Vietnam-era veteran, was undersecretary of the Navy. Sue earned her Ph.D. in clinical psychology, training in a Veterans Administration hospital. Sue objected strongly to U.S. policy in the Vietnam War. She attended the Memorial Fund's reconciliation seminar. At one point, referring to questions I had asked, she said:

> I'd like to push back to something that you said, Jack. I've got my nerve up to talk about that male/female thing which Jack has been goading us to talk about more. I think that one of the reasons it's difficult today to deal with masculinity and the masculine role and the feminine role, and who's got which role, is precisely a combination of two things. One is a feeling, certainly that I have always had and I suspect most women have, of guilt. Of being safe. We went through that generation never having to worry about student deferments. We had to worry about our men. We never had to worry about our physical safety. What really felt very strange, it was all so very nice I wasn't about to give it up. But it made me feel guilty. And I think one of the reasons that I and I suspect the rest of the women in the room feel very ambivalent about the draft, and *if* you draft *who* you draft, has to do with what is the special role of men and women. Is there a specialness for each sex? And does it have to do with fighting? And should it? Personally I thought there

should be a draft for men and women, if there was
going to be one. I voted very heavily in favor of registration for both men and women inside the Carter
Administration.

I always suspected that during Vietnam the men I knew
felt a little resentful of the fact that they had to go
through the difficult decisions and the contortions. It's
a combination of that and fear; a fear for the men we
love and a fear for our children. And it is a very
complicated set of reactions and frankly I'm not surprised that we find it difficult to deal with, because
we haven't sorted out either personally or as a society
how we feel about how different men and women
ought to be.

Susan Jacoby, in *The Wounded Generation,* traced some seeds
of anger in discussing the draft and the prospect of a future war:
"Who can deny that there is a kind of biological insanity in
sending women into combat? . . . The whole issue makes women
uncomfortable, but there is no way around it unless you believe
there is no need for an army. . . . If we lose all awareness of
the role of women as potential childbearers, what sort of society
will be left to defend?" Susan supports a draft and a peacetime
Army, and seems willing to accept drafting women for noncom-
batant jobs. But she concludes, "My own views on the military,
particularly on the matter of a peacetime draft, are not typical
of women as a group (if there is a typical group of women). For
many women who came to maturity during the Vietnam era,
anything connected with the military can be a bitter pill to swal-
low."

The most severe anger and denial among women regarding
these issues is aroused by the idea that the Vietnam veteran has
been a proximate instrument of the fulfillment of their dreams.
This may be misinterpreted. My hypothesis does not diminish
the resourcefulness of women leaders. The important result is
the signal creativity of America in fashioning a true partnership
between woman and man.

## SILENCE

The technology of birth is fungible. Sperm banks can be used in place of fathers, and petri dishes can be used for conception in place of the womb and the mother.

Woman without man and man without woman make for a kind of silence. With the advent of genetic technology Susan Jacoby's question about the biological insanity of sending women to war may be obsolete. Who needs woman? Who needs man? Who needs child? Who *needs* husband? Who *needs* wife? *Why bother with woman and man?* The questions are obvious. They are the questions posed by the sexual equality and genetic discoveries of the sixties. If there are no ready answers, then silence is as natural as silence about the men who returned from Vietnam.

Being alone in Vietnam in the masculine Army culture, I thought a lot about women and sex. In light of my journey at Virginia Seminary, I think Michael Blumenthal is right. We are not here *just* for "fun." In the early 1970s, Art Mosley gave me a letter I had written to him from Vietnam. I wrote, "the only measure, the only treasure" is what we give or make possible for others. I was not wholly right. It is instead a two-way street. There is treasure in what we do and make possible for ourselves. The standard should be to provide for ourselves the way we provide for other people. I agree with C. S. Lewis, speaking through the character Aslan. At the end, all love endures, a sum is enhanced by our acts of love. Brokenness and evil are judged, healed, and redeemed. They do not endure.

We were made for love and to be in relation with others. In my opinion, that is close to the reason why we are here. Maybe it is an expression of the reason. And we live in these bodies. Relationships include our bodies. We dance. Parades at West Point express commitment to country, and to ancient promises, constantly renewed. Even in the cloister, the nun expresses herself with her body, in kneeling. My thought is that intimate relationships include expression through our bodies. In the Nicene Creed the body is important. At the resurrection we have a new body. A *body,* to express love. It must be capable of intimacy. I do not think we will choose to genetically alter the way most humans express love through sex, although we may be able to.

The tension in the sexual differences between woman and man leads to much pleasure. The evidence is that the female-male tension in sex is for the majority very pleasurable. Its power may be one reason why a minority choose to avoid heterosexual intimacy. Also, Debbie Fallows' writing reminds us that children flower in the presence of a mother and father. Growth is different, not so rich, in the absence of one or both parents.

Women and men in our generation are mulling over the institution of marriage. The *Washington Post* on August 3, 1983, ran an article by thirty-five-year-old California artist and writer Robert Ferrigno. He said, his culture is characterized by "low-rent apartments, diplomas stapled to the wall next to the Flint-stones glassware, loud parties to celebrate the snaring of a federal grant and love affairs that last about as long as atomic particles zipping through the nuclear accelerator at Stanford University." He wrote about what women want in marriage, in his view. "Now there are articles about how women have had enough sensitive men; they want tough guys." His theory is that "women need men less than they ever have, and men are finally realizing how much they need women." Fathers are not technologically needed. Ferrigno feels that marriage is our culture's "rite of passage." Bearing a child is another rite of passage. (I had always thought, I would rather go to war than bear a child, even before I watched Elisa bearing Katie and John. Now, *that* is pain and risk.)

For twelve hundred words Ferrigno dances with words and the subject of marriage. He is probably right in his conclusions, "I don't think men and women will be happy together until men no longer *need* women. No longer need them for validation of manhood, for a crying towel, for a housekeeper, for a mother, or because they are incomplete without them." He looks for men "to grow up," concluding "when the desperation leaves, the good times may arrive. But it may take a long time for men to learn that lesson—and to grow up."

Sam Brown says that plunging into the war protest was a "rite of passage." It seems that growing up includes major risks. Can there be risk without commitment? To "grow up" includes expressing the capacity to love, I think. Jeanne Edmunds seems to be right in saying that a result of our generation's passage through youth and the sixties and early seventies "was a loss of the ability to be truly intimate. . . . if we can't be truly intimate, and if we don't appreciate the value of truly intimate friendships and love relationships, we will never be happy." The separations that run among our generation are part both of the symptom and cause of the loss Jeanne articulates. The loss seems to be evident in Robert Ferrigno's column. In his twelve-hundred-word piece about marriage, he uses the word "love" only once.

## TIES
Professional working ties among women and men have become more evident, as the consequence of the equal-opportunity revolution that was fed by the Vietnam War and the turbulence and movements of the last twenty years. While the turbulence has been an important cause of separation of women and men, the professional and working partnerships provide potential channels for recognition and discussion of the issues of separation and professional competition. These discussions might occur in the course of the natural camaraderie and friendship of the workplace.

From a historical viewpoint, the new working partnership among women and men in the various vocational settings of our generation is startling. At the United States Securities and Exchange Commission, I saw the partnership develop in five years. By 1978 the law schools had fielded so many able women lawyers that the junior professional staff at the SEC was over a third and perhaps nearly half women. There were very few women senior managers. There had never been a women commissioner on the five-member Commission. By 1983, there had been two women commissioners, Roberta Karmel and Barbara Thomas.

This is happening usually at a slower pace, elsewhere in business and law firms. People who work together form friendships. My hope is a simple one: in diffuse and countless businesses and in diffuse and countless conversations over the next decade, the female and male leaders in our generation will understand that the turbulence of the sixties and seventies had men and the idea of manhood paying a material amount of the up-front cost of making women equal. There is health in a generational assimilation of how we got where we are. It could generate a healthy readjustment of societal concepts about masculinity and femininity. Top management should be aware that the emergence of the women's movement has the effect of stretching out the gap of time it will take military veterans to "catch up" those lost years on the career ladder. Management will have to take care to spot junior women and men who have weathered military service among the competitive and usually more senior crowd of their peers.

There are other ties among women and men that can diminish the separation. Increasingly, women are examining the issue of what happened in our generation during our youth. These women particularly include scholars, novelists, and journalists who were involved in sixties movements and now have the resources and skills to step back and begin to integrate the experiences we have all been through. Sara Evans is an example, with her book *Personal Politics*. Myra MacPherson of the *Washington Post* is an established writer in this area. Marcia Landau works in the VVLP. At WGBH television in Boston, the team that assembled the weekly series on the Vietnam War depended on professionals Kathryn Pierce and Margaret Roth. At the Vietnam Veterans Memorial Fund, Sandie Fauriol and her assistant Karen Doubek managed the fund raising for the Memorial and planned and managed the citywide week-long National Salute to Vietnam Veterans in Washington. The political fight over the Memorial design became the part of the battlefield onto which we Vietnam veterans at the Fund were called. The creative and substantive achievement of attracting the money and celebrating the week was implemented by women. The fight should have been discouraging. For every favorable article, foes of the design fashioned another one attacking it. But at the height of the bad press, Sandie Fauriol popped in one day and told Jan Scruggs and me that since the attacks on the design the Fund's contribution rate had nearly doubled, to fifty thousand dollars a week: "It's OK! The papers are spelling our name right!"

These women have learned about the dynamics and effects among our generation of idealism, war, protest, and fights for equality. They have incredible insight to offer.

*If death is to come tomorrow, what would I do today? In our generation, as young adults we begin to see families and friends face cancer and unexpected illness. In her work as an Episcopal priest, Elisa seems each week to be called to some place of turmoil. Two kids watching their parents divorce. A father in his thirties succumbing to cancer. A couple with children whose business is on the rocks, and neither parent has a job. Sometimes I think that there is no one in our generation who is not facing bankruptcy, divorce, or cancer. Karen Gray, thirty-eight years old, was a banking officer for the National Savings and Trust Bank in Washington, D.C. With the help of her husband, Douglas, she fought cancer for years, yielding in the struggle one part of her body then another, and then in August, 1983, her spirit. Karen never left her bank work. At Katie's homecoming from the intensive care nursery in 1977, we needed five hundred dollars a week for nurses, with a debatable prospect of medical-plan reimbursement. Karen was our banker. She helped us weave the fabric of loans and repayments and quickly cashed medical-plan checks that have held us together economically. So that is what Karen chose to do, when told that she dies in the coming day. She chose relationships and helping. I see Katie and I am often reminded of Karen. In the week and the hour of her death the priest of the church by her side was a woman, the Reverend Vienna Cobb Anderson, who said it is all right to die. Woman symbolizes that there are things worth living for, and Vienna was witness to the ancient promise of new life.*

# CHAPTER SEVEN

*There was, I see in retrospect, much
of which I was unaware, and to some
extent my lack of awareness was not
innocent; I despise admitting it, but
upon reflection I find I am a scandal
to myself.*

W. Taylor Stevenson
*Anglican Theological Review*
Issue on the Effects on
America of the Vietnam War

*I look in the mirror and do not like
what I see—a walking lie, a hypocrite. . . .
disesteem is fundamental to the whole
category of human discontents. If self-
esteem is strong enough, anger will be
more appropriately handled and the self-
damaging aspects of human difficulties
will be obviated.*

C. FitzSimmons Allison
*Guilt, Anger, and God*

# SEPARATIONS: SELF FROM SELF

An important part of the larger separation of man from man and woman from man in our generation is the natural reluctance that individuals have in recognizing or discussing some intensely personal act or insight, which is carried in silence as a burden or treasure. This reluctance creates a kind of separation of self from self. The treasure could be a creative idea which needs only enunciation to become real. Albert Einstein said, "To imagine is everything." But the image has to be seen and shown. The burden could be some act of which we feel ashamed. Such a personal burden is lightened in several ways. We might be accepted by others in spite of the act. Or that act, regardless of how we ourselves judge it, is really no cause for shame. Or we may realize that we've overreacted, that the act is not as terrible as we'd initially thought. Others can help us realize that we've overreacted. If we're fortunate, we find others who can draw us out, and we learn about ourselves. This often happens gracefully, by chance, but there are examples of intentional and organized settings, like the outreach centers for Vietnam veterans opened by the Veterans Administration and the Disabled American Veterans and the "consciousness-raising" groups in the women's movement during the sixties and seventies. It is possible for creative or healing discovery to take place in complete solitude, but the more usual experience involves others.

These insights which we keep hidden or do not yet see, when aggregated across our generation, are also a cause of the severe divisions among us. A lot of women may have mixed feelings about the Vietnam War, and remain silent. The silence increases the separation from women which some veterans, or nonveterans, may feel. Or a lot of nonveterans may feel some sheepishness about their decisions regarding military service. In general, they stay silent. The silence increases the separation from nonveterans which veterans feel.

The separations among us bottle up creativity. These separations keep able people apart, yet people working together are needed to implement creative ideas. Individual burdens can spark but also hamper creative ideas. Diverse kinds of separations of self from self seem to be consequences of the movements and events of the sixties and seventies. Since they also aggregate to form the larger separations among us, each of us needs to think about and try to recognize them. For example, the fierce progress of the women's movement has brought to many women the burden of constant tension of allocating time between profession and children. The wealth and health of so many black Americans have contributed to a tension among blacks that is very evident in the eighties: like women, blacks are not so uniform in their objectives and views that unanimity or even consensus on issues is automatic.

Over July 4, 1979, Jan Scruggs announced that he had raised $144.50 in his drive to create a National Vietnam Veterans Memorial. He and Bob Doubek had started the Vietnam Veterans Memorial Fund in April. The announcement constituted their first national coverage. On vacation in Pawley's Island, South Carolina, I walked out in the morning to a vending box and bought a paper. Standing in the sunshine by a beach house, I read about Jan and Bob. I felt a tremendous pull of identification with Jan's dream.

> Friendship arises . . . when two or more . . . discover that they have in common some insight which . . . others do not share and which, till that moment, each believed to be his own unique treasure (or burden). The typical expression of opening Friendship would be something like, ''What? You too? I thought I was the only one.''

C. S. Lewis wrote this description. *Jan? You too?*

> It is when two such persons discover one another, when, whether with immense difficulties or semiarti-

culate fumblings or with what would seem to us amazing and elliptical speed, they share their vision—it is then Friendship is born.

Sam Brown, Christopher Buckley, James Fallows, and Susan Jacoby are certain that the interconnected events of the sixties and seventies were formative, divided us, and need to be examined. Surely, many of us agree. *You too?*

> Friendship is born. And instantly they stand together in an immense solitude. . . . Friends find this solitude about them, this barrier between them and the herd, whether they want it or not. They would be glad to reduce it. The first two would be glad to find a third.

So I called up Jan. I joined him and Bob. That is how we started. They articulated an idea. They drew me out. To imagine is everything. *I see the image too.* The image marshalled my remembered hurts on coming home from Vietnam. It marshalled the lessons learned in building the Southeast Asia Memorial at West Point. The image was at the same time healing and creative. I was carrying a burden I had only vaguely sensed: what do I do with my memory of the war years and coming home? What is my vocation now that I am a lawyer? Jan's announcement helped me form the question and answer it. As controversy developed over the design of the Memorial, we found that much of it was generated by fellow Vietnam veterans who, as we did, considered the potential importance and power of the Memorial as a symbol.

> The man who agrees with us that some question, little regarded by others, is of great importance can be our Friend. He need not agree with us about the answer.

## HURTS

I am witness to the separation of self from self. Serving in Vietnam on senior general staff, I assumed that the war and service in Vietnam affected my interior life not at all. Well, it did, as I realized later in reflecting on my life in the early seventies. I was in Vietnam 1969–70. Elisa and I married in 1973. Not until late 1975 did I begin to tell Elisa that the memories of my dead friends were painful ones, and I had to talk about them.

For five years, I followed society's rule that a part of life—my life—was to be excised. The reasons for this compliance are doubtless complex. There is Taylor Stevenson's suggestion that many in our generation, without realizing it, felt defiled by the war. The Watergate scandal for two years overshadowed Vietnam, in the end distracting the government during the time when the final 1975 assault on South Vietnam was happening. (The Watergate ''Plumbers'' operation itself had grown out of efforts to stop national-security-information leaks. To that extent, Watergate can be viewed as, in some degree, a consequence of the fiery protest and debate over the Vietnam War. If the war may have made Americans feel defiled, there is no question that the Watergate break-in and cover-up did.)

Some men who did not serve also appear to have undergone such separation of self from self, as they take a hard look at their actions of the last decade and consider the tasks and international dangers of the present decade. Christopher Buckley, James Fallows, and Michael Blumenthal have expressed these concerns. Blumenthal questions his manhood by suggesting that those who did wear the uniform may be better men. Buckley says, ''It's still confusing to me.'' Fallows concludes:

> I think there was in almost all the people at least a modicum of this feeling that they were doing their duty too, and the problem now is that, because there were also these other elements which *most of them look back on with some chagrin, with some shame,* that most people have not been able to honestly sort out the things they should be proud about and advertise as values to their children, to other people, and the things they should honestly regret. *And so it is the unspoken and unanalyzed nature of these things which I think is the big roadblock to your knowing more of these people and their being willing to hear what you have to say* [italics added].

The experiences which Jim associates with chagrin and shame are hurts—who would choose to disclose them? Yet hurts, even more than grand ideas, show a person's humanity. Making friends is easier when the pretense of flawlessness is set aside. My own embarrassment was not complicated. I was the Long Binh scrounger. I begged, borrowed, and otherwise appropriated assets so that our computers could talk to each other. I did not seek battle command. I was afraid to die. Until 1977, I felt like I had bought my life at the price of not meeting the West Point standard, the one met by my West Point classmates, the men whom Rick Atkinson called my "blood brothers" in his Pulitzer prize-winning series on the class. Starting in 1977, I began to see, as I conversed with others, that my Army education, including the study of Napoleon at West Point, the time at Harvard, and the Pentagon assignment had tempered my judgment. The war for me was life and death, because I was going. But by 1969, a certain pattern was evident to my Army eyes: the soldiers' individual sacrifice and commitment—such as Tommy Hayes' sacrifice and commitment—was not matched by a parallel level of political sacrifice and commitment at home. This was not like the war my dad went to. In a way, by going into the war zone first, Tommy had thrown himself on a grenade whose shrapnel was marked for me, too. At Tommy's funeral, a classmate infantryman, wounded and decorated for valor, said bitterly with fist clenched, "This war is bad. We can't go after enough enemy." I was not sure what he meant. I knew he was upset and bitter. The question which is naturally open is how a troop unit under my command would have fared, how I would have fared. The answer is, I don't know. Not having the answer was a loss. It was one thing to grieve over, to say goodbye to.

I wonder if the heated debate among women about the time to set aside for child rearing is similar as an emotional issue. It is a very personal question, and there is more than one right answer. So is the question of how a working couple divides or shares the labors of child rearing and family support. Both of these questions are pertinent to the successful women's movement. The answers include sacrifices, as we change old assumptions about married life, relocate to a spouse's new city of employment, or alter our jobs in some way so that we may nurture our children.

Our lives in the sixties have shaped our reaction to the present. What do the Peace Corps volunteers from Latin American countries now feel about their country of assignment, given the turbulence on the South American continent? Jerry Sternin was my friend at Harvard and a Peace Corps volunteer in Nepal. So is Winifred Hill. Their personal investment in the country is high. The Soviet invasion of nearby Afghanistan has been a shock. I think that returned Peace Corps volunteers, as they follow events in their assignment countries, are as keenly aware as any in our generation that there are things worth dying for, that peace and war are not unconnected opposites.

During the Vietnam War, two incidents happened which illustrate other aspects of pain that endure. An elderly colonel told me about meeting the father of a lieutenant just killed in battle. The casket with the body had just been flown home. The father wanted to make sure that it was his son's body in the casket. One reason was to remove any doubt about identification of the body. Another was to help say goodbye to his son. Elisa tells me that the bereaved are encouraged to view the body, when possible and appropriate, because the seeing helps make the death "real." Thus grief begins and later denial will tend to be diminished. The father was afraid of his reaction, so he asked the colonel to accompany him. The sight of his son's dead body was terrible. The colonel held the reeling father. The return of a son's body is a little-discussed part of the war. C. D. B. Bryan's book about Peg and Gene Mullen is an exception.

Also during the war, a platoon leader crouched at night in the middle of a defensive perimeter constructed by his men far out in the field. Under fierce hand-to-hand attack they were being overrun. One of the platoon's defensive precautions within the perimeter was to place explosives around cans of fuel. In the heat of the overwhelming attack, the lieutenant detonated all the explosives. The earth erupted. Eardrums ruptured. Some of his own men were killed. The enemy withdrew. He was able only to begin talking about the incident after ten years. He keenly feels the burden of losing his own men. Even some men cited for valor in battle feel continuing pain for not performing with one notch more efficiency, so that one more friend's death would have been avoided. Health requires that these kinds of incidents be talked through with those of us who care. That is a primary value of the outreach centers and is a vital reason for dialogue.

In *The Wounded Generation* there are glimpses of two more sources of contemporary pain. Wallace Terry covered the Vietnam War for *Time* and produced an award-winning documentary on black GI's in combat, *Guess Who's Coming Home*. Janice Terry, his wife, made eighteen trips to Vietnam from her home in Singapore, visiting every war zone. Both are black. They report that by the war's peak in 1968, blacks, eleven percent of the American population, comprised fourteen percent of the combat deaths: "There was little to support the charges of some black leaders that black soldiers were being unwillingly used as 'cannon fodder.' Most black soldiers, in 1966 and 1967, were eager to prove themselves in combat and agreed that the war was worth fighting to halt the spread of communism." *The blacks earned respect in battle:* "It becomes clearer . . . that the black soldier would forevermore be respected not only by the enemies of his uniform but by his white comrade-in-arms—even those who wore Ku Klux Klan costumes, burned crosses, and waved Confederate flags on the fields of Vietnam." But in America, the respect bore little fruit. That is the hurt. One study in 1977 showed that twenty-eight percent of black veterans surveyed were unemployed; the corresponding figure for white veterans was three percent. The war protest, women's movement, and environmental movement drained some of the resources of the civil rights movement. Then in a terrible poetry, Marine veteran Allan Bakke prevailed in his reverse-discrimination case, in a sense pitting veteran against veteran. Although the case alleged reverse discrimination in an Affirmative Action program, in effect it also pitted one veteran's urgent need to catch up on lost years of civilian educational and work opportunity against black veterans' claim to respect for honest service, since blacks were helped in Affirmative Action programs. Blacks gave up the same years Bakke did, and they faced the same shunning. But the events of the war years simultaneously heightened their sense of respect and claim to respect while eroding America's ability to honor the claim.

The Terrys also interviewed Carolyn Paton, an older black psychologist who joined the Peace Corps in 1964. She went to the Caribbean in 1967 and stayed until 1970. She revealed something about Peace Corps life in the late sixties:

> The war impacted on me as a Peace Corps country director in light of the changes in the nature of the volunteers we got in the field. In the early '60's the people who joined were pretty much idealistic, dedicated young Americans who thought that they could truly help Third World people. Toward the later '60's we were getting the drug people and the Vietnam draft dodger. . . . it was a tacit understanding that if you served in the Peace Corps you could avoid going to Vietnam. I was very, very concerned about the level of people we were getting, especially whites who were patronizing or unconcerned and insensitive to the needs of Third World people. Another problem that we had was that many young people we recruited wanted to use their position in Third World countries to speak out against Vietnam and embarrass host nations. The most widely publicized incident of this type was when an American in Chile wrote a letter back to *The New York Times* as a Peace Corps volunteer opposing the Vietnam War.

She also revealed something about blacks serving in Vietnam:

> [Y]ou learned to be responsible for yourself and what it means to have power. You never forget that. And I think a lot of the black Vietnam veterans who came back did not simply go back to the hills and pick up that hoe and climb behind that mule, because Vietnam gave them a chance to experience power. And it cost. A hell of a lot, but I think we are a different group of people as a result of that experience.

## ANGER, GUILT, AND DENIAL

Carolyn Paton, the gray-haired observer of the sixties, has no pretense of flawlessness in assessing Peace Corps life. I wish she had been at Tom Pauken's confirmation hearings or at the

VVLP hearings, to calm us all down. It occurs to me that part of the anger among the Peace Corps volunteers and sixties activists involves a heated denial that good could emerge from the military service they protested or that the law of human fallibility operated in their own ranks.

Elissa Melamed entitled her book about aging among women *Mirror Mirror*. The imagery of mirrors is a way of expressing truths about ourselves. The mirror can be an alter ego or the response of a friend who listens to us. Or it can be a statement at a congressional hearing by someone perceived to be a foe. Mirrors can be frightening. One of Saint Paul's images of the Last Judgment is of no longer seeing in a mirror dimly, but coming face to face with ourselves, with truth, with the Creator who knew us while we were still in the womb.

Mirrors in these different guises can make people angry. They bring guilt to the surface. Christopher Buckley originally titled his reflections in *Esquire,* "Hell No, We Didn't Go!" The face of the Vietnam Veterans Memorial is so polished that it is a near-perfect mirror. Faces, clouds, even the distant Capitol dome, Washington Monument, and Lincoln Memorial are clearly reflected. When a crowd stands in front of the Memorial, I sometimes imagine the reflected images as the dead men, looking back at us. A sea of faces, like in Michelangelo's *Creation* or *Last Judgment*. That it is a vast mirror makes the Memorial evocative. I think it also disturbs many people. During the design controversy, there were pleas for a white surface, which reflects not at all, and for substitution of the names with a fixed single image, which diminishes introspection. Christopher Buckley found the Memorial evocative. It helped inspire his *Esquire* article.

It takes time to decide to look in the mirror. It can take years.

## SILENCE

Jim Fallows mentioned to me that his Harvard friends rarely mentioned his 1975 article, "What Did You Do in the Class War, Daddy?" They certainly read it; it was published and republished nationally. The feelings laid bare in the article are intensely personal. They have to do with manhood, rites of passage, and perceptions of sexual and political power. A direct result of his article was friendships with Vietnam veterans. In his revelations we understood that he was like us, in that he hurt and the circumstances of the hurt mattered greatly. His disclosure of a personal burden drew friends from an unexpected quarter.

Still, silence about the experiences and consequences of the sixties movements remains the personal preference of many blacks and women, veterans and men who did not wear the uniform.

Many very able women and men have discussed these matters with me and said they preferred more time to mull them over before expressing themselves publicly. An example is Virginia Bensheimer, editorial writer for the *Louisville Courier-Journal*. In 1981, a friend showed me an editorial on the Memorial: "The intent can only be to honor the dead, who gave their country the ultimate gift, without unduly glorifying the conflict about which many Americans still have painfully conflicting emotions: . . . Must a war monument be like every other war monument to speak its message of respect and honor?" In the wording and objectivity I sensed a woman's hand and said so. I called the newspaper. The author is Virginia. I think that many of us like Virginia will have a lot to offer when we begin to express ourselves on the larger issues of how the events of the sixties and seventies are shaping us now.

The silence is natural and not permanent. It reflects in part the operation of the grief process in the early stages of assimilating a loss. And the truth is complicated and will take time to figure out. It took many Vietnam veterans *years* just to figure out how to live and grow with some interior peace in post-Vietnam America, much less to begin to verbalize what in fact is going on.

## TIES

In time, those among us who articulate the particular hurts or new ideas rooted in our past will strike chords of response. The VVLP is a narrow example. Christopher Buckley's *Esquire* essay refers to Jim Fallows' "Class War" article and to the research by Arthur Egendorf in the *Legacies of Vietnam* federal study. Fallows attended Harvard College and is a Democrat. Buckley is a Republican from Yale College, and Egendorf is a

Vietnam veteran and Harvard College graduate. These men are gifted, serious thinkers and writers who agree that it is important even if painful to begin to explore how divisions have been created among us.

To some extent, the ties among our generation will be used and strengthened by the writers like Ginny Bensheimer and Christopher Buckley. Working together is a vehicle for renewing those ties, as in the camaraderie found in the WGBH series on Vietnam, the VVLP, and the Memorial Fund. I think the force for renewal will be potent in organizations formed of members of our generation. The conglomeration of people at the Memorial Fund supports the point.

Jan Scruggs grew up in rural Maryland, near Bowie. He volunteered to join the Army and serve in Vietnam. He was a private and a combat soldier at nineteen. He walked his share of hours as point man in patrols. He developed the seasoned soldier's eye for spotting insincerity, poor planning, and bad leadership. The North Vietnamese nearly killed him, leaving a load of shrapnel parked at various places in his body. Bob Doubek comes from Chicago and is proud of his Czech roots. His family manufactures cookies. Prudent and thorough, he was an Air Force intelligence officer ("spook") in Vietnam, then became a lawyer. Michael Shannon Davison, West Point 39, rose to four-star rank and Field Force Command in Vietnam through service in World War II and Korea. Classmates of his died in the Bataan Death March and in Japanese prison camps. With a son in the class of 1964, few men better understand the West Point classes of the sixties. West Point has a Century Club. It is a club for men who have walked one-hundred hours of punishment tours (marching with rifle in dress uniform, back and forth across the paved barracks courtyard). As chief of discipline and military training, he oversaw Joe Zengerle's selection to the Club. He oversaw hours walked by John Wheeler, Lucian Truscott, Art Mosley. Over six feet tall, he is a lithe skier, compassionate, and spare in speech. "Big Mike," cadets called him. He tells a joke on himself. In 1979, in comes his friend, the equally tall black brigadier general   George B. Price, the brother of Leontyne Price: ("I don't sing in no choirs; she don't fight in no wars.") Price, in deep, rumbling voice: "General, I've met a private you should meet. He's going to build a Memorial for Vietnam veterans. He has Senator Mathias and Senator Warner interested." Davison: "That's fine, George. Be glad to. Say, George, *how do you talk to a private?*"

In entering Yale Law School, my fantasy was to work my way up to partner in a law firm. I pictured the fellowship of professional equals rolling up their sleeves and together solving problems. I like the picture, with its spirit of community. But I met Mac, and that led to securities law and world-hunger articles and the offers of government work. Then I read the article about Jan. He, Bob Doubek, and I combined our skills. We were partners. Every skill I had was tested. General Davison gave us his advice as we saw how easily our own objectivity could disappear. A creaky private, a Chicago cookie scion, a dented captain, and a tough old general.

I found what I wanted, but with a surprising twist. I was partner in a Memorial firm. It was wildly improbable, something I could not have predicted. The work was personally healing for all of us because it involved relating some ignored parts of the national as well as our individual past to the present and the future. The experience made me think about faith. Christianity itself rests on an improbable story. The story can be debated, but *who would have dreamed up such an improbable story?* Surprises carry the ring of truth. Our partnership also taught us that we were not the focus. The job and certainty of obstacles were so intimidating that we *knew* we each were vulnerable. The community of effort had to be our focus.

If the Memorial brings healing, than I think God's hand touched us as a group. If God succeeded through such an assortment of nuts and bolts, consider what more He could do through a less wacky crew.

*At a lunch counter in 1976, I told Art Mosley that Elisa and I were having a baby. He considered. "That's very, very heavy," he said. (More than he knew; at birth Katie was eight pounds three ounces and John seven pounds eleven ounces. We didn't know we would have twins for months after the lunch.) Was my exposure to Agent Orange responsible for their birth defects?*

*In the week after the births, Elisa was in her hospital room recovering from surgery. We awaited the verdict on John's heart. Katie was in intensive care and might die. A christening in church at three or four weeks' age might not be possible. Edgar Romig came over from Epiphany Church. He stood by me and Katie, in her crib with all the wires. "Name this child," he said. "Katherine Marie Wheeler." He touched her forehead: "Katherine, I baptize you in the name of the Father, and of the Son, and of the Holy Spirit. . . . You are sealed by the Holy Spirit in Baptism and marked as Christ's own forever." I slept alone at the house. I awoke at 4:30 a.m. to call the hospital. "Is my daughter still alive?" She might have brain damage. I remember showering once, exhausted. I leaned against the tiles in the flow of water and wept. I prayed that Katie would live long enough for me to swing her on a swing in sunshine someday, and have a mind that knew that I loved her.*

"Sir, a child of mine lies paralyzed and racked with pain."

"I will come and cure her."

"Sir, who am I to have you under my roof? You need only to say the word and the child will be cured. I know, for I have myself been under orders, with soldiers under me. I say to one, 'Go,' and he goes; to another, 'Come here,' and he comes; and to my servant, 'Do this,' and he does it."

*Art asked me during those days what I did to sustain hope. I told him about my prayer the morning I wept in the shower. I never told anyone else.*

# CHAPTER EIGHT

*Lanford Wilson's play is one of the few*
*in recent years to paint a picture of the*
*1960's generation, a decade later, in colors*
*that are both true and touching. . . . Their*
*lives have been shaped by Berkeley, pot,*
*protest, the Vietnam War and the liberation*
*of our sexual mores. Ken, a homosexual who*
*lost both legs in Vietnam and now lives*
*openly with his male lover, can even refer*
*to himself as "Super Fag," and no one bats*
*an eye. Gwen sniffs coke, discusses her sex*
*life and indulges all her raging neuroses as*
*a wealthy copper heiress who really wants*
*to make it as a country-western singer.*

David Richards
Review of *Fifth of July*,
*Washington Post*
May 21, 1983

*It sometimes happens that a single image,*
*a tiny radioactive particle . . . has the*
*power to start a chain reaction in millions*
*of brains. Sometimes a still picture or*
*even a phrase can flash through the*
*nation with the same effect. The process . . .*
*[is] not logical, rational, or consistent.*

Godfrey Hodgson
*America in Our Time*
Discussion of reporting
of Tet '68

# STEREOTYPES AND AVOIDANCE

Why does Lanford Wilson choose to put his Vietnam veteran into a wheelchair, chop off his legs, and bar him from approaching women? And why does he debilitate his female lead with neurosis? It is my opinion that these depictions represent fear. It is fear of the health in Vietnam veterans and in women. It is fear of potency and authority evidenced and earned in a hard way by Vietnam veterans. This reflects some fear of how the past really was and how it really affects the present. To move radioactive metal, break it into pieces and shield it. Break his legs and protect the women. The more afraid one is, the more fearsome others become. The more hurt, angry, and worthy of punishment one feels, the more natural it is to to replace oneself as the hurt, angry, and guilty one. Jan Scruggs tells the story of a Vietnam-veteran amputee approached by a war protester who says, "It serves you right." Wilson creates Ken and Gwen. Why does David Richards applaud?

Lanford Wilson is a poet, and so is David Richards. They have an inner ear that picks up truth. The truth is that health in others can be threatening, especially given any personal imperfection we find in ourselves. It is also true that health in ourselves can be threatening. Becoming well can mean giving up some familiar and even comfortable patterns. These are some of the reasons some congressional staffers and veterans view the VVLP with alarm. These are some of the reasons some politicians are edgy as women claim full partnership with men.

So the poet may instinctively, either consciously or unconsciously, choose images that avoid the nervousness in the audience. The play's images are stereotypes, like a cripple or a gifted but neurotic person. The avoidance of sensitive subjects lets the audience relax so that at least some communication can occur.

There is voltage in the idea of healthy masculinity because the idea runs counter to the assumptions of the sixties and seventies—dirty war, dirty men. I think that part of the message of Lanford Wilson's play is that in the early 1980s there is so much voltage in the idea of healthy masculinity, including masculinity of Vietnam veterans, that the voltage has to be "stepped down" in the transformer of a play, the way high city voltage is stepped down by the transformers near our houses. The idea of strong and healthy femininity also has high voltage, and has been stepped down by stereotypes about feminist stridency or about the allocation of time to husband's and children's needs.

In this instance, a stereotype is not necessarily an unflattering image. It is instead an image for softening, mediating a truth, and presenting the truth in a way that audiences find attractive. Scriptwriters or journalists might instinctively believe the truth to be too strong for direct presentation, or, for a time, any presentation at all. The situation changes over time, as writers' perception both of the subject and of public receptivity changes. The use of images or stereotypes in this manner is avoidance, and sometimes it is healthy. It can be more constructive to offer a digestible truth than a larger truth that will not reach an audience. The images used and the process of avoidance can vary among our institutions. Avoidance is probably most prevalent in politics, news and media commentary, since they represent the nonfiction and practical side of life, where change and truth are most threatening. There is somewhat less avoidance in school curriculums, since the academic setting involves a sense of cushion and distance from reality. The arts tend to arrive at the direct truth first.

The stereotyping and avoidance can be bold and stunning, as in the complete negation or exclusion of a truth, or it can be subtle as artists (again, either consciously or subconsciously) employ a fascinating progression of symbols and settings to ease a truth into the public consciousness.

## POLITICS, NEWS, AND COMMENTATORS

Mel Krupin's is where professional Washington meets for lunch: ample room, ample menu, comfortable decor, and spirited management. Everybody goes. It is a tradition. There are booths and tables, signed caricatures of city notables, and Redskins posters. There is a framed note on the wall honoring Stu Stiller, the young lawyer who gave the uproarious lectures on criminal law in my D.C. bar-exam cram course. We laughed, so we learned. He died a few years later. Just before the bar exam he told us one of his Rules to Remember: "You don't always get what you want in life, but usually, with work, you get what you need."

In early 1983 I called David Broder, the political columnist for the *Washington Post*. In planning the *Century Generation* monthly report on how events of the Vietnam era shape America, I had pieced together some thoughts about his 1980 book on our generation, *Changing of the Guard*. We met over the phone. He offered lunch. The maitre d' said, "Ah, Mr. Broder's guest. This way." David appeared, warm, gentle, a patient listener, and with evident affection for our generation. He is national political correspondent and an editor for the *Post*. In 1973 he won the Pulitzer Prize for Distinguished Commentary. Two hundred and sixty papers carry his political column. He is often on TV and travels to lecture. He has been called "the single most influential voice in American presidential politics" and "the high priest of political journalism." He emphatically agreed that the divisions among our generation are important and need examination. He offered his help. He had listened to my theory about his book. He said, "That's a fair criticism."

His book examines the way our generation is poising itself politically for the tasks of national leadership in the coming decades. The book examines the networks that operate among our age group—organizers (like Tom Hayden and Sam Brown), the New Right (like Phil Gramm and David Stockman), labor and business leaders (where our generation is only just emerging), public-interest lawyers and reformers, women, Hispanics, and blacks. Some of these groups cut across party lines, although, with the exception of the New Right, most are Democratic rather than Republican. But they share common interests that can be tighter than party bonds and they stay in touch within their networks. Broder's assertion is that one indicator of our generation's future is the dynamics of the network that each of us feels bonded to.

The book completely omits ex-soldiers as a key political network of leaders. Among the ten million men who wore the uniform, especially the three million who returned from Vietnam, the shared hardships, values, and friendships are strong. The network is active, and it includes brotherly counselors who served in Korea, like Peter Braestrup and Ralph Wadeson.

The title *Changing of the Guard* is a military metaphor. At West Point, change of guard was a formal matter, ceremonial in character. Its formal name is Guard Mount. Given the imagery of the book's title, the omission of bonding among veterans is ironic. For example, World War II service is a common thread among senior national leaders. The qualities nurtured in wartime service—wisdom and the spirit of sacrifice and love of country—are distinct from single-issue politics. Broder points out that Congressman Phil Gramm replaced Olin ("Tiger") Teague, "a wounded World War II veteran who had served [in the House] for thirty-two years and who had, in fact, been the sponsor of the War Orphans Act under which Gramm, the son of a disabled veteran himself, had gone to college." In five pages at the book's beginning Broder lists veterans recently elected to Congress. In these several ways Broder walks right up to the obvious but remains silent.

*There should be a network here, given the bonding. And if there is not one, that is of even greater political significance, for it marks a sea change in the underlying currents of respect, authority, compassion, and power in America.*

There has been no sea change. The Vietnam soldiers are no exception. Preliminary evidence is shown in their cohesion and leadership in creating Federal Express, the National Vietnam Veterans Memorial, and the Vietnam Veterans Leadership Program, among other achievements.

Also disturbing is Broder's chapter "Women," discussing the new feminine political network. For most young Americans, the potential for full man-woman partnership in all career fields amounts to the most striking tension within our generation. Controversy about the integrity of homemaking as a vocation is an example. What will society be like when perhaps half *and more* of the senior administrators are women? The book does not analyze deeper aspects of bonding, sex, and power.

One important factor is that David writes from a perspective outside the generation. He accurately portrays what is visible. The currents that are felt but not visible, and which have not electrified the political field, are too intangible to detect. The currents of leadership and creativity emergent in the generation are larger than politics, and will govern politics, so it will take a process of some years of inquiry and examination to understand what is happening. Another factor is that David casts his net a bit under, and just over, the Americans who came of age during the sixties and early seventies. The scope includes people fifty years old in 1980. Had the analysis zeroed in on the actual baby boom, roughly those who reached twenty-one during the Vietnam War years, the influential effects of wartime events would have been more evident, including the separations present in the early eighties. The sixty million of us in the Vietnam generation—the Century Generation—are the core of Broder's story and overshadow the book's diffuse twenty-five-year span of people.

Other commentators, such as James Reston, George Will, and Ed Yoder have all evinced interest in the issues but have not explored them. Mary McGrory, Phil Geyelin, Suzanne Garment, Jack Anderson, Colman McCarthy, Hugh Sidey, James Kilpatrick, and Ellen Goodman reported the Memorial Fund story and in conversation have also shown interest in the deeper issues of separation and convergent creativity, including the story of creativity among Vietnam veterans.

## SCHOOLS

In colleges and universities there tends to be a division of labor between the departments of political science and history, in which more recent events, like those of the Vietnam period, are taught in the political science department. But the practice is not uniform. Alan Brinkley's successful course at Harvard is in the history department. Especially in these departments, there is resurgent research, teaching, and student interest in the events of the Vietnam War period. Fox Butterfield's February 13, 1983, *New York Times* cover story, "The New Vietnam Scholarship," reports this interest, with the observation, "Until quite recently, Vietnam has been a giant black hole in American academia."

The *New Yorker*'s August 1, 1983, letter from its "young friend" shows interest that succeeding generations have in the political passions of the sixties. According to Butterfield's story, though, the researchers are still few in number, and contribution from departments of sociology, psychology, English, and anthropology are nascent.

Butterfield reports an important fact: few academics were in Vietnam. Many protested the war. Stephen Vlastos, war protester, Princeton '66, is professor of history at the University of Iowa, teaching "The Vietnam War in Historical Perspective." "He is candid about his antiwar sentiments," reports Butterfield, quoting Vlastos: "It's the reason I'm teaching the course." Is he teaching the whole story? Is he discussing his personal sentiments? Looking squarely at the war years as a disciplined and objective scholar must be extraordinarily difficult, like being a harpooner on the small dories launched by the whaling ships of old. What beast is there, and how deep will it sound? Will the rope sear and then drown me? But there is help. As the VVLP shows, there are very able Vietnam veterans all over the country who will volunteer to aid teachers with courses on the sixties and the American future. Butterfield reports, "One of the most imaginative new classes is at the University of Louisville, taught by an unlikely duo: a former hawkish artillery officer in Vietnam, Richard N. Pfeiffer, and a confirmed antiwar activist with a Ph.D. in East Asian history." Pfeiffer is vice president of an industrial supply firm. Andrea McElderry, the Ph.D., is an associate professor of history. She says, "Until I met Richard, I was sure of my views about Vietnam. He has made me rethink them, and I have influenced him, too. I couldn't have taught the course the same way with my Asian specialist colleagues, because all of them were getting 2-S student deferments during Vietnam."

It is signal to me that in Butterfield's report it is a woman who is bridging the gulf between men who wore the uniform and men who did not, so that students can judge all the evidence for themselves. If, for males who protested the war or did not wear the uniform, the questions about the war years may touch nerves connected to masculinity, power, and loyalty, then females would find the questions less hard to broach. As threatening as the questions may be to women, the most fiery crucible of personal decision in the sixties was war. Do I go? Am I afraid? Who is sure he wants to remember that furnace and peer into the mirror at the final product? *But there may be health in doing so and health in the image we see.*

## THE ARTS

The depictions of veterans from Lanford Wilson's paraplegic and homosexual Ken through the tortured but sympathetic men in *Coming Home* and *The Deer Hunter* and the gregarious figures in *The A-Team, Magnum,* and *Rage of Angels* demonstrate the push and pull as artists depict the man from Vietnam. The film *Apocalypse Now* has a secret in it, I think. Its depiction of the technology of battle is technically accurate. Phil Caputo told me that the helicopter assault scene was so real that in the theater he became briefly disoriented; *he was in the helicopter again.* However, the secret is that the distant jungle city, the heart of darkness, to which the soldiers traveled was America. America was the darkened heart we came home to. What else could the savage assemblies, music, dancing, and soldier slaying in that dark city possibly have depicted, if not America of the sixties and early seventies?

Art is imagery and poetry. William Shatner is Hollywood's Captain Kirk of the starship *Enterprise* in *Star Trek.* His friend is the loyal and powerful first officer, Spock, played by costar Leonard Nimoy. Spock, from a strange place. A powerful friend. In 1983, Shatner became T. J. Hooker, senior police lieutenant who takes care of his men. All are compassionate about the hurts of the city. Hooker's friend and sidekick is Officer Vince Romano, Vietnam veteran, played by costar Adrian Zmed. In a sense, Spock has become Romano. In the arts, the soldier is now being given an identity other than as a soldier. He is a policeman or a private eye or a politician. One purpose of the National Vietnam Veterans Memorial is to separate the warrior from the war. The warriors did not create the war or prolong it. Ultimately, Vietnam veterans will carve their own image.

Stereotypes are to some extent two-way streets. Vietnam veterans themselves use them as a safe way to express some part of themselves. On our coming home, America beheld us with stony silence. The media characterized veterans as hurt and angry. So that was the reflection of ourselves we could acceptably show: anger, and, only indirectly, compassion, wisdom, or creativity. Lewis Bruchey led long-range recon patrols, and received the Silver Star for valor in forty-seven missions. His poem, "Cold, Stone Man," ends:

> Save your
>    judgment,
> Your sorrow,
> Your pity,
> Your prayer.
>
> For I am
> A cold, stone man
> Of Vietnam.
> Beware! Beware!

This is an example. Lewis is married, passionate, and compassionate. He was showing to America the only part of himself that I think America would appreciate at the time, or would choose to see.

But stereotypes are exasperating. Blake Edwards is a successful stand-up comedian, a Vietnam veteran. One of his stories goes something like this: "Hey, you know I was in Vietnam. Going was bad. Coming back was bad. Guy comes up to me and says, 'You Vietnam veterans are all the same! Violent, angry, irrational!' So I pulled out a pistol and shot him." Yet the stereotypes also are a creative stimulus; the subjects can react to express the larger truth about themselves. Tom Pauken testified that stereotypes were a main reason he took the VVLP idea to the president:

> I have been distressed since the time I returned from Vietnam, to see the image of the Vietnam veterans portrayed as losers, fools, or dope addicts. Now, there is an additional new mythology—it is Vietnam veterans as guilt-ridden victims, ashamed of their service. I think it is important to recognize that more than

8o percent of the Vietnam veterans, even with enormous difficulties, have come home and have made the successful transition back to civilian life. They are doing well. I think that we need to help some of those successful Vietnam veterans restore a sense of pride and self-worth to all veterans. This will be accomplished by mobilizing this massive body of successful veterans as volunteers to help those who still need a hand. In this small way, we who did return can help fulfill our debt to those who did not.

*Norman Mailer, James Michener, Kurt Vonnegut, and Herman Wouk are originals and, incidentally, veterans. So are Phil Caputo, John Del Vecchio, Tim O'Brien, and James Webb. And Jan Scruggs. When Tom Pauken brought me into ACTION to form the VVLP he told me, "Winnie will arrange it. Talk to her." Winifred Pizzano, deputy director of ACTION. An experienced young woman Republican, she knew Washington politics, including budget politics. There would be no VVLP money without her help and insight. She is an original. The VVLP story. I could never have made it up.*

*We are each of us, every one, an original.*

# PART III
# TO COME

In the future day, which we seek
to make secure, we look forward to
a world founded upon four essential
human freedoms.

The first is freedom of speech and
expression—everywhere in the world.

The second is freedom of every
person to worship God in his own
way—everywhere in the world.

The third is freedom from want
—which, translated into world
terms, means economic under-
standings which will secure to
every nation a healthy peaceful
life for its inhabitants—
everywhere in the world.

The fourth is freedom from fear
—which, translated into world
terms, means a world-wide
reduction of armaments to such
a point and in such a thorough
fashion that no nation will be in
a position to commit an act of
aggression against any neighbor
—anywhere in the world.

*Franklin D. Roosevelt*
*January 6, 1941*

# CHAPTER NINE

*Whom shall I send?*
*Who will go for me?*

Call to Isaiah
*Old Testament*

*"Do you love me?"*
*"You know everything;*
*you know I love you."*
*"Feed my sheep."*

Jesus and Peter
*New Testament*

# LEADERSHIP, AUTHORITY, AND RESPONSIBILITY

"Leadership" is a word, like "honor," which seems awkward in the 1980s. Michael Barone wrote in an August 25, 1983, *Washington Post* column about the public wariness shown in opinion polls on United States policy in El Salvador and Nicaragua, "This skepticism reflects a general tendency to disbelieve leaders today." I am not sure that the tendency was so absent in the past. Lincoln was vilified in the press. Nevertheless, the tendency is strong today, and, Barone continues, it grows in part out of the public's "deep-seated feelings and searing personal experiences" arising from the "vivid historical experience of Vietnam."

In a pluralistic society, anger and dissent can be tough on leaders. James Webb said, "we are going to be at each other's throats, and that's beautiful, because it's creative." Given the anger from the sixties and early seventies that resides in the public memory, going for "each other's throats" can get out of hand. The controversy over the design of the Vietnam Veterans Memorial is a clue that this is true, especially some of the bitter denunciations of the hope that honoring Vietnam veterans could help foster national reconciliation in wake of the war. Webb concluded his hope with the condition, "as long as we can sort of hold the outer fabric together." If the condition means anything it must mean at least that there be an effort to diminish excesses of anger and vilification directed at opponents in political and social debate.

In Vietnam, on the night Bruns Grayson told me about his travail in applying to colleges, we went back to his hootch in his company area. Showing me the books he read, he selected a volume. He turned on a small reading light, and I settled on a footlocker, my head against the wall. It was after midnight. He read from a poem.

> Things fall apart; the centre cannot hold:
> Mere anarchy is loosed upon the world,
> The blood-dimmed tide is loosed, and everywhere
> The ceremony of innocence is drowned.

He ended,

> And what rough beast, its hour come around at last,
> Slouches toward Bethlehem to be born?

Years later, Godfrey Hodgson would cite these lines in *America in Our Time,* saying with regard to the public memory of the sixties, "Not a few have thought of the lines from Yeats' poem *The Second Coming.*" When in 1973, at Bruns' request I wrote to the Rhodes Scholarship interview committee about him, I dwelled on the poetry he read and how the poem seemed to apply to American life in 1970. The "centre" became a hard place to be.

Hodgson reported that "consensus had yielded to schism." Bill Jayne remarked on this to the veterans who gathered to discuss writing on November 11, 1982. The workshop invitation had explained that the purpose was to encourage Vietnam veterans to write, beginning with one-thousand- to three-thousand-word publishable papers:

> "The topic can be any topic under the heading "Commitment to Country" or either of the subheads "Commitment to Remember" and "Commitment to Serve." The intent is to relate explicitly your experience in and after Vietnam to the questions of where our country should go in remembering the events of the war years, or of your view of certain national problems, in light of the personal seasoning you have undergone as a person who fought, returned, and continued your vocation.

Citing Paul Fussell's reflections on World War I in *The Great War and Modern Memory,* Bill wrote a letter to me on the discussion group he had chaired:

> I presented this concern in terms of what you called "Commitment to Country." In other words, it seems that the Vietnam War was for many Americans the same sort of polarizing event that World War I was for Western Europe, in particular, and the "intelligentsia" of Western Civilization in general.
>
> The experience has left us with a legacy of pronounced polarization, a binary view that reduces questions of policy to two opposing views: One is opposed to the black, submerged Vietnam Veterans Memorial or one is an "antiwar" apologist bent on destroying the fabric of American society; one is opposed to the national resource policies of the Reagan Administration or one is an enemy of the environment bent on destroying our natural heritage; one is a proponent of the "nuclear freeze" or one is a mad militarist bent on the destruction of life on the planet.
>
> As a veteran, I felt that my experience of commitment to country, my concrete experience of citizenship, allowed me, paradoxically perhaps, to avoid this "imaginative habit." Having seen firsthand the destructiveness of war itself, the destructiveness of the imaginary habit of the binary view carried to its extreme actualization, I felt a particular urgency in the task of avoiding the binary view.

This is the condition that produces Jim Fallows' speculation that anticipation of being "yelled at" inhibits men who did not wear the uniform from discussing the consequences of national and personal decisions made during the Vietnam era.

One means to down-scale the enmity and anger Jayne diagnoses is to carry out a careful commitment to remembering, in the sense of exposing the influential experiences and memories that continue to shape us most significantly. This would be a step toward making it easier for leaders to find a consensus among us on key issues. It will help make it easier for members of our generation to address successfully the larger question which, in our youth, we posed for ourselves, as identified by Hodgson in remarks by *Time* editor-in-chief Hedley Donovan:

> We look out on this world of 1969 as a deeply con-
> fused country. It is easy to say that it is the cruel
> question of Vietnam that has got us so mixed up. . . .
> But I believe the causes of our confusion go much
> deeper than Vietnam. Indeed the Vietnam experience
> . . . has in a sense masked a more fundamental change
> in the underpinnings of American foreign policy. That
> change, very simply, is the loss of a working consen-
> sus, for the first time in our lives, as to what we think
> America means.

People tend to forget that John Kennedy had been responsible for early commitments in Vietnam, and that Lyndon Johnson felt he had some obligation to honor those commitments. Kennedy's sweeping panorama in 1961 of American purpose, power, and willingness to pay any price was a leader's grand vision. That vision encouraged us to fly to the moon and to launch the Peace Corps. It also landed us in Vietnam. Doubtless, the contrast between the national vision in 1961 and the national division in 1969 makes America judge its leaders harshly, particularly in light of Watergate and the "binary view." Leadership is important in all areas of life, not only politics. In his column, Michael Barone brought up a point that makes many leadership situations exasperating: "On every difficult policy question, public opinion is inconsistent. Ordinary people are maddeningly unwilling to resolve these inconsistencies: that's what they hire public officials to do."

Two aspects of leadership for our generation have been obscured by the trends of the sixties and seventies. Dusting them off and keeping them in mind will enable prospective leaders and constituencies to define the kinds of American purposes we are willing to fulfill. One aspect is authority. The other is responsibility.

## AUTHORITY

The Episcopal Church in the United States is administered by a presiding bishop assisted by an executive council of lay people. While at Yale, I served a term on the Executive Council's Committee on Social Responsibility in Investments, and after several years off the Committee, was reappointed in 1982. At one of the 1983 meetings, a consultant in her thirties reported that many church groups are against militarism. In her voice and manner was what I perceived to be the attitude, "All things military are all bad." I asked her what she meant by the term "militarism." Her response was, "A hierarchical structure." The implication was that power is suspect and so is structure. As Edwin Yoder has argued in his writing, in the popular mind, institutions have become especially suspect, and the consultant's response struck me as evidence for Yoder's view.

Yet part of the exercise of leadership is authority, the power of leaders to implement their decisions. Structure and hierarchies are often an effective way for leaders to exert authority. In the business world, this is an accepted framework. It is accepted as part of the life of most religious denominations. But it is not so widely accepted in the life of American politics or social movements. David Broder sensed this in his many interviews with members of our generation, and he found it disquieting: "Much of the question about their leadership potential turns on the issue of how comfortable they are with the exercise of power. The pervasiveness and the fervor of their anti-bureaucratic sentiment was striking." Not having examined the network among men who wore the uniform or returned from Vietnam, Broder concluded about the young leaders he met, "Most of them have spent much of their lives, at this point, on the outside, lobbing bricks—real or verbal—at the establishment. In those movements, as Dick Celeste pointed out, authority was so decentralized, the command structure so loose, that even local leaders could 'do their own thing.' " Broder cites President Carter as such an "entrepreneur," and characterizes Congress as "535 individual entrepreneurs." He concludes, *"None of these individualists . . . is eager to accept the discipline involved in any hierarchical power structure"* [italics added].

Extreme individualism is a bar to commitment. It is a bar to the "small death" of self inherent in giving of oneself to another or to a group. It is also true that in extremes of commitment and organization, individuals lose their identity and their capacity for innovation suffers. But the current balance in American political and social life seems to be tilted heavily toward extremes of individuality. The separations among us caused by the events of the war years must be one explanation, since the separations tend to prevent us from trusting and subscribing to authority, from accepting our common purpose, and from esteeming others.

## RESPONSIBILITY

At the Supreme Court building on July 19, 1983, the American Institute for Public Service presented the annual Jefferson Awards. The award is a gold medal, and the Institute is a private institution. Jan Scruggs earned one for his work on the Vietnam Veterans Memorial. He invited me to the ceremony. There were television cameras in the small room. I felt proud for Jan and the Fund. Among the guests, I saw Justice Byron White, Senator Robert Taft, Senator Richard Lugar, and Jan's fellow recipients, including Kirk Douglas, Paul Volcker, and Helen Hayes.

There was also Candy Lightner. On Saturday, May 3, 1980, a drunk driver ran down and killed Candy's thirteen-year-old daughter, Cari, while she was walking to a school carnival. The driver had been arrested four times for drunk driving and had received four slaps on the wrist. *Who wants to talk about how our children are killed by drunks?* Candy founded Mothers Against Drunk Drivers—MADD—an organization of victims' families and interested citizens. Her organization has spread nationally, and is one of the most visible citizens action groups in recent years. Due to MADD's efforts, driving under the influence laws have been tightened in twenty-six states. MADD now has over two hundred chapters in forty-three states. In the Supreme Court, Candy showed us how much the memory of her daughter moved her. At the rostrum, and with an apology to all of us, she held out her medal, looked up and said, "This is for you."

Candy Lightner confronted Cari's death and felt a responsibility. Being a personal witness to a tragedy often imparts a sense of responsibility to provide help and healing. *If she does not act, who will?* Jan Scruggs saw the Vietnam War film *The Deerhunter* and felt a responsibility. This sense of responsibility for correcting the wrongs that personally grieve us is strong in our generation, as the activism of the sixties demonstrates. It is a force which counters the fashion against authority. As more and more writing from our generation examines and diminishes the separations and disesteem we feel, as there is frequent communication among us, we will form a consensus around issues which concern us and leaders will emerge around these issues. The improvement may be modest, but the malaise and fractiousness of the seventies are such severe impediments to a healthy community life in our country that modest improvement would be beneficial.

One aspect of being a witness to a hurt is that it gives authority. Christopher Buckley ended his *Esquire* article, "I should have been there, if only to bear witness." The speaker has his *own* authority because he is witness to his own interior life.

Part of the value of Vietnam veterans is the authority they command by virtue of their experience. Buckley's attitude suggests this authority, as does the advice to the Vietnam-veteran candidate by the political adviser in *Rage of Angels*. Godfrey Hodgson quotes Carl Kaysen about the memory that the intellectuals of the Kennedy administration had of World War II: "There we were, captains and majors, telling the whole world what to do." Vietnam veterans have their memory, of military successes and denial and rage at home. They are personal witness to Yeats' poem. By having endured and even in many cases creatively prospered through their experiences, they are accorded deference and power. "Spooky" means powerful. "Spooky" is the name of an airplane, the mightily armed C-47 in Vietnam. Michael Herr wrote in his book *Dispatches* about the many machine guns on the C-47. "It was awesome, worse than anything the Lord had ever put down on Egypt, and at night, you'd hear the Marines talking, watching it, yelling, 'Get some!' until they grew quiet and someone would say, 'Spooky understands.' "

On June 13, 1982, Kurt Vonnegut, like Michael Blumenthal, a poet, a person who sees, said, "What makes the Vietnam veterans so *spooky?* We could almost describe them as being 'unwholesomely mature.' They have never had illusions about war" [italics added]. This was part of an address at the Episcopal Cathedral of St. John the Divine in New York City, presided over by Bishop Paul Moore, wounded in battle as a Marine infantry commander in the Pacific and cited for valor, who became one of the most effective priests of the church in attacking urban poverty. Going and then coming home made many Vietnam veterans suddenly vastly mature. It took getting used to. It was a form of empowerment. I think Vonnegut senses the power and calls it "spooky." He does not know what to expect. For one prediction, he could look to the bishop.

There is a responsibility in the authority that Vietnam veterans are accorded. The authority can be dissipated in rash or selfish preoccupations, and it can be dissipated in blind anger at the past. But it can also be used in bearing witness to the American past and applying our witness to the reality of the present and the future. Many Vietnam veterans have begun the creative examination of our past that each woman and man of our generation could similarly undertake with the same benefit for us all. We can find an alternative to the harsh "binary" world described by Bill Jayne. We can join Bill Jayne in looking for a third way. In his *Legacies of Vietnam* report, Arthur Egendorf concluded:

> Vietnam veterans should be a concern to policymakers not only because of their need, but of their potential contribution to a renewed national identity. The soldiers who carried the brunt of the battle have become the veterans who, more than most of their fellow citizens, feel the urgency of finding meaning in the sacrifices of the war years. While their official tour of duty is over, these men continue to perform a valuable service to their country by working through war experiences. American society ultimately gains from their efforts to derive significance from the confusion and pain still associated with that conflict.

In recent years, public discussions of American relations with other countries have frequently posed a choice between forgetting or remembering the Vietnam experience—putting it behind us or clinging steadfastly to it as an instance of what we must avoid at all cost. Our study of individual Vietnam veterans has revealed that a significant minority of these men have begun to explore a third way. They do not block out the pain and horror of the past. But neither do they insist that a fixed set of conclusions, drawn from their experience, be applied rigidly to all future situations. Working through past experience means, according to their example, to allow deeper, more encompassing and more flexible perspectives on the war to develop through reflection and dialogue. If the country as a whole wishes to derive important lessons from its experience in Vietnam, and also be open to seeing when a given lesson may not apply, it would do well to acknowledge and encourage Vietnam veterans as among those leading the way.

*Parenting is a form of leadership. It is a form of leadership where personal example is especially important. Children learn from the adults who spend time with them. The personal proximity of a parent is a powerful factor, powerful in presence, powerful in absence. Jeff Rogers was nearly killed in a situation of personal leadership. Frozen on the mountain slope under fire, no trooper would move. He led them up the ridgeline to safety by personal example, and attracted the bulk of enemy fire. The investment of self in showing by example is compelling. It shows a kind of love. It commands respect and earns authority. Witnessing such an example can inspire a sense of responsibility, to live up to and to show the same example. Sons tend to father as their fathers did. Perhaps the same is true for daughters and mothers. Jesus led by personal example. Personal example compelled attention to his message. The women and men he spent time with were drawn to become leaders. He said He was the Son of God. There are two choices, with no choice in between. One is that He was insane. Does insanity foster love like Peter's? Mary Magda-*

*lene's? Paul's? Martha's? The remaining choice is his story, the Nicene Creed. His claim left no room for an in-between position. Sometimes at night, going to sleep, I imagine what I would say, if I could go back to Galilee two thousand years ago and listen at the lakeside. I would speak up. And say what? Would I know Aramaic? I would sound odd in English. "Who is my enemy?" The Samaritan, nigger of the New Testament, is my neighbor. OK. But there is "Love your enemies." Who is my enemy? Besides turning the other cheek and praying for the enemy, how do I love an enemy? Surely friends and enemies are not to be known and treated identically? Teach me to know my enemy. Please, a parable about enemies. I live in a country and a time where it is unfashionable to believe there are enemies. Lead, kindly Light.*

*I know what I would expect to hear. "What troubles you? Why do enemies preoccupy you? I heard you in Dean Wood's office. I heard you in Professor McDougal's office. I heard you beside Katie's crib. Have you given thanks? Follow me. You will know an enemy soon enough."*

# CHAPTER TEN

*Let us suppose we possess parts of a novel
or a symphony. Someone now brings us
a newly discovered piece of manuscript
and says, "This is the missing part of
the work. This is the chapter on which
the whole plot of the novel really turned.
This is the main theme of the symphony."
Our business would be to see whether the
new passage, if admitted to the central
place which the discoverer claimed for it,
did actually illuminate all the parts we
had already seen and "pull them together." . . .
Something like this we must do with the
doctrine of the Incarnation. Here, instead
of a symphony or a novel, we have the
whole mass of our knowledge. . . . In the
Christian story God descends to reascend. . . .*

*So it is also in our moral and emotional
life. The first innocent and spontaneous
desires have to submit to the deathlike
process of control or total denial: but
from that there is a reascent to fully
formed character in which the strength
of the original material all operates but
in a new way. Death and Rebirth—go down
to go up—it is a key principle. Through this
bottleneck, this belittlement, the highroad
nearly always lies.*

C. S. Lewis
*Miracles*

# SPIRIT

At Katie's and John's birth I was anxious, like most parents. As Joe Zengerle said, the assumption of a smooth delivery with no hitches is easily rebuttable. As events cascaded during the next days I felt like I was in a vast, empty, and long tunnel. It was hellish. Everyone's voices seemed to echo. Elisa, Katie, and John were each in a separate ward. The correctability of John's heart murmur was in doubt. Every time Katie inhaled, there was a cry as she wrested air over her constricted vocal cords. It hurt to hear her. It must have hurt to breathe. We awaited the brain-damage test results. Katie was rushed by ambulance from Georgetown Hospital to Children's Hospital. Elisa and John remained in the wards at Georgetown. I stayed up much of each night with Katie. The week was like a long fall downstairs. It brought me to the exhausted prayer in the shower, and to my focus on what mattered most, to be able to communicate my love to Katie, for her to understand that I loved her.

As Karen Gray approached death, the occasion surely made her focus on what mattered to her most. She sought Elisa's and Vienna's companionship. In 1982 she became a communicant in the Episcopal Church, at St. Alban's parish in Washington, D.C. From the perspective of 1962, that was a surprising moment: two women priests usher in a new communicant, blessed by the Right Reverend John T. Walker, black, and bishop of the Church.

The profound moments in life awaken in us the ancient questions, like whom do we love? And why do we love? What in us even causes us to raise such questions? Surprises also nudge us toward similar wonder. Wordsworth called these nudges intimations. Professor McDougal surprised me. I did not expect the warmth of his reception or the power he gave me to chart my own legal education. The first paper I wrote for him was my plan for the next two years at law school. On the lower right corner I typed, from the movie sound track of Kazantzakis' *Zorba the Greek,* the dialogue where Zorba asks the student:

> "Why do the young die? Why does anybody die? Tell me."
> "I don't know."
> "What's the use of all your damn books? If they don't tell you that, what the hell do they tell you?"
> "They tell me . . . about the agony of men who . . . can't answer questions like yours."

## RESTLESSNESS

Another nudge toward wonder is an emptiness sometimes felt even when we have what we say we want. Augustine called it restlessness.

I think that restlessness, rather than exigency, characterizes the more common daily experience in our generation. In many ways the great movements of the sixties were successful, even successful in a revolutionary sense. And even most Vietnam veterans have things they longed for in-country, like a peaceful sleep, a woman's intimate love and children, being home in America. Nevertheless, many of us in the generation feel separated, either from others or a part of ourselves. The separations contribute to restlessness in each of us if only from the strain of estrangement we occasionally or frequently feel. In any event, there seems to be little sense of fulfillment based on the success of the causes we supported in the sixties. We want *more.* Even parents are restless with their children. We want them to grow or behave. There is a theological term of art called the incarnation. It means that God is *the* Heroic Materialist, in that He created *everything,* woman, man, relationships, gold, and then became a human part of the creation. The incarnation means that the things we see and touch are good, that God made them and shared in them as a human, but also that there is more to life than what we see and touch.

George C. Rosenwald and Jacquelyn Wiersma uncover examples of this restlessness in a survey of fifteen women who "had previously been committed to domestic work as housewives and mothers and had then made a decision to launch themselves on a different career.'' Rosenwald is a professor of psychology at the University of Michigan, and Wiersma is clinical assistant professor of psychology at the University of Minnesota. They argue that, while the women's movement has made strides, the combination of rhetoric and high expectations about the new careers open to women obscure how hard life can be in those careers. This includes a kind of binary problem similar to the one diagnosed by Bill Jayne: the women feel pushed to be all of one thing (career) or all of another (mother, wife). Society offers no forgiving middle ground: ''One may view the resistance they encounter as a measure of 'role breadth' that is, of societal or communal tolerance for acceptable variations within a role. Beyond these limits, the person attempting to *alter* the role is tallied as having *abandoned* the role.'' [italics added.]

This is the experience of many Vietnam veterans. They seek to *alter* their role of commitment to country among peers who have insisted they abandon their memory and persona as Vietnam veterans. It is true of nearly all former military people that entry into civilian life is accompanied by a continued sense of obligation in public service. But restlessness attends new roles.

## LETTER TO VALENTINA
My own experience as a Vietnam veteran with my own role changes, has been that faith makes restlessness bearable and even dissipates restlessness. My own faith is Christian. I think that the people most perplexed by Christianity are our peers in the Institute of the U.S.A. and Canada, in Moscow. The Institute is powerful. It is the official Soviet think tank for observing and explaining America to the Soviet hierarchy. It is the brainchild of Soviet Americanologist Georgi Arbatov. I love the Russian language and studied it at Hampton High and West Point. Tommy Hayes and I took Russian together our plebe year. Once for fun I translated the Harry Belafonte song ''Jamaica Farewell'' into Russian. I also translated ''Scarlet Ribbons'' and ''I Love Paris.'' After running through the English nursery rhymes, I sang my Russian songs to Katie in the hospital. Knowing the language yields some feel for the culture. Solzhenitsyn is insistent that the Russian culture and the Soviet state are not identical. Russia,

with its deep Christian roots, scares its government, and that is one reason the State stresses imaginary or real threats to the mother country posed by other nations. The Czars did the same thing. The threat to country tends to rally Russians to the State. Many of the grandparents of our Russian peers were baptized Christians. There is still an echo of Christianity in the family memory of Russians our age.

For the younger Russian staff in the Institute, Christianity must be puzzling. From their point of view the diversity in the United States makes prediction notoriously hard. I imagine these women and men our age poring over *Time, Newsweek, U.S. News & World Report*. The newspapers. Some probably travel or study in America under various arrangements. *Over half of America is affiliated with a church.* We are one of the most deeply evangelized nations in history. What is going on? I fantasize that there is one particular analyst in the Institute, an exceptionally able woman named Valentina. She is thirty-nine, born in 1944 while her father fought on the German Eastern front. Her husband is an administrator in the secret police. Both did well in the competition for schooling, met in Moscow, and enjoy a prized possession—a good apartment with access to a good school for their two children. Because she is bright and objective, Valentina senses that Christianity is an important component in American life. Understanding Christianity, though, must be hard in the confines of Soviet libraries, even those in the Institute. So, as a favor, in my mind's eye I compose this letter to Valentina.

Washington, D.C.
April, 1984

Dear Valentina,
I write in English. Yours is better than my Russian. I am a former soldier, like your father. Christianity in America is a puzzling concept to your group in the Institute, especially the idea that any of your American peers see anything weighty in Christianity, as far as their personal lives are concerned. In addition, the USSR and USA are the two most powerful nations on earth, with immense capacity for good and evil. It seems to me that, both as an expert on America and as a Russian, you might like the offer of friendship and explanation in this letter.

Religious commitment is an important current in American and world Life. Consider the public concern over the censure of Hans Küng or the considerable commentary on the recent changes in the Episcopal Prayer Book. The pope's travels draw a broad response. Our president professes religious faith, and in this he is not alone among world leaders. There are important religious voices in the pro-life/pro-choice debate on birth control. The Sinai accord, Lebanon's travail and the grim news from the Far East remind us that religious ideas have consequences.

Americans have diverse beliefs about God, and some believe in no God. But the same can be said about Keynesian economics. The point is that religious faith profoundly affects many Americans. Our understanding of God is important to understanding ourselves as a country, to explaining ourselves to others and in sorting out what we as individuals ought to do.

Other sets of beliefs that significantly inform American life— say, on economics, military spending, or education—receive exacting attention from you. One would expect this also to be true in regard to the central theological questions.

In fact, the import of the First Amendment to our Constitution is that freedom of the press and religion are among the ultimate strengths, as well as sanctuaries, of a free people.

Right now, the stakes of foreign policy seem again, as in the early forties, to be whether free speech, free press, and free worship have a future in the world. Shall Americans boldly extend these ideas to new places on the globe? Shall we even defend them where they now flourish?

The answers will be reflected in our individual choices. To some extent those choices will be affected by faith. The view of life through a theological lens shapes and colors the way we approach and interpret all of life, from world affairs to relations with neighbors.

This religious perspective needs full understanding by important observers like you. The need is to search the substance and importance of key Judaic, Christian, and Islamic ideas. For example, one beginning would be an awareness of the Christian view of historicity, sin, and vocation as one basis for interpreting world news. These ideas are powerful in the context of our time. They are powerful Judaic and Moslem ideas as well.

God acts in history. This idea radically shapes the Christian's thought. God created this world and the universe. That He acts in history and created us expresses the underlying truth that God loves us and has a purpose for this world and each of us.

In history, it was the Christian monk Cyril who created an alphabet so the Gospel could be spread in Russia. Your alphabet is the Cyrillic alphabet. In history, Aleksandr Solzhenitsyn was doubly lost, in the Gulag and in a cancer ward. He was doubly lost, like biblical Jonah, who was in a beast's belly beneath the sea, but who lived to prophesy. Now Solzhenitsyn writes as a free man in Vermont.

For the Christian, God's central act was the life, self giving, and suffering of Jesus, culminating in the Resurrection: by that act God showed us that the terrible things we see now are not the last word.

The crumpled body at Kent State is not the last word. Nor is the grave of the soldier, the Iowa son, back from Vietnam. Nor is the mutilated child of Iran, Cambodia, or El Salvador. But the Resurrection means that our own acts, although certainly redeemed in our resurrection, will transcend time. By them we will be judged in a setting in which each of us is individually accountable.

God's judging points at the powerful idea of sin. Sin is our separation from God. A notable part of sin is pride: putting oneself in the center of the world and behaving accordingly. History, the Inquisition in Spain for example, suggests how easily pride can swamp the aims of an institution or those who work in it.

It is tempting to treat sin as an arcane word, harmless in its present import. But it is no mere sentimental part of the Christian lexicon. It tells us that there is evil in this world. Without the concept of sin and its resultant warning of evil, the terrors of war—including nuclear war and forced starvation and genocide—are without logic. But the notions of pride and defiant evil make it possible to understand the creation that includes these terrors. They are wounds caused by the misuse of freedom. They are proof that we need God's saving acts.

For the Christian, this describes our state. This is plainly a broken world, but one already redeemed by God. This faith frees us from angst and fear, an immense liberation. We are free to do what is right. But that leaves the practical question: especially in today's time and today's history, what do we do? To this, Christianity supplies the idea of vocation.

"Vocation," by its root word, means "call." It denotes the powerful idea that God, if we let Him, calls and leads each of us, usually with struggle and surprise, in our life work. This includes not only the gross sense of basic career choice, if one is fortunate enough to have such a clear-cut choice, but the more telling details of day-to-day choices and the occasional crisis of a major personal or professional choice.

Perhaps of all major Christian ideas, the idea of vocation is the most urgent for Americans. This is because it poses for us the task of inviting, in prayer, guidance that does not come from the self. The prayer is "Thy Kingdom come! Thy will be done!" It means just that.

It is not a modern idea. But for the Christian the prayer is the inescapable honest response to the God who loves this world and has redeemed each of us forever. In detail, though, what is the Christian who is a thoughtful American citizen doing right now? In focusing on this question, the apparent first obstacle is the act of prayer. How are modern people to pray, let alone pray in the belief that there will be a recognizable answer?

The Christian community gives abundant answer. It reports the experience of people who say that their prayers do have identifiable answers. This accumulation of testimony comes under the theological rubric of "witness." It comprises weighty evidence, hard to ignore in any analysis at the Institute.

But the question of whether anyone listens and answers in prayer is not really the urgent first question. The urgent question is whether the modern Christian-American wants to know the answer that follows honest prayer.

The answer could point to unpleasant tasks. The answer could point to sacrifice. It could point to new work. It could point to danger. It could point away from or to the battlefield. It could point to the truth.

This is what I believe. *Chto dumayetye,* What do you think? I feel that I am not that different from you or your husband. In fact I worked in the Pentagon for a year in the role of a Soviet planner, to test American defenses. I once translated "Scarlet Ribbons" into Russian. I will trade you my Russian translation of "Scarlet Ribbons" for your Russian translation of "California Girls."

I hope this letter helps you fashion an understandable picture of America. The Institute has power. I hope your voice is heard.

Sincerely,
John Wheeler

*Willingness to change is important. Ed Timperlake told me that, especially in crisis, there is a psychological momentum that says, "If I wait, things will be OK." This momentum can be fatal to pilots in emergencies. Ed knows. Right at takeoff on a solo jet flight as a student pilot one fire light of four went on. Then another. He was at three hundred feet, in pitch night. Then a third. "I am going to die unless I act." He ejected as the plane veered and exploded. The parachute opened, swung twice, hit a tree, and put him in a swamp. Two backwoodsmen approached him. "You know where that airplane wreck is?" Ed emerged from the mud. "I AM the wreck," he said. The guess is that only half the pilots confronted with the sudden display of lights act fast enough. There is a deadening tendency to wait one more second. Sometimes change must be discontinuous. Sometimes the present situation must be abandoned. Like Army parachuting. But one common thread in all change, continuous or discontinuous, is willingness to honor the signal calling for change.*

# CHAPTER ELEVEN

*All great civilization has been in
a certain measure a civilization of
the Dialogue. The life substance of
them all was not, as one customarily
thinks, the presence of significant
individuals, but their genuine inter-
course with one another. Individuation
was only the presupposition for the
unfolding of the dialogical life.*

*War has always had an adversary who
almost never comes forward as such,
but does his work in the stillness. This
adversary is speech, fulfilled speech,
the speech of genuine conversation
in which men understand one another
and come to a mutual understanding.*

Martin Buber
*Pointing the Way*

# WORK

Few people are as articulate as Stephen Rosenfeld about the "messiness" and complications of the patterns of fact in life. In conversation and in his *Washington Post* editorials and columns he teaches a great respect for the gradations and intricacies in attitudes and situations. His approach uncovers distinctions that show possibilities for understanding and agreement where none might have been apparent. Like Bill Jayne, he can discover a middle way and avoid polarized yelling. It was a lunch conversation we had that led to the *Post*'s creation of *The Wounded Generation* material. He took the idea to editors Al Horne and Dick Harwood. By the same token, Stephen has cautioned that a sense of generational specialness does not explain all things, and is an idea that must compete with other views of American life. He also cautions about being premature in drawing conclusions about the American passage through the Vietnam era. In his March 11, 1983, column he wrote that the "wounds" of Vietnam "are still too raw. No usable consensus yet exists from which Americans might draw a common meaning."

With Stephen's caveats in mind, it is still apparent that there is a sufficient inventory of effects of the interconnected events of the war years to warrant some generalization. In fact, we can itemize evidence of these effects and we can then focus on that which is positive in our experience.

There is some basis for optimism. One reason is the spirit of hope and fullness of life that surges in our own culture. There are glimpses of this hope and sense of life. The enthusiasm of veterans who gathered at the November 11, 1982, writing workshop reflected optimism and confidence as did the enthusiasm that created the Vietnam Veterans Memorial Fund and the Vietnam Veterans Leadership Program. So does Rick Eilert's story. Technological creativity is also a sign, in the proliferation of new business ventures that employ the computer, space science, and genetics breakthroughs of the sixties. The ventures represent economic risks we are taking, born out of some optimism about the future. Another sign is the generous attention given to quality programming for children's television, including the evolution of "The Muppets" characters from *Sesame Street* teachers to superstars. There are also the positive depictions of Vietnam veterans, as in the Romano character of "T. J. Hooker."

Television offered another glimpse which I found hopeful. A few years ago, in the midst of the "malaise" ascribed by President Carter, I turned on the set to discover a made-for-TV move, *Amber Waves*. It related the story of harvest time in the Midwest, through the eyes of a family that drove the huge combines. They traveled from farm to farm with the big machines. The recurring image was of the combines moving like a formation of ships through the crops. The family's son had gone to Canada rather than serve in Vietnam, creating a breach in the family friendship with a clan whose son was brutally wounded or killed in Vietnam. With his son in Canada, the father takes in and redeems a young man who needed work and some hard knocks in order to grow up. Love evolves between surrogate son and the family daughter. It was a gentle and simple story, spare in dialogue and with vivid imagery of vast fields, hot sun, and blue sky. One day on the road father and surrogate son stop for fresh bread in an out-of-the-way bakery. They eat the loaves outside, in the sun. Amber waves of grain. Their daily bread in the sweat of their brow. Work and hope sufficient to fill the family's life, in the midst of the brokenness of the Vietnam era. It was a nationwide broadcast, with ample sponsors.

## EVIDENCE

In writing this book, I've included evidence for the following effects and conclusions. The effects and conclusions are, in turn, evidence of the work our country, and especially our generation, needs to undertake.

- The events of the Vietnam era created complex separations among the generation of Americans that came of age during the Vietnam War years. Notable is the separation of self from self.

- Vast creativity surges in our generation, a creativity in many ways deepened and matured by the heady and harsh events of the sixties and early seventies. The sense of separation bottles up this creativity to some degree.

- The single most creative outcome of the turbulence of the war years is the emerging equality and partnership of woman and man throughout our culture.

- In television and movies the Vietnam veteran is emerging as an attractive figure who is strong and who cares about other people.

- The immense successes and remaining frustrations of the civil rights movement, women's movement, war protest, environmental movement, and the Peace Corps and VISTA contributed significantly to these separations. For example, Affirmative Action programs, especially for women, have collided with efforts of Vietnam veterans to ''catch up'' on the years lost on the career ladder due to military service.

- The Vietnam War and war protest were at least catalysts for the social upheaval and change of the late sixties and early seventies. The sequence includes the deadly effectiveness of the American forces in-country, the media portrayal of the war, including visits to North Vietnam, the political calculations made by North Vietnamese leaders about American commitment in light of the media portrayals and the war protest, the public reaction to the new experience of televised death and daily visual updates from the battlefield, the ignition of protest, the ''movement training ground'' provided in civil rights and war protest work, and the overwhelming ''all bets are off'' attitudes toward institutions and traditions under which every fundamental assumption of American life was up for reexamination. In this sequence the American man in Vietnam, as carrier of the war, in effect was instrumental to quickening women's equality.

▪ In America of the 1980s there is a double standard operating against men, by which society applauds a woman's femininity *and* her professional achievements, while society finds nothing to affirm in masculinity. Men are affirmed in their professional roles and in the measure to which they reflect the feminine qualities that men do have. Like most double standards it is subtle in most individual instances but massive in collective societal effect. One cause of the evolution of this double standard is the rough equation of war with manhood and the conclusion, "dirty war, dirty man."

▪ The masculine expression is suppressed in American culture, as part of the double standard that operates against masculinity. Masculinity is a lost idea in America. This is a fundamental imbalance that undermines the male roles of husband, father, and soldier. It weakens the cultural fabric. Femininity expresses the idea that there are things worth living for. Masculinity expresses the idea that there are things worth dying for. Because of unresolved guilt and grief over Vietnam and of the lost idea of masculinity, our generation has diminished its ability to defend America and is psychologically unable to implement a military draft even if plainly needed. *Nuclear deterrence is weakened.*

▪ A key (and still overlooked) determinant of American presidential politics in our lifetime will be the effects of the events of the Vietnam era. The divisions and need for healing are so fundamental that they will be an important factor at the center of the political process *of a struggle for the generation's soul.*

▪ Because of the cascade of revelations of the Vietnam era, public service, both elective and appointive, is a vocation that is vastly diminished in social esteem. This weakens our cultural fabric.

Finally, there is a special possible effect:

▪ Vietnam veterans might have been significantly exposed to dioxin through ingestion of water supplies in base areas cleared by use of defoliants informally obtained—scrounged—from the Air Force. *If* research confirms the dangers of dioxin, it magnifies the risks and possible harm to Vietnam-veteran fathers and the children they conceived.

These interconnections and consequences of the Vietnam era, even if only roughly defined, show a need for further research and discussion, to uncover more fully the impact of the period upon each of us.

Most important is the evidence of strength and creativity in our generation. Successful business ventures and the arts of the seventies offer proof of these qualities. There is more general proof. At Yale Law School, Myres McDougal and Harold Lasswell assessed communities by the conditions of eight key societal variables. Applied to our generation, there is great strength in each aspect: wealth (the economic inheritance of our country); skill (training, as in crafts or the professions); enlightenment (deeper knowledge and research, as in a liberal education); rectitude (faith and sense of moral obligation—that a person feels guilty discloses a sense of spiritual or moral obligation); well-being (sense of personal integrity; quality and accessibility of health care); respect (recognition of merit and avoidance of discrimination on the basis of race, color, sex, and factors other than merit); power (the desire and capacity to mobilize to control outcomes of events, as foreshadowed in the activism of the sixties); affection (capacity for interpersonal bonding).

## FOR OURSELVES
By these criteria our generation is endowed with mighty potential. The area for the most immediate work encompasses well-being, respect, and power. The separations among us disclose an unease among many women and men as they recall the route they traveled in the sixties and early seventies. Most significantly, the separations among our generation affect our power. The separations diminish our desire and capacity to combine to influence national and world events.

The first urgent step in the work before us is dialogue and research. There is evident and immense need for more Sue Woolseys, Lynda Zengerles, Michael Blumenthals, Christopher Buckleys, and James Fallowses to continue the dialogue among us on these matters. There is a need for novels, studies, and films to correct and refine the rough picture of us presented in this book. Doctoral dissertations and formal private-foundation and government research will contribute greatly to this dialogue. Our past shapes our present. We can govern the effects of the past by understanding the effects. For example, any who feel needless shame who will examine the causes of the shame can then appreciate the needlessness of their feeling. And any whose shame might be accurately felt can purge this feeling by examining it and putting it into proper perspective. *Why journey to the year 2000 with such burdens?*

Our work needs to be:

- based on the idea that a generation of humans is a vital subject of study and policy, *as the generation lives its life*
- organized
- systematic
- intensive
- aimed at getting people talking
- continued, updated, and refined throughout the lifetime of the generation

It will cost money. Congressional, White House, business, academic, and foundation leaders must each delve into the health and status of our generation.

*With potential cohesion and power unique in history, we have a responsibility to use that cohesion and power.* The inquiry needs public hearings and foundation grants as a major undertaking in our institutions.

The main questions with respect to the effects of our passage through the Vietnam era are:

- What are the divisions among us?
- What illusions do we have?
- Are female and male workers, professionals, and leaders working together for constructive purposes?

- Are we fulfilling our potential and our obligations as a uniquely large and powerful generation?
- What are our children learning from us?

Children in kindergarten in the 1983–84 school year are the college class of the year 2000. In *The Wounded Generation* there is this exchange:

STEVE HOWARD: The kids come in their Calvin Kleins. They're shooting space invaders. They're shooting rockets. They're shooting tanks. And all they worry about is getting their initials on those game machines. That's all little brothers and sisters are thinking about. Getting their initials for the best score. Do you get my point?

MALIK EDWARDS: Well, I don't need to eat the whole pie to see what it tastes like.

HOWARD: We got to teach the children. Do you get my point, Blood?

EDWARDS: Steve, what are you talking about?

HOWARD: Don't you see? There's war in those game machines.

## FOR OTHERS

There is also work which involves our personal needs but has more to do with what each of us gives to others. Like Ed Timperlake in the cockpit of the burning plane, we face one particularly important signal: *almost nobody speaks of unified community, creativity, and sacrifice.* Consider the cases of West Germany and Japan after World War II where these qualities reinvigorated those countries. Instead, the rhetoric of the potential leaders among us is combative, bartering over some fixed sum for us. It is as if we want our 1950s Christmas morning to be perpetuated. There is a balance between these two views in American life. The tilt at the moment is away from community, creativity, and sacrifice. Former presidential counselor Lloyd Cutler has written that divisiveness is so prevalent that under the

Constitution a president cannot "form a government" capable of creating and implementing any coherent policy. *What are we here for?* "I have a dream." OK. What will we *do* when the dream comes true? What are we here for?

Reporting on the November 1982 workshop, Mark Treanor summarized a feeling of all of us there: "[We] felt that the real reason for us being together and wanting to write, was because of our concern for our country's future, not because of Vietnam. . . . it seemed to each of us in that room that what we were addressing and the problems that we wanted to begin to attack were much bigger and of much greater importance than the fact that each one of us had served in Vietnam." I think this is a common hunger among many women and men in our generation. Why would it be unique to Vietnam veterans?

From my work helping to launch the Presidential Commission on World Hunger, I know that American technological sophistication in relation to hunger is one splendid example of the potential available to us. In a world of six billion souls, the nose-diving cost of computer memory storage makes it theoretically possible to record each name, just as in 1969 by computer in Vietnam we kept track of each of our soldiers each day. Technologically, and in theory, we could know, always, what child, or village, or region in the world is hungry, or will be hungry. Crop information satellites allow such projections. In fact, the key bottleneck in world hunger in both 1974 and 1984 is *not* world food *production,* it is food *distribution.* As the population expands, the world can grow sufficient food probably at least through the year 2000. The real issue is one of ships, trucks, prices, payments. The problem of hunger can be solved with long lead times of information about bad local crops and detailed population information and efficient distribution. So computers and satellites can make a material and creative difference in our hands.

## KEEPING TRACK

There are concrete signs to watch for in measuring the effect of a dialogue among our generation on the permanent, significant, and cumulative influences on us of the events of the sixties and early seventies.

- In presidential campaigns an emerging awareness both of the divisions and the potential of our generation.

- In presidential campaigns, an increasingly generous and comprehensive view of the potential of America's contributions to the world. One sign would be solid planks on world hunger in both major party platforms.

- Recognition in Congressional hearings and in federal research funding of the long-range importance of the dynamics created among our generation by the events of the Vietnam era.

- Increased discussion in the media by individuals of the choices they made in the Vietnam War years.

- Increased number of Vietnam veterans who openly affirm their pride in the choices they made during the war years.

- Systematic and comprehensive studies of the specific tensions created in the generation as a whole by the successes of the war era movements, such as the way professional couples in the generation are handling child-rearing logistics, and comparative statistics on income and business placement among the various segments of the generation, including men who wore the uniform, men who did not, and women.

- Comparative statistics on political activism and success among the segments of the generation.


*There is a surprise when I look back. My work includes a consistent theme of building a basis for dialogue about the shaping effects of the war years. The Memorial at West Point. The Memorial on the Mall. The VVLP. The Wounded Generation. The Anglican Theological Review. The Century Generation. This book. It is a happy surprise, so it is likely the answer to a prayer. It would be the prayer uttered in August of 1971 in Dean Wood's office. Just the vocation one would have expected: financial law, world hunger, and the effects of the Vietnam era. An obvious combination! But the three labors intricately support each other, a mystery for which I am grateful.*

# CHAPTER TWELVE

*Being a realist today
makes one an optimist.*

Herman Kahn

# PREDICTIONS

In spring of 1983, James Reston, Sr., decided to visit the Vietnam Veterans Memorial. We met at his Washington office prior to our cab ride over to the Mall. He asked about its history, and I explained how I met Jan Scruggs and Bob Doubek and how we organized the Fund's work. I studied him. I wanted to learn.

He was the reporter who covered my *dad*'s war in Europe, before I was born. He has watched America evolve since that war. I read his columns in the *New York Times* all the time I was at West Point. I had a question for him. It was a sunny day. Mr. Reston took out a Brownie camera and snapped pictures. "How did you find and check the names?" he asked. I told him. He said he was moved by the design. Walking back to Constitution Avenue I asked him if he had any predictions about the next twenty years. He considered, then said, "The things people are most afraid of usually don't happen."

## LIKELY TO HAPPEN

The immense richness of our youth and the partially dashed expectations in young adulthood incline me to describe our generation as a mature and potentially cohesive creative force. Because of our tendency to try to find insight in ourselves and because of the idealism ingrained in us while we were young, I believe we will realize that cohesion and be responsible for major innovations in the world.

The contributions of women will be original. Learning the consequences of full partnership between woman and man will be an adventure. The individual freedom and power of the thirty million women in our generation are unique in history. As imperfect or incomplete as their power and freedom may be, the power and freedom are great and on a par with men. There will be women vice presidential candidates. A woman will earn the Presidency.

We will form a comprehensive bipartisan assault on world hunger, one that perhaps only our generation, in our country, has the will and resources to carry out.

The culture will confirm the emerging strong and compassionate television film image of the Vietnam veteran as representative of most actual Vietnam veterans. One signal of confirmation will be a greatly increasing emergence of Vietnam veterans as part of the leadership in the various activities of our society. Concomitantly, some adults among us, daughters and sons, will be proud that however terrible it was, their fathers were willing to go into uniform. They will develop this attitude from the culture and from their own parents.

I think that sheepishness and edginess in discussing the interconnections and consequences of wartime events will mount and then dissipate. Discussion and exposure of a national topic tends to evolve that way.

The dialogue among us will temper our national illusion that we have no enemies. Some analysts foresee as much as another century of tug and push between the United States and the Soviet Union, on numerous world fronts, with no nuclear devastation, but with some constant abrasion. Douglas MacArthur was a genius, in many ways the creator of modern Japan. I think he is right that we must prepare for engagements in which American military will sacrifice their lives.

In the next two decades we will inspire some form of national youth service. Most men and women will give about two years of their youth to fight such ills as drug abuse, environmental decay, city deterioration, and also, stand ready to defend the nation.

Discussion about separations in our generation will restore the balance between feminine and masculine ideas in our culture. There will be for us things worth dying for. We will work to make it not so, but we will come to allow that some of our sons—and daughters—may fight in battle.

## NOT LIKELY TO HAPPEN

The most destructive result feared in confronting our past is vast recrimination. The seasoned reporter Robert G. Kaiser on November 28, 1982, published a *Washington Post* article, "We Can't Bury 'Nam Under the Memorial." He wrote, "Looking back at the '60's and '70's now, we seem to have jumbled together Vietnam, urban riots, campus chaos, assassinations, generation gaps and Watergate, as if those years were just a bad time full of bad events. But most of these events had common origins— in Vietnam. The war was one of those great matters that change the course of history. . . . Our politics is flat and sterile, and few Americans turn to government to solve what they consider major problems." Kaiser calls for an accounting of those who made the decisions about Vietnam. He says, "There will be some kind of reckoning." Kaiser is right. Inquiry is needed. The tone though could cause principals in the Vietnam years to fear harsh public judgment. But my faith is in common sense and generosity. Harsh judgments are simple judgments. The interconnections of the events of the war years are so intricate and complex that no such simplicity will suffice. Dialogue will uncover surprises and the truth. And forgiveness, first of all of ourselves.

*Elisa and I learned in late February of 1977 that John's heart should heal itself, as he grew. Whatever problem there may be would not diminish his growth. The brain damage test on Katie was negative. Once, holding Katie in the ward with a gastrostomy tube leading into her tummy, to feed her, and the tracheotomy tube leading into her trachea, to help her breathe, Elisa noticed the child in a nearby mother's arms turn white, as white as this page. The nurses and doctors rushed in. They pulled the curtains. Elisa told me she thought, "I can't save Katie. If she needs to die, then she will die. She is God's child in this life and the next. I can live without her. I can let go. I can even bear your going, Jack. But I cannot bear loss of God's love or of God's presence in my life."*

*Katie and John are in kindergarten now. College class of 2000. The "trach" tube requires a medical nurse to accompany her in school. Well, her teacher, Tim Welsh, was introduced to*

*Katie's nurse, Mary Horton. One thing led to another. Soon they'll be married. Elisa and I will attend the ceremony in St. Columba's and Katie will be the flower girl. John carries the ring. Surprise. A wedding and the commitments therein. The bone of life. Woman and man. Mary and Timothy. Jesus performed his first miracle at a wedding. Evenings at the dinner table Katie tells me what happens at school. She ends her report, "True life, Daddy!" True life.*

# EVENTS,
# 1959-1975

## 1959

**Jan. 2:** Fidel Castro's "26th of July Movement," launched in 1953 against Dictator Fulgencio Batista's rule, succeeds as Castro's guerrilla troops storm into Havana.

**Apr. 5:** U. S. Naval Research Laboratory announces a 300 percent increase in atmospheric radioactivity in eastern U. S. after the U.S.S.R.'s 1958 nuclear tests.

**Apr. 7:** Lorraine Hansberry becomes the first black to receive the New York Drama Critics Circle Award for her first play, *A Raisin in the Sun.*

**June 11:** Postmaster General Arthur E. Summerfield calls *Lady Chatterley's Lover* by D. H. Lawrence an "obscene and filthy work," and bans it from the U. S. mails.

**June 18:** A three-man U. S. federal court finds the Arkansas law, under which Governor Orval Faubus closed the Little Rock public schools, unconstitutional.

**Aug. 1:** Vice President Richard M. Nixon tells the Soviet people, on radio address in Moscow, they will live in tension and fear if their leaders try to advance Communism outside the U.S.S.R.

**Aug. 12:** Police hold back a mob of segregationists with clubs and fire hoses, as two newly integrated high schools in Little Rock reopen.

**Sept. 15:** America spends thirteen days watching "Mr. K." visit the U. S., as Soviet Premier Nikita Khrushchev says Communism will prevail.

**Nov. 9:** In the first of such announcements in America, U. S. Health, Education and Welfare Secretary A. S. Fleming warns housewives against buying cranberries contaminated with herbicides, causing a nationwide panic.

**Dec. 19:** Walter Williams, the last remaining veteran of the American Civil War, dies in Houston at the age of 117.

## 1960

**Feb. 1:** The first "sit-in," inspired by the Rev. Martin Luther King, Jr. to end segregation of restaurants and stores, takes place in Greensboro, N.C.

**Mar. 16:** President Eisenhower endorses Nixon as his successor.

**Mar. 25:** New York Judge Charles Clark says *Lady Chatterley's Lover* can go through the mails, after all, because the public shouldn't be kept "in blinders."

**Apr. 27:** The Episcopal Church endorses southern sit-ins.

**Apr. 28:** The Southern Presbyterian Church okays marital sex relations without procreative intentions.

**May 5:** Cold war tensions increase as Khrushchev announces the Soviet capture of Francis Gary Powers after the pilot's unarmed U-2 spy plane was downed over Russian territory. Two days later, the U.S. admits to the spying and four days later says such flights will be discontinued.

**May 21:** Professor Landrum Shettles of Columbia University announces that human sperm exists in two varieties: one with round heads that produce males, and the other with oval heads to produce females.

**Sept. 10:** Thirteen Arab nations establish OPEC in Baghdad.

**Sept. 12:** John F. Kennedy says the public welfare, not the Vatican, would guide his actions if he wins the presidency.

**Sept. 26:** John F. Kennedy and Nixon begin television debates, which many will call the deciding factor in the 1960 election.

**Nov. 8:** America elects John F. Kennedy, the first Roman Catholic and the second youngest President in history. Texas Senator Lyndon Baines Johnson is elected as Vice President. The tally will show a victory of 49.7 percent to 49.6 percent, the closest margin in U.S. election history.

## 1961

**Jan. 3:** The U.S. breaks diplomatic relations with Cuba.

**Jan. 20:** John F. Kennedy is inaugurated, saying to Americans, "Ask not what your country can do for you—ask what you can do for your country."

**Feb. 22:** The National Council of Churches endorses birth control as a means of limiting one's family.

**Mar. 1:** President Kennedy creates the Peace Corps and asks for American volunteers to help underdeveloped nations abroad.

**Apr. 17:** Anti-Castro Cuban exiles, trained by the Central Intelligence Agency, invade the Bay of Pigs in Las Villas Province, Cuba. Poor planning, bad luck, and Cuban jets squash the invasion within two days.

**Apr. 24:** President Kennedy, badly embarrassed, admits U.S. involvement in the Bay of Pigs.

**May 5:** America's first spaceman, Alan B. Shepard, Jr., makes a fifteen-minute suborbital flight into space on Freedom 7 as 50,000,000 Americans watch on television. "What a beautiful view!" he says. Shepard followed Soviet Cosmonaut Yuri A. Gagarin's secret orbit on April 12.

**May 9:** Newton Minow, chairman of the Federal Communications Commission, calls television a "vast wasteland" and says TV programming should meet Americans' needs, not just "cater to the nation's whims."

**May 14:** Busloads of racially mixed "Freedom Riders" on a trip from Washington, D.C., to New Orleans designed to protest racial segregation of bus terminals, are attacked by mobs of whites.

**Aug. 13:** The Berlin Wall, built by the Communists overnight, denies East Berliners freedom of movement into the West.

**Sept. 1:** Russia ends a three-year ban on atmospheric testing of nuclear weapons, with an atom blast over Siberia.

**Sept. 8:** The American Medical Association cites "statistical evidence" linking smoking and heart disease.

**Sept. 15:** The U.S. resumes atomic testing in Nevada.

**Sept. 22:** The Interstate Commerce Commission orders all interstate railroad and bus terminals to be desegregated, effective November 1.

**Oct. 6:** Kennedy says every American should receive Civil Defense protection from thermonuclear attack, and urges all families to build fallout shelters.

**Dec. 5:** Kennedy calls for a massive national program of physical fitness, declaring that America has become a nation of "spectators" rather than athletes.


## 1962

**Feb. 10:** The Soviets release Francis Gary Powers in exchange for Russian spy Rudolf Abel.

**Feb. 14:** Kennedy says U.S. troops in Vietnam may fire to protect themselves, but they are not combat troops.

**Feb. 20:** John H. Glenn, Jr. becomes the first American astronaut to orbit the Earth.

**June 25:** The Supreme Court rules against prayer and bible reading in public schools, calling it religious activity forbidden by the Constitution.

**Aug. 17:** Dr. Frances O. Kelsey of the Food and Drug Administration receives a gold medal for preventing the U.S. distribution of Thalidomide, a tranquilizer found to be responsible for fetal deformities.

**Oct. 1:** Black student James H. Meredith enrolls at the University of Mississippi as federal troops hold back rioters.

**Oct. 22–24:** Kennedy tells the nation that Russia has placed missiles and air bases in Cuba, and orders a sea and air "quarantine" of the island. "Brinksmanship" becomes a household word as twenty-five Russian ships steam toward Cuba.

**Oct. 27:** Khrushchev agrees to remove Russian missile bases in Cuba, under U.N. supervision.

**Nov. 4:** Kennedy halts U.S. atmospheric nuclear tests, but says underground tests will continue.

**Nov. 20:** Discrimination in federal housing projects is banned by the President.


## 1963

**Feb. 14:** Kennedy proposes VISTA (Volunteers in Service to America), a domestic Peace Corps.

**Mar. 14:** The first large "pop art" exhibition opens at the Guggenheim Museum.

**May 2:** Young blacks, led by Martin Luther King, Jr., begin a drive against discrimination in Birmingham, Ala. Their sit-ins are followed by confrontations with police using fire hoses and dogs to attack demonstrators, and hundreds are arrested.

**June 10:** Kennedy signs legislation requiring equal pay for equal work regardless of sex.

**June 12:** NAACP Field Secretary Medgar W. Evers is murdered by a sniper as Evers walks from his car to his home in Jackson, Miss. Mass demonstrations follow.

**June 25:** The U.S., Great Britain and the U.S.S.R. sign a treaty banning nuclear testing in space, the atmosphere and under water.

**Aug. 28:** 200,000 civil rights demonstrators, in a Freedom March on Washington, D.C., demand immediate legislation assuring equal rights and opportunities. Martin Luther King, Jr. tells the peaceful throng, "I have a dream."

**Aug. 30:** Washington–Moscow telephone hotline opens amid hopes it will reduce the risk of accidental nuclear war.

**Sept. 15:** A dynamite bomb explodes during Sunday service at the 16th St. Baptist Church in Birmingham, Ala., killing Denise McNair, 11, and Carole Robertson, Cynthia Wesley, and Addie Mae Collins, all 14. Their murders help consolidate public opinion in favor of civil rights.

**Oct. 11:** The U.S. Commission on the Status of Women reports to President Kennedy that discrimination against women exists in America.

**Nov. 1–2:** A military coup in South Vietnam follows severe repression, and the fiery suicides of Buddhist monks. President Ngo Dinh Diem is killed during the revolt. By now, 16,000 American military advisers are serving in the war-torn country, and the U.S. government recognizes the provisional government of South Vietnam.

**Nov. 22:** President Kennedy is assassinated and pronounced dead at 1:00 p.m. in Dallas. Lyndon Johnson is sworn in as the thirty-sixth President two hours later at Love Air Field in Dallas.

**Nov. 24:** Lee Harvey Oswald, accused assassin of President Kennedy, is shot and killed before millions of television viewers while he is in the custody of Dallas police. Nightclub owner Jack Ruby is arrested for his murder.

**Nov. 25:** Schools, offices and businesses nationwide are closed as America mourns, watching on TV as JFK is buried with full military and state honors at Arlington National Cemetery.

**Nov. 29:** President Johnson names a commission headed by U.S. Chief Justice Earl Warren to investigate the assassination of President Kennedy.

## 1964

**Jan. 8:** President Johnson in his State of the Union message declares the "war on poverty" and civil rights to be the major issues of the day.

**Jan. 9–11:** Twenty-three people die in Panama Canal Zone riots touched off by the flying of the U.S. flag.

**Feb. 2:** The Beatles, England's sensational revolutionary rock group, are mobbed and pelted with jelly beans at a Carnegie Hall concert.

**Mar. 4:** Johnson announces the appointment of ten women to major government posts.

**Mar. 14:** Jack Ruby, convicted of the murder of Lee Harvey Oswald, is sentenced to death by a Dallas jury.

**June 21:** Young civil rights workers Chaney, Goodman and Schwerner disappear near Philadelphia, Mississippi.

**July 2:** Congress passes the Civil Rights Act of 1964 and Lyndon Johnson signs it in a televised ceremony the same day, greatly increasing federal powers to combat racial discrimination in voting, education, employment, federally assisted programs, and public facilities and accommodations.

**July 18:** Major race riots break out in Harlem, leaving several people dead and causing property damage in the millions.

**July 28:** Ranger VII begins relaying the first close-up pictures of the moon before crashing into its surface.

**Aug. 2:** U.S. destroyer *Maddox* is attacked by North Vietnamese PT boats in the Gulf of Tonkin.

**Aug. 4:** The FBI discovers a shallow grave in Mississippi, containing the bodies of the three civil rights workers missing since June.

**Aug. 5:** Johnson orders U.S. planes to bomb North Vietnamese targets.

**Aug 7:** The U.S. House and Senate approve the Gulf of Tonkin Resolution granting presidential authority to order retaliatory attacks in Vietnam. Only two members of Congress vote against the resolution.

**Sept. 3:** Congress creates a permanent national wilderness system by placing nine million acres of virgin land under government protection.

**Sept. 27:** The Warren Commission reports that no domestic or international conspiracy was responsible for the assassination of President Kennedy and concludes that Lee Harvey Oswald acted alone.

**Oct. 14:** Civil Rights Leader Martin Luther King, Jr. receives the Nobel Peace Prize and donates his award money to the civil rights movement.

**Oct. 16:** The People's Republic of China explodes its first atomic bomb.

**Nov. 3:** Lyndon Johnson and Hubert Humphrey are elected President and Vice President in a landslide vote as the Democrats increase their majorities in both houses of Congress.

**Dec. 5:** Johnson affirms U.S. determination to fight Communism in Vietnam as he presents the U.S. Medal of Honor to U.S. Army Captain Roger Donlon.

**Dec. 24:** Two Americans die in the Christmas Eve bombing of U.S. Officers Quarters in Saigon.

## 1965

**Jan. 2:** Civil rights leaders begin a massive voter registration drive during which 3,000 people are arrested.

**Jan. 4:** President Johnson pledges improved education, crime prevention, national beautification and development of poverty-stricken areas, in his State of the Union message to Congress.

**Jan. 18:** Clashes between whites and blacks registering to vote reach their height in Selma, Alabama.

**Jan. 23:** Buddhists begin demonstrations in South Vietnam, forcing out Premier Tran Van Huong.

**Feb. 7:** The U.S. bombs North Vietnam after Viet Cong attacks in South Vietnam, including the U.S. base at Pleiku.

**Feb. 13–17:** Violent anti-U.S. demonstrations erupt in Latin

America, Europe and Africa in the wake of U.S. bombings in North Vietnam.

**Feb. 21:** Black Nationalist Malcolm X is assassinated as he addresses his Afro-American Unity organization in New York City.

**Mar. 8:** The U.S. Supreme Court rules that any conscientious objector with a sincere belief in a Supreme Being may be exempted from combat training and service.

The first American combat troops arrive in Danang, South Vietnam, bringing more than 3,500 Marines.

**Mar. 21:** Martin Luther King leads 3,500 marchers from Selma to Montgomery, culminating in a rally of 25,000 people at the State Capitol on March 25.

**Mar. 24:** The University of Michigan holds its first "teach-in" on Vietnam.

**Mar. 25:** Civil rights worker Viola Liuzzo is shot and killed in Alabama.

**Apr. 24:** The ruling junta in the Dominican Republic is overthrown.

**Apr. 26:** U.S. Defense Secretary Robert McNamara estimates that the cost of the Vietnam War is now $1.5 billion annually.

**Apr. 28:** 400 U.S. Marines land in the Dominican Republic to help U.S. citizens return to America. By May 2, the U.S. committed 14,000 troops to help prevent the "spread of Communism" in the Western Hemisphere.

**May 15:** Teach-ins on Vietnam are held on scores of American college campuses.

**June 7:** The U.S. Supreme Court rules that an 1879 Connecticut law forbidding the use of contraceptives is unconstitutional because it violates the right of privacy. By now, American doctors are freely prescribing "the pill."

**June 14:** President Johnson's day-long Festival of the Arts and Humanities at the White House is boycotted by artists and intellectuals, led by the poet Robert Lowell, in opposition to the Vietnam War.

**June 17:** The first mass bombing raid in Vietnam takes place as Guam-based B-52s attack a Viet Cong concentration thirty miles north of Saigon.

**July 1:** There are civil rights clashes at Bogalusa, Louisiana.

**July 28:** Johnson announces increases in troop strength in Vietnam to 125,000 men and doubling of the draft to 35,000 per month to support the Vietnam War.

**Aug. 6:** The U.S. Voting Rights Act of 1965 becomes law.

**Aug. 11–16:** The Watts ghetto in Los Angeles explodes into riots after police stop a black motorist suspected of drunk driving; 35 people are killed, hundreds are wounded and $200 million in property is destroyed.

**Oct. 14:** The Defense Department issues the largest draft call since the Korean War.

**Oct. 15–16:** There are antiwar demonstrations in cities from New York to Berkeley and several men burn their draft cards.

**Nov. 9–10:** Thirty million people in the Northeast U.S. are left in the dark by the first massive power blackout in American history, caused by a failure at a Niagara Falls generating plant.

**Nov. 20:** U.S. casualties, after a week-long battle in the Ia Drang Valley in Vietnam reach 240 dead, exceeding for the first time the weekly toll in the Korean War.

**Nov. 27:** The National Committee for a Sane Nuclear Policy organizes a 25,000-person antiwar rally in Washington as old-line antinuclear groups join academics to oppose the war.

## 1966

**Jan. 12:** President Johnson says, in his State of the Union message, the U.S. will remain in Vietnam until aggression there ends.

**Jan. 18:** The first black Cabinet member, Robert C. Weaver, takes office as the Secretary of Housing and Urban Development.

**Mar. 2:** U.S. troop strength in Vietnam reaches 215,000; McNamara announces another 20,000 troops are on their way there.

**Mar. 10:** A Green Beret camp in the Ashau Valley falls to Communists after a 72-hour siege, with 200 U.S. and South Vietnamese soldiers killed or wounded.

**Apr. 6:** Hispanic leader Cesar Chavez and the National Farm Workers Union win their first victory on being named official bargaining agent for Schenley Industries, a major California grape grower. Chavez and the union had been on strike since September, 1965.

**Apr. 30:** Communist China begins a cultural revolution as Premier Chou En-lai calls on the Chinese to wipe out all vestiges of bourgeois ideology.

**May 14:** The Student Nonviolent Coordinating Committee (SNCC) elects Stokely Carmichael its chairman; the black militant urges SNCC to embrace "black power" and violence in a split between pacifist followers of Martin Luther King's Southern Christian Leadership Conference and militants like Carmichael and Floyd McKissick of the Congress of Racial Equality (CORE).

**May 15:** The White House is picketed by 10,000 antiwar protesters who pledge to vote only for antiwar candidates.

**June 3:** Twenty graduating seniors walk out of commencement exercises at Amherst College in protest against Defense Secretary McNamara's receiving an honorary degree. Exercises at New York University, Brandeis University and other schools are scenes of similar antiwar protest throughout the month.

**June 6:** James Meredith is shot and wounded during his solitary walk from Memphis to Jackson, Miss. to encourage voter registration.

**June 11:** McNamara says U.S. troop strength in Vietnam will soon reach 285,000 and announces that 2,000 U.S. soldiers have died there since the beginning of the year.

**June 29:** The U.S. ends its policy of avoiding major North Vietnamese cities in bombing raids, as American planes attack Hanoi and Haiphong oil installations, highways and bridges. Within a week, two-thirds of the Communists' oil supply is destroyed.

**July 10:** Martin Luther King demands an end to Chicago discrimination in housing, schools and jobs and an end to police brutality during a mass rally at Soldiers Field.

**July 13:** Chicago makes more news as drifter Richard Speck stabs and strangles eight student nurses in a dormitory apartment.

**July 18–23:** Blacks riot in Cleveland's Hough ghetto.

**Aug. 1:** Charles Whitman kills his mother and his wife, then kills thirteen other people and wounds thirty-one from a perch in a tower at the University of Texas at Austin in a vicious one-man murder rampage. Whitman is himself then killed.

**Aug. 6:** In New York, 200 people stage a sit-in at the headquarters of Dow Chemical, manufacturer of napalm and the toxic defoliant Agent Orange.

**Aug. 26:** Martin Luther King cancels plans to march on the white Chicago suburb of Cicero after he wins concessions in housing rights from the Chicago Real Estate Board.

**Sept. 4:** Robert Lucas of CORE charges King with selling out to whites and takes marchers into Cicero; violence erupts as angry whites attack them, leaving many wounded and arrested.

**Sept. 23:** Military officials announce that U.S. planes have begun defoliating huge areas of jungle to destroy cover used by Communist troops.

**Nov. 8:** Ronald Reagan wins the California governorship.

Massachusetts voters elect Republican Edward W. Brooke the first black U.S. Senator since Reconstruction and the first ever elected by popular vote.

**Dec. 15:** Walt Disney, 65, creator of images and archetypes that had helped shape a generation of Americans and influence the world's view of America, dies in Los Angeles.

**Dec. 30:** Several hundred student body presidents and college newspaper editors reportedly organized by Allard Lowenstein sign an open letter to President Johnson, protesting the Vietnam War and warning that "Unless this conflict can be eased, the United States will find some of her most loyal and courageous young people choosing to go to jail rather than to bear their country's arms." *The New York Times* publishes it as a news article on page one.

**Dec. 31:** A New Year's Truce, immediately violated, begins in Vietnam.

## 1967

**Jan. 9:** Black Democrat Julian Bond takes his seat in the Georgia House of Representatives, after the U.S. Supreme Court rules he cannot be refused his place for making statements against the Vietnam War and in defense of draft-card burning.

**Jan. 16:** Former paratrooper Lucius Amerson takes the oath of office as the century's first black sheriff, in Tuskegee, Alabama.

**Feb. 13:** After an exposé is published in the magazine *Ramparts,* The National Student Association (NSA) admits taking more than $3 million from the Central Intelligence Agency since 1952, causing a furor on college campuses and deepening academics' distrust of the government.

**Mar. 28:** U.N. Secretary-General U Thant announces that the North Vietnamese have rejected his proposal for a general truce in Vietnam and says the U.S. and South Vietnam will accept it only with qualifications.

**Apr. 15:** A crowd variously estimated at between 100,000 and 400,000 marches from Central Park to the United Nations Building in protest of the Vietnam War. 150 men burn their draft cards.

**Apr. 21:** Svetlana Alliluyeva, daughter of Joseph Stalin, arrives in New York after defecting from Russia.

**May 11:** The 100 millionth telephone is installed in the U.S. Americans now have half of all the phones in the world.

**May 15:** The Supreme Court rules that children who are arrested are entitled to the protection of the Bill of Rights, even as are adults.

**May 19:** U.S. planes strike the heart of Hanoi in Vietnam.

**June 3:** What would come to be called "the long, hot summer" of the worst race riots in America's history, begins as Boston's black Roxbury ghetto explodes into violence. Blacks battle police after a "Mothers for Adequate Welfare" sit-in.

**June 5–10:** In the "Six-Day War" with the Arabs, Israel emerges the victor, taking the Sinai and Gaza Strip from the United Arab Republic, Old Jerusalem from Jordan and border areas from Syria.

**June 12:** The U.S. Supreme Court unanimously rules that no state can prohibit interracial marriages.

**June 17:** Communist China explodes its first hydrogen bomb.

**June 23–25:** In the New Jersey college town of Glassboro, President Johnson and Premier Kosygin have ten hours of talks on topics including the Middle East.

**July 6:** The secessionist Republic of Biafra is attacked by federal troops as civil war rages in Nigeria and hundreds of thousands there continue to die of famine. News photos of starving Biafran children awaken Americans to a new appreciation of the scope of world hunger.

**July 12–17:** Blacks in Newark riot and fire at police from roof-tops, leaving 26 dead and 1,300 injured.

**July 17:** A United Nations patrol takes up positions near the Suez Canal to supervise an Israel-United Arab Republic cease-fire.

**July 23–30:** Detroit is trashed in six days and nights of violence, as 43 people are killed, many are injured, and 5,000 are left homeless. The violence begins when police raid a party for two veterans, just home from Vietnam.

**July 27–28:** President Johnson forms the National Advisory Commission on Civil Disorders to be headed by Illinois Governor Otto Kerner, Jr.

**Aug. 3:** Johnson announces a maximum limit of 525,000 on American troops in Vietnam.

**Aug. 17:** From Havana, militant black leader Stokely Carmichael broadcasts a message that American blacks should arm themselves for "total revolution."

Under-Secretary of State Nicholas Katzenbach tells the Senate that the 1964 Gulf of Tonkin Resolution gave the President authority to commit troops without a declaration of war.

**Sept. 7:** McNamara announces the U.S. will create an antiinfiltration barrier of land mines, barbed wire and electronic devices between North and South Vietnam.

**Sept. 28:** Walter E. Washington becomes the first black to head a major city government in the U.S. as he is sworn in as Commissioner of the District of Columbia, a post equivalent to mayor.

**Oct. 2:** Thurgood Marshall takes his oath as the first black appointed to the U.S. Supreme Court.

**Oct. 3:** Woody Guthrie, 55, dies in New York City, after a life spent composing songs and music that influenced a generation of folksingers and rock stars from Bob Dylan and Joan Baez to the Beatles, Rolling Stones, Simon and Garfunkel and many others. Meanwhile, the Beatles' revolutionary album "Sgt. Pepper's Lonely Hearts Club Band" remains at the top of the charts.

**Oct. 9:** Student radicals mourn the death, announced today by the Bolivian army, of Cuban Guerrilla Revolutionary Ernesto "Che" Guevara, who had told them that revolutionary peoples' struggles against the Establishment would be won only with "two, three, many Vietnams."

**Oct. 14:** The U.S. charges the North Vietnamese with the mistreatment of prisoners of war, in violation of the Geneva Convention guidelines.

**Oct. 21–22:** Thousands protest the Vietnam War in a massive March on the Pentagon sponsored by the National Mobilization to "shut down the war machine," and 647 people, including Norman Mailer, are arrested after a clash with the police.

**Nov. 7:** By unanimous vote in its General Assembly, the United Nations adopts a Rights for Women declaration, calling on governments, organizations and individuals to work toward equality and the rights of women in "employment, politics, education and cultural life." The action is hailed by the National Organization for Women and others in the newly resurgent feminist movement in the U.S.

**Nov. 16:** The Johnson administration announces a $300 million slum-clearance program for American cities.

**Nov. 21:** The population of the United States, despite declining birth rates, reaches 200 million.

**Nov. 22:** After weeks of fighting and 290 of their number killed, Americans take Hill 875 in Dak To, South Vietnam.

**Dec. 14:** Stanford University biochemists announce they have produced a synthetic form of DNA, the genetic substance that controls heredity.

**Dec. 20:** U.S. troops in Vietnam now number 474,300.

**Dec. 31:** Americans listen to the announcement that 9,378 military have been killed during the year in Vietnam.

## 1968

**Jan. 1:** Calling for global peace, the United Nations inaugurates an International Year of Human Rights.

**Jan. 3:** North Vietnamese troops surround the Marine base at Khe Sanh as U.S. troops kill 329 to repel the attack.

**Jan. 5:** Dr. Benjamin Spock, who wrote the book that helped parents raise the Vietnam Generation, the Rev. William Sloane Coffin of Yale, and two other antiwar protesters are indicted for conspiring to aid and abet draft resisters.

**Jan. 18:** Black actress and singer Eartha Kitt stuns a White House ladies' luncheon when she states that discussion of the U.S. domestic problems is pointless while the Vietnam War rages.

**Jan. 21–22:** 20,000 North Vietnamese forces redouble attack on U.S. base at Khe Sanh.

**Jan. 30–31:** Communists launch massive Tet Offensive on Saigon, including the U.S. Embassy, and thirty-seven other major cities and provincial capitals of South Vietnam including Hue, Vietnam's ancient capital, and the Marine base at Khe Sanh as the Viet Cong carry the war to major population areas of the South. U.S. casualties are heavy, consolidating public opinion against the conduct of the war. The U.S. now has 550,000 troops in Vietnam; 14,500 will die in combat during 1968.

NBC-TV and The Associated Press transmit a film seen by millions of Americans, showing South Vietnamese National Police Chief Nguyen Ngoc Loan shooting a Viet Cong suspect in the head. The photo later is argued by many to be the single most important image in causing the shift of opinion against the war.

**Feb. 1:** Nixon declares his candidacy for the Presidency.

**Feb. 13:** Johnson orders 10,500 more combat troops to Asia.

**Feb. 16:** Major cutbacks in occupational and graduate-student draft deferments are announced.

**Feb. 24:** After twenty-five days of bitter fighting, with more than 11,000 civilians and U.S. and Communist soldiers killed, allied forces recapture Hue from the Viet Cong and North Vietnamese.

**Feb. 29:** "White racism" is blamed by the President's National Advisory Committee on Civil Disorders for riots and urban unrest; the Kerner Commission urgently calls for more aid to black ghettoes in American cities, but concludes that the nation is moving toward "two societies, one black, one white—separate and unequal."

**Mar. 12:** Supported by a "children's army" of student volunteers, Senator Eugene McCarthy of Minnesota campaigns in the snow in the New Hampshire Democratic Presidential Primary and astonishingly captures just under 50% of the vote. This shocks the political establishment, the press and the nation, all of whom sense in the outcome a clear mandate to end the war.

**Mar. 16:** Senator Robert Kennedy, sensing Johnson's vulnerability, announces his own candidacy for President and begins campaigning hard on a broad platform of liberal planks.

U.S. troops report killing 128 of the enemy in a Vietnamese hamlet called My Lai 4.

**Mar. 31:** President Johnson stuns the nation with his television announcements that he has called for an immediate halt to the bombing of North Vietnam above the 20th parallel and that he will not seek, and will not accept, his party's nomination for the presidency for a second full term.

**Apr. 3:** In a speech in Memphis before a planned march in support of striking black workers, Martin Luther King, Jr. tells his followers that God has allowed him to "go up to the mountain." Says King, "I've looked over and I've seen the promised land. I may not be there with you, but we as a people will get to the promised land."

North Vietnam offers to talk about beginning peace talks.

**Apr. 4:** Standing on the balcony of his room at the Lorraine Motel in Memphis, the thirty-nine-year old King is assassinated by a sniper in the early evening. Within hours, and for a week thereafter, black ghettoes in Washington, Boston, Detroit, Philadelphia, San Francisco, Toledo and 120 other American cities are in flames with riots, arson and looting that leave 46 people dead, 2,600 injured and 21,000 arrested. In Chicago, Mayor Richard Daley instructs the police to "shoot to kill" arsonists, and to "shoot to cripple or maim" anyone caught looting.

**Apr. 5–6:** American relief combat forces reach Khe Sanh, and help end the bloody seventy-seven-day siege.

**Apr. 8:** Coretta Scott King takes her husband's place at the head of a line of 45,000 civil rights demonstrators in Memphis, one day before King is to be buried.

**Apr. 9:** More than 200,000 mourners, including Robert Kennedy, march behind his mule-drawn casket at the funeral of Martin Luther King in Atlanta.

**Apr. 23:** Students for a Democratic Society (SDS) leader Mark Rudd and other dissident student leaders seize five buildings at Columbia University, hold several university officials hostage several hours, and occupy President Grayson Kirk's offices to begin a week-long takeover of the university in protest of the school's "racist" plans to build a gym in Morningside Heights on land needed by the neighboring black community, and in protest of the war in Vietnam.

**May 2:** The Poor People's March on Washington, planned by Martin Luther King, begins under the leadership of King's lieutenant, the Rev. Ralph Abernathy. Later in the month 3,000 marchers camp in a "Resurrection City" on the Mall but the demonstration is plagued by rain, mud and indifference from a public weary of ghetto riots.

**May 13:** The Vietnam War Peace Talks open in Paris as United States Chief Delegate W. Averell Harriman, calls for restraint by the North in return for a total bombing halt and North Vietnam Chief Delegate Xuan Thuy accuses the U.S. of "monstrous crimes."

**May 27:** The U.S. Supreme Court rules that the ban on burning draft cards is constitutional and that, pursuant to a 1965 amendment of the Selective Service Act, destroying a draft card can be prosecuted as a crime.

**June 3:** Pop artist Andy Warhol is shot and seriously wounded by Valerie Solanis, self-proclaimed female chauvinist.

**June 4:** Having lost the Oregon primary to McCarthy, Robert F. Kennedy wins the California primary.

**June 5:** Robert Kennedy, age forty-two, is shot three times by Jordanian born Sirhan B. Sirhan in a kitchen at the Ambassador Hotel in Los Angeles, after a triumphal victory speech. Kennedy dies the next day and the nation is once again thrown into despair, frustration and grief.

**June 7:** More than 150,000 come to mourn Kennedy as he lies in St. Patrick's Cathedral in New York City.

**June 8:** Kennedy's funeral train reaches Washington and he is buried at Arlington National Cemetery. Authorities seize ex-convict James Earl Ray in London and charge him with the murder of Martin Luther King.

**June 14:** A verdict of guilty is returned in the Spock conspiracy case.

**June 23:** The Vietnam War becomes the longest war in American history.

**June 24:** Twenty-four police disperse demonstrators at "Resurrection City" in Washington, D.C., and close the campsite.

**June 27:** U.S. forces withdraw from Khe Sanh.

**July 15:** A Russian Aeroflot jet lands in New York and Pan American Boeing 707 leaves for Moscow as the U.S. and Soviet Union open commercial flights between the two countries for the first time.

**July 19:** James Earl Ray is returned to the U.S. and jailed in Memphis.

**July 25:** Pope Paul VI reiterates the Roman Catholic Church's condemnation of artificial birth control methods.

**Aug. 5–9:** Richard Nixon is nominated for President at the Republican National Convention in Miami; Maryland Governor Spiro T. Agnew is tapped as his running mate. Their platform calls for progressive "de-Americanization" of the War in Vietnam and increased law-and-order.

**Aug. 7:** Riots in the black ghetto of Miami begin, leaving three dead and hundreds injured.

**Aug. 10:** Senator George McGovern, Democrat of South Dakota, announces his candidacy for the Presidency.

**Aug. 20–21:** Czechoslovakians weep and jeer as Russia invades their country with 200,000 troops and hundreds of Soviet T-54 tanks, ending the movement toward liberal reforms there.

**Aug. 26–29:** In the midst of most violent national party convention in American history, Vice President Hubert Humphrey and Sen. Edmund Muskie, from Maine, are nominated by the Democrats for President and Vice President. On the streets, Chicago Mayor Richard Daley's 12,000 police and National Guardsmen beat and club antiwar demonstrators and news reporters in a nightmarish battle televised throughout the world.

**Oct. 18:** U.S. track stars Tommie Smith and John Carlos are suspended from competition at the XIX Olympiad in Mexico City for giving the black power salute during the playing of the National Anthem, at the ceremony in which they are awarded their victory medals.

**Oct. 31:** President Johnson announces full halt to all American bombing of North Vietnam.

**Nov. 1–4:** The Vietnamese National Liberation Front, the Viet Cong, joins the Vietnam peace talks in Paris.

**Nov. 5:** In the slimmest margin of victory to date in American electoral politics, Nixon defeats Humphrey for the Presidency.

**Nov. 26:** South Vietnam ends its boycott of the Paris peace talks.

**Dec. 1:** The National Commission on the Causes and Prevention of Violence calls police action during the Democratic National

Convention "a police riot" and warns of increasing tendencies toward violence in the country.

**Dec. 4:** The American Medical Association formulates and announces a new standard of death: when the brain ceases to function and death is irreversible.

## 1969

**Jan. 16:** After weeks of debate and a rising chorus of international derision, conferees at the Paris peace talks agree on the shape of the negotiating table, and discussions begin in earnest two days later.

**Jan. 21:** A U.S. Government report says chronic hunger and malnutrition are widespread in America.

**Feb. 8:** A massive oil spill off Santa Barbara on the California coast finally ends, and the cleanup of forty miles of beaches begins.

**Mar. 4:** The U.S. Defense Department says it is shipping lethal nerve gas by rail and says it is spending $350 million annually on chemical and biological weapons.

**Mar. 10:** James Earl Ray receives a ninety-nine-year prison sentence for the assassination of Martin Luther King.

**Apr. 3:** U.S. combat deaths in Vietnam reach 33,641 since Jan. 1, 1961, more than the 33,629 killed in the Korean War.

**Apr. 9:** 300 students protesting the war in Vietnam occupy the main administration building at Harvard University and evict eight deans; 400 state and local police clear the building the next day.

**Apr. 23:** Sirhan Sirhan is sentenced to death in the gas chamber for the assassination of Robert Kennedy.

**May 20:** Hamburger Hill is captured by U.S. troops after ten days of savage battle; Congress members denounce such "senseless" assaults and the Hill is recaptured days later by Communists.

**May 22:** A Canadian official says his country has admitted many U.S. draft evaders and says Canada will also admit deserters who qualify as immigrants.

**June 6:** The FBI tapped the telephones of Martin Luther King, a federal court in Houston reveals, although such taps are authorized only to protect "national security."

**June 8:** President Nixon announces that 25,000 U.S. troops will be pulled out of Vietnam by August 31.

**July 11:** A U.S. court of appeals overturns the convictions of Dr. Spock and three others on charges of aiding draft resisters.

**July 19:** Senator Edward Kennedy of Massachusetts, tells the police in Edgartown, Martha's Vineyard, that Mary Jo Kopechne had died when his car plunged off a bridge on Chappaquiddick Island ten hours earlier.

**July 20:** First humans step onto the surface of the Moon as Astronauts Neil Armstrong and Edwin Aldrin, Jr. emerge from their module Eagle near the Sea of Tranquility.

**Aug. 15–18:** In what many would later term the "last hurrah" of the love and peace movement, 500,000 young people throng Max Yasgur's farm in upstate New York for the Woodstock Music and Art Fair. Rain, mud, drugs and three deaths do not quell the spirit of music and cooperation.

**Sept. 24:** The trial of the "Chicago Eight" opens with Judge Julius Hoffman presiding; the defendants, radical leaders of the protesters during the Democratic Convention, disrupt proceedings and Black Panther Chairman Bobby Seale is ordered bound and gagged in the courtroom.

**Oct. 15:** Following a Gallup Poll reporting that 58 percent of Americans oppose the war in Vietnam, a massive national Vietnam Moratorium Day is held across the country, marked by vigils and demonstrations; Nixon ignores the event and Agnew calls its participants an "effete corps of impudent snobs."

**Nov. 11:** Veterans Day rallies in support of U.S. policies in Vietnam are held throughout the country.

**Nov. 13:** Vice President Agnew accuses the news media of being an "unelected elite" controlling what Americans think.

**Nov. 16:** News reports say more than 450 villagers had been massacred by Lt. William Calley and his infantry troops at My Lai on March 16, 1968; the Army begins an investigation.

**Nov. 22:** A single gene, the basic unit of heredity, is isolated by Harvard scientists, opening up a new era of genetic research and, some fear, control.

**Nov. 25:** Nixon says the U.S. will not engage in biological warfare and will not make "first use" of lethal and incapacitating chemicals. Tear gas and defoliants are not included.

**Nov. 26:** Nixon signs into law a bill allowing for a lottery for Selective Service draftees, the first drawing to be held December first.
**Dec. 4:** Police storm a Chicago apartment and kill Illinois Black Panther Party Chairman Fred Hampton and another party leader; the American Civil Liberties Union charges they have been murdered.
**Dec. 15:** President Nixon announces reduction of U.S. troops in Vietnam to 434,000 by April 15, the third reduction since he took office.
**Dec. 31:** It is announced that 9,500 U.S. soldiers have been killed in Vietnam during the year.

## 1970

**Feb. 18:** Five defendants in the "Chicago Eight" trial acquitted of major charges from riot at the 1968 Democratic National Convention. Convictions on lesser charges later overturned.
**Feb. 26:** The U.S. Army responds to protests by announcing it will no longer conduct surveillance of peaceful civilian demonstrations and will discontinue keeping files on civilians who might be involved in riots.
**Feb. 28:** The Nixon administration memorandum proposing "benign neglect" of racial issues is leaked to the press. Its author, Nixon Domestic Advisor Daniel P. Moynihan, explains that he meant only that blacks would be better served by more temperate discussions of racial issues.
**Mar. 16:** The *New English Bible* is published, translated by Protestant scholars directly from ancient texts. It is praised for its modernity by some, criticized by other for lacking the rich dignity of the *King James* version.
**Apr. 1:** Cigarette advertising is banned from radio and television as of January 1, 1971 by federal law.
**Apr. 20:** President Nixon says he will bring 150,000 troops home from Vietnam by early next year.
**Apr. 22:** Growing public concern over oil spills, strip mining, noise pollution, smog, radioactive fallout, pesticide abuses, the destruction of wildlands and redwood trees, the supersonic air transport, the Alaska oil pipeline and other forms of environ-

mental destruction culminates in a massive nationwide "Earth Day" observance that attracts millions, legitimizes the environmental movement and introduces concern for the ecology into the American consciousness and vocabulary. The ecology movement becomes a major political force and a cultural alternative as hundreds of thousands of young people go "back to the land" in rural communes.

**Apr. 29:** A major offensive against the North Vietnamese and Viet Cong positions in Cambodia is launched by more than 20,000 U.S. and South Vietnamese troops.

**May 2:** U.S. college campuses erupt in protest.

**May 4:** In a shocking event many would later analyze as the death knell of the period of 1960s activism, National Guardsmen fire into a crowd of antiwar demonstrators at Kent State University in Ohio, killing four students and wounding nine.

**May 8:** Deep domestic divisions caused by the Vietnam War widen as peace demonstrators marching through New York's Wall Street are beaten bloody by hard-hat construction workers.

**May 9:** Huge crowds amass in Washington, D.C., New York, and other U.S. cities to protest the expansion of the war into Cambodia and the killing of the students at Kent State. More than 450 U.S. colleges close down in protest.

**May 15:** Two students are slain at Jackson State College in Mississippi as state and city police open fire on demonstrators.

**June 13:** President Nixon appoints a nine-member Commission on Campus Unrest headed by former Pennsylvania Governor William Scranton to study the causes of campus violence; it will conclude that prospects for social tranquility are gloomy because of growing intolerance for opposition views.

**June 24:** The U.S. Senate votes eighty-one to ten to repeal the Gulf of Tonkin resolution.

**June 29:** The U.S. withdraws all forces from Cambodia.

**June 30:** The Senate adopts the Cooper-Church Amendment barring U.S. military personnel from Cambodia.

**July 4:** Thousands convene in Washington, D.C. in "Honor America Day" rallies in support of U.S. domestic and foreign policy.

**Oct. 4:** Janis Joplin, the leading female blues-rock singer of the era, dies at age twenty-seven of a drug overdose.

**Nov. 2:** The U.S.S.R. and the United States resume Strategic Arms Limitation talks in Helsinki, Finland.

**Nov. 12:** The court-martial of Lt. William L. Calley, Jr. begins at Fort Benning, Georgia. Calley is accused as the principal in the alleged massacre by U.S. troops of Vietnamese civilians at My Lai.

**Dec. 2:** The Environmental Protection Agency begins its first day of existence as William D. Ruckelshaus is sworn in as its first director. The EPA's charge is to handle and supervise federal pollution control efforts.

**Dec. 21:** The U.S. Supreme Court rules that eighteen-year-olds may vote in federal elections.

**Dec. 26:** The White House announces a phase-out of herbicide operations in Vietnam.

## 1971

**Feb. 11:** Sixty-three nations sign a treaty prohibiting the installation of nuclear weapons on the floor of the world's seas.

**Mar. 1:** As more species of whales are placed on the endangered list, Commerce Secretary Maurice Stans issues an order ending the licensing of U.S. commercial whale hunters.

The "Weather Underground," a loosely organized group of radical terrorists, claims responsibility for the explosion of a bomb in a rest room in the Senate wing of the U.S. Capitol. $300,000 in damage is reported.

**Mar. 8:** The Supreme Court rules that any draft exemption granted on the grounds of conscientious objection must be based on the claimant's opposition to all wars, not just the current war in Indochina.

**Mar. 25:** FBI files leaked to U.S. newspapers, reveal that the agency has engaged in widespread surveillance of black and antiwar militants and has sought to create a climate of fear intended to discourage their activities.

**Mar. 29:** Lt. William Calley is convicted of premeditated murder of twenty-two Vietnamese civilians and is sentenced to life in prison, reduced August 20 to twenty years. Calley appeals.

**Apr. 7:** Nixon announces that 100,000 additional U.S. troops will be withdrawn from Vietnam by the year's end.

**Apr. 20:** In a series of decisions, the U.S. Supreme Court rules that ending *de facto* school segregation by means of busing children between school districts is constitutional.

**May 3–5:** Police arrest more than 12,000 people who have been engaged in massive antiwar protests in Washington, D.C., including Vietnam veterans who have deposited their military decorations on the steps of the Capitol on April 23. The police action is both praised and condemned.

**June 11:** Fifteen native Americans are forcibly removed from Alcatraz Island in San Francisco Bay, which they had seized nineteen months earlier, claiming ancient treaty privileges to unused federal lands. The American Indian Movement (AIM) will grow in strength and number, radicalized and politicized by this year's publication of the history of American Indians' loss of their tribal lands, Dee Brown's *Bury My Heart at Wounded Knee.*

**June 13:** *The New York Times* begins publication of the *Pentagon Papers,* the popular name for a top-secret *History of the U.S. Decision-making Process on Vietnam Policy,* begun during the Johnson administration. The federal government's attempts to stop publication of the *Papers* are overturned by a Supreme Court decision on June 30, holding that the government cannot impose prior restraint on published materials.

**June 28:** Former Defense Department official Dr. Daniel Ellsberg announces that he had leaked the *Pentagon Papers* to *The New York Times;* he is later indicted for theft and possession of secret documents.

**July 28:** The U.S. Army announces a major drive against narcotics use by troops in Vietnam and says virtually all U.S. servicemen there will be tested for heroin use.

**Sept. 22:** Captain Ernest L. Medina is cleared of all charges against him, stemming from the My Lai massacre.

**Sept. 30:** The U.S. and U.S.S.R. sign agreements designed to reduce the risk of accidental nuclear war.

**Nov. 6:** Despite the protests of environmental and antiwar groups, the U.S. explodes a powerful underground nuclear bomb in a test on the Alaskan island of Amchitka.

**Nov. 12:** Nixon announces troop reductions of 45,000 in Vietnam, to leave 139,000 there by February, 1972.

**Dec. 26–30:** The U.S. conducts massive sustained air attacks on military targets in North Vietnam.

## 1972

**Jan. 7:** Nixon announces his candidacy for a second term as president.

**Jan. 13:** Nixon says U.S. troop levels in Vietnam will be decreased to 69,000 by May 1.

**Jan. 25:** Nixon reveals that his National Security Advisor, Henry Kissinger, has held secret peace talks in Paris since August 1969. He offers a total cease-fire in Indochina, new presidential elections for South Vietnam and withdrawal of troops.

**Feb. 21:** Nixon arrives in Peking for historic meetings with Chinese leaders including Mao Tse-tung and Chou En-lai, during which they will pledge a new era of peaceful coexistence.

**Mar. 22:** With Senate approval Congress proposes the Equal Rights Amendment to the U.S. Constitution, calling, in proposed Amendment XXVII, for equality of rights under the law which "shall not be denied or abridged by the United States or by any State on account of sex." Hawaii ratifies the amendment the same day; after nearly a decade of bitter struggle the amendment will eventually fail in ratification, in a most serious setback of the new women's movement in the U.S.

**Mar. 23:** The U.S. halts Paris peace talks, claiming the North Vietnamese are unwilling to cooperate.

**Mar. 30:** North Vietnamese troops launch a major spring offensive and attack military bases throughout the South.

**Apr. 16:** The U.S. resumes massive bombing of North Vietnam; protest erupts across U.S.

**May 8:** Nixon orders mining of Haiphong and other North Vietnamese harbors.

**May 22:** Nixon arrives in Moscow, the first U.S. President to visit the Russian capital. He and Leonid Brezhnev sign accords on space, environmental cooperation and strategic arms limitations.

**June 5:** A United Nations Conference on Human Environment draws 1,200 delegates from 114 nations.

**June 17:** Five men are arrested at 2:00 a.m. in Democratic National Committee headquarters in Washington, D.C. and are charged by police with second-degree burglary. The next day, Carl Bernstein and Bob Woodward, young reporters at the *Washington Post,* begin working on the story, which will unfold into a scandal that will bring down President Nixon and many of his men.

**July 10–13:** Senator George McGovern of South Dakota, running on a peace platform, wins the Democratic nomination for President at the national convention. His running mate, Senator Thomas Eagleton of Missouri, will be replaced during the campaign after disclosures that he has undergone hospitalization for nervous exhaustion.

**July 13:** The Paris peace talks on Vietnam resume after a ten-week hiatus.

**Aug. 8:** The Democratic National Committee approves Sargent Shriver to replace Thomas Eagleton as the party's vice-presidential candidate.

**Aug. 12:** The last U.S. ground troops leave Vietnam; 43,500 service personnel, pilots and advisers remain.

**Aug. 21–23:** Richard Nixon and Spiro Agnew are renominated.

**Aug 22:** Thieu cancels democratic elections in South Vietnam.

**Oct. 26:** Henry Kissinger announces that "peace is at hand" in Vietnam; Radio Hanoi announces a breakthrough in the peace talks.

**Nov. 1:** President Thieu objects to the peace agreement terms.

**Nov. 7:** Massachusetts is the lone dissenter as forty-nine states go for Nixon-Agnew. Triumphant Nixon begins his second term, secure in the support of the "Silent Majority" of Americans.

**Dec. 13:** Paris peace talks end without agreement.

**Dec. 18:** Nixon resumes full-scale bombing in Vietnam "until such time as a settlement is arrived at."

**Dec. 30:** Bombing is halted above the 20th parallel in Vietnam; the Paris Peace Talks are set to resume January 8, 1973.

## 1973

**Jan. 11:** Judge John J. Sirica of the U.S. District Court in Washington, D.C., opens the trial of the defendants allegedly caught bugging and burglarizing the Democratic Party national headquarters at the Watergate complex.

**Jan. 15:** Citing progress in the peace talks, Nixon suspends the bombing and mining of North Vietnam.

**Jan. 22:** In the *Roe v. Wade* decision, the U.S. Supreme Court affirms a woman's constitutional right to an abortion by ruling that in the first third of pregnancy, the decision must be left to a woman and her physician. The court allows increasingly stringent restrictions to be imposed by the states in the latter months of pregnancy.

**Jan. 23:** Nixon announces an agreement for "peace with honor" in Vietnam.

**Jan. 27:** The American involvement in Vietnam officially ends with a cease-fire agreement signed in Paris calling for withdrawal of all U.S. troops, release of American prisoners of war and the creation of a four-nation commission to supervise the truce.

**Feb. 12–13:** The first 116 of 456 U.S. servicemen known to be held prisoner in North Vietnam are released in Hanoi.

**Feb. 27:** 200 supporters of the American Indian Movement seize the hamlet of Wounded Knee on the Oglala Sioux Reservation in South Dakota and resist efforts to evict them by a show of armed force.

**Mar. 2:** A treaty banning the commercial trade of 375 species of endangered wildlife is signed by eighty countries in Washington.

**Mar. 29:** The remaining known POWs fly out of Hanoi; the last American troops leave South Vietnam.

**Apr. 7:** A week-long housewives' boycott against the purchase of meat comes to an end as the women pledge to continue protest against high food prices.

**Apr. 30:** Nixon announces the resignation of top administration officials touched by Watergate: Chief of Staff H. R. Haldeman, Domestic Affairs Assistant John Erlichman, Attorney General Richard Kleindienst and Presidential Counsel John W. Dean III.

**May 11:** Federal Judge William Byrne dismisses the U.S. government's charges against the *Pentagon Papers* defendants Daniel Ellsberg and Anthony Russo, Jr.

**May 12:** The United Nations reports that six million Africans living along the southern edge of the Sahara Desert are in danger of dying of starvation after a five-year drought.

**May 17:** Millions of Americans watch the opening of the Senate Select Committee on Presidential Campaign Activities hearings under the chairmanship of Senator Sam J. Ervin, Jr., of North Carolina. They watch the hearings throughout the summer, as the entire story of sabotage, dirty tricks and secret tape recordings unfolds on television.

**June 22:** Nixon and Brezhnev sign new agreements to avert nuclear war.

**July 21:** France ignores a ruling by the International Court of Justice at The Hague and explodes the first nuclear test in its current series in the South Pacific, despite protests from many nations.

**Aug. 6:** Vice President Spiro Agnew admits he is under investigation for possible violations of law, including income tax evasion, extortion and bribery, allegedly committed by the law-and-order champion over a ten-year period. Agnew maintains his innocence but eventually pleads "no contest" to tax evasion and agrees to resign from office in exchange for immunity from prosecution. He resigns the Vice Presidency October 10.

**Oct. 2:** President Nixon orders mandatory allocations of propane and distillate fuels to avert a potential energy crisis in the U.S.

**Oct. 6:** The Middle East erupts into war as Egyptian forces cross the Suez to attack Israeli troops, and Syria attacks Israel in the Golan Heights.

**Oct. 12:** Nixon names Republican House Leader Gerald R. Ford of Michigan to replace Spiro Agnew as Vice President.

**Oct. 20:** In a "Saturday Night Massacre," President Nixon fires Special Watergate Prosecutor Archibald Cox; Attorney General Elliot Richardson resigns in protest and Solicitor General Robert Bork replaces Richardson on an acting basis.

**Oct. 21:** Kuwait, Bahrain, Qatar and Dubai complete a total embargo on oil shipments from Arab countries to the United States. The move signals the end of America's complacency about cheap and plentiful light, heat and gasoline.

**Oct. 27:** A United Nations peacekeeping force begins arriving in Egypt.

**Nov. 12:** Egypt and Israel sign a cease-fire accord, temporarily halting the Mideast War.

## 1974

**Jan. 23:** The U.S. Interior Department permits construction of the Alaskan oil pipeline, long delayed by environmentalist lawsuits.

**Feb. 3:** Mao Tse-tung launches a New Cultural Revolution in China.

**Feb. 13:** Alexandr I. Solzhenitsyn is deported by the Russians in reprimand for his book *The Gulag Archipelago, 1918–1956,* a work revealing the brutalities of the Soviet penal system and political repression. He takes up residence in the U.S.

**Mar. 1:** The Watergate grand jury indicts seven Nixon aides, the former Attorney General and two Nixon campaign aides on charges of perjury, conspiracy and obstruction of justice.

**Apr. 16:** The sentence of Lt. William Calley, convicted for murder in the My Lai massacre, is reduced by half.

**July 14:** The Gallup Poll finds that inflation is the most worrisome issue faced by Americans.

**July 24:** The U.S. Supreme Court unanimously rules that President Nixon must hand over subpoenaed documents and tapes, as evidence in the trial of six of his former aides.

**July 27–30:** The House Judiciary Committee approves three articles of impeachment against the President, charging him with obstructing justice, abusing the powers of the presidency and defying legitimate subpoenas for evidence.

**Aug. 5:** Nixon releases tape transcripts implicating him in the cover-up of the Watergate burglary.

**Aug. 8:** The nation holds its breath as the President announces he is guilty of "some misjudgments" and will resign.

**Aug. 9:** President Nixon becomes the first U.S. Chief Executive Officer to resign; Vice President Gerald Ford succeeds him after Nixon bids a tearful farewell to his staff and the nation.

**Aug. 14:** The Episcopal Church rules invalid the July 29 ordination of eleven women as priests, stirring an outcry from women.

**Aug. 19:** A United Nations conference on world population opens in Rumania.

**Sept. 8:** President Ford grants Nixon a "full, free and absolute" presidential pardon for any and all crimes Nixon may have committed in office.

**Sept. 25:** The conviction of Lt. William Calley is overturned because of prejudicial pretrial publicity.

**Oct. 14:** The prosecution of five former Nixon aides begins in the Watergate cover-up scandal.

**Nov. 5:** A United Nations conference opens in Rome to discuss ways to prevent and alleviate worldwide famine and starvation.

**Nov. 8:** Eight Ohio National Guardsmen are acquitted of charges in the Kent State killings.

**Nov. 9:** The Reverend Alison Cheek becomes the first woman to celebrate Communion in a U.S. Episcopal Church.

**Dec. 30:** The Watergate jury begins deliberations that end two days later with convictions of four former top Nixon aides.


## 1975

**Feb. 21:** Haldeman, Ehrlichman, Mitchell and Robert Mardian are sentenced to varying terms in prison for their roles in the Watergate cover-up.

**Mar. 18–20:** South Vietnamese troops abandon seven provinces to the Communists.

**Apr. 1–3:** North Vietnam takes control of major coastal cities in the South as troops there flee.

**Apr. 30:** South Vietnam surrenders to the Viet Cong and Communist forces as Saigon falls; the United States, in a scene of mass panic, airlifts many military and service personnel and civilians during the hours before the surrender.

**May 12:** The U.S. freighter *Mayaguez* is seized in the Gulf of Thailand by Khmer forces and Ford is faced with his first real crisis as President. On May 14, fifteen U.S. servicemen die in an attempt to free the ship and its thirty-nine crewmen.

**June 12:** *The New York Times* reports that two million Cambodian refugees are fleeing oppression in the cities and hiding in the countryside.

**July 2:** A world conference on women's rights and the status of women concludes in Mexico City; delegates from 113 countries approve a ten-year plan for increasing women's political and social roles in the international arena.

**July 17:** For the first time, American and Soviet spacecraft link in orbit.

**Sept. 5:** President Ford is the target of an assassination attempt by twenty-six-year-old Lynette "Squeaky" Fromme, a devotee of convicted murderer Charles Manson.

**Sept. 14–18:** Moslems and Christians battle in Beirut, leaving one hundred dead and the city nearly destroyed.

**Sept. 22:** President Ford escapes a second assassination attempt when Sara Jane Moore shoots at him in San Francisco. She and Squeaky Fromme both get life sentences.

**Sept. 27:** OPEC nations raise oil prices ten per cent, causing havoc in the world economy.

**Nov. 18:** The Senate committee announces it has learned that the FBI had mounted an ongoing and extensive campaign throughout the 1960s, to discredit civil rights leader Martin Luther King, Jr. by prying into his affairs by means of illegal bugging and surveillance.

**Dec. 31:** On the eve of America's 200th year, Harvard's Daniel Bell asks, "What happened to the American Dream?"

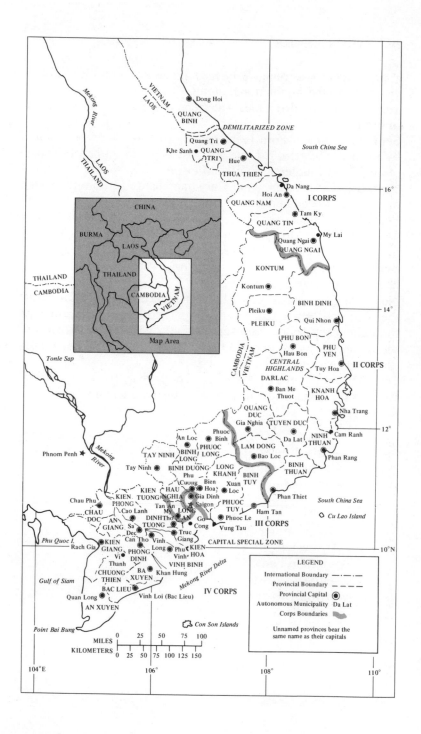

# REMEMBRANCE

This book tells about several men who
gave their lives in Vietnam. Their names
are located on the Vietnam Veterans
Memorial on the Mall in Washington, D.C.
Starting at the center, the names progress
outward along seventy panels on the east
wall toward the Washington Monument.
They then continue to progress inward
seventy panels toward the center along the
west wall, so that a kind of circle is formed.
The panels are like pages of a book. The
book has a beginning and an end, opened
to be read on the Mall.

| NAME | RANK | SERVICE |
| --- | --- | --- |
| ROBERT H. CRUM, JR. | 2d Lieutenant | Army |
| RODNEY MAXWELL DAVIS | Sergeant | Marines |
| EMILIO A. DE LA GARZA, JR. | Lance Corporal | Marines |
| DANIEL FERNANDEZ | Special Fourth Class | Army |
| THOMAS JAY HAYES IV | Captain | Army |
| WALTER NEVILLE LEVY | 2d Lieutenant | Marines |
| MICHAEL EUGENE MULLEN | Sergeant | Army |
| FRANK ANTHONY RYBICKI, JR. | 1st Lieutenant | Army |
| HECTOR SANTIAGO-COLON | Special Fourth Class | Army |
| ROBERT BENNETT SWENCK | Major | Air Force |

| DATE OF BIRTH | DATE OF CASUALTY | HOME | PANEL NO. | LINE NO. |
|---|---|---|---|---|
| 4-20-41 | 5-22-66 | Houston, Texas | 7E | 100 |
| 4-7-42 | 9-6-67 | Macon, Georgia | 26E | 8 |
| 6-23-49 | 4-11-70 | East Chicago, Indiana | 12W | 121 |
| 6-30-44 | 2-18-66 | Los Lunas, New Mexico | 5E | 46 |
| 9-8-43 | 4-17-68 | Arlington, Virginia | 50E | 29 |
| 11-10-38 | 9-18-65 | New York, New York | 2E | 87 |
| 9-11-44 | 2-18-70 | La Porte City, Iowa | 13W | 29 |
| 2-10-44 | 5-9-67 | Balboa, Panama | 19E | 74 |
| 12-20-42 | 6-28-68 | New York, New York | 54W | 13 |
| 3-18-33 | 11-25-71 | Louisville, Kentucky | 2W | 72 |

# FURTHER READING

## CULTURAL CHANGES IN THE SIXTIES

Dickstein, Morris. *Gates of Eden: American Culture in the Sixties*. New York: Basic Books, 1978. Analyzes the radical 1960s from the point of view of art, literature and music.

Hodgson, Godfrey. *America in Our Time: From World War II to Nixon—What Happened and Why*. New York: Doubleday, 1976. An excellent cultural and historical analysis of the upheavals of the 1960s, in a context of an examination of American political ideologies by an objective British observer.

Jones, Landon Y. *Great Expectations: America and the Baby Boom Generation*. New York: Coward, McCann & Geoghegan, 1980. Offers an illuminating analysis of the sixties as the inevitable creation of the most populous and affluent generation in American history.

Lipset, Seymour and Altbach, Philip, eds. *Students in Revolt*. Boston, Mass.: Houghton Mifflin, 1969. Studies the student movement and examines its concepts and objectives.

Teodori, Massimo, ed. *The New Left: A Documentary History*. Indianapolis, Ind.: Bobbs-Merrill, 1969. Contains the germinal writings of the radical thinkers that created the antiwar movement and contains a useful chronology, bibliography and insightful commentaries.

Viorst, Milton. *Fire in the Streets: America in the Nineteen Sixties*. New York: Simon and Schuster, 1980. Offers an insightful historical overview of the events of the sixties, from the Freedom Rides, to the Days of Rage in Chicago, and the deaths at Kent State University.

## CIVIL RIGHTS

Carmichael, Stokely and Hamilton, Charles V. *Black Power: The Politics of Liberation in America.* New York: Random House, 1967. A germinal work which argues that political unity is the only tool by which blacks can gain an effective share in the total power of the society.

Kerner Commission Report. *Report of the National Advisory Commission on Civil Disorders.* Washington, D.C.: U.S. Government Printing Office, 1968. The report of the official investigation of the federal government into the causes of urban unrest in America.

Lewis, Anthony. *Portrait of a Decade.* New York: Random House, 1964. An account of the civil rights movement from 1954–1964 as compiled from *The New York Times* coverage by a veteran reporter.

Lewis, David L. *King: A Biography,* 2nd ed. Champaign, Ill.: Univ. of Illinois Press, 1978. By general consensus, the best biography of the civil rights leader and contains excellent detail and background material.

Meier, August and Rudwick, Elliott, eds. *Black Protest in the Sixties.* New York: Quadrangle, 1970. A compilation of essays, articles and addresses of the many of the voices of the 1960s analyzing the black revolution.

Muse, Benjamin. *The American Negro Revolution.* Secaucus, N.J.: Citadel Press, 1970. Gives a general history of the civil rights movement.

Silberman, Charles. *Crisis in Black and White.* New York: Random House, 1964. This is still perhaps the best book to read for an understanding of the background of the struggle for black rights.

## WOMEN'S RIGHTS

Bird, Caroline. *Born Female*. New York: David McKay, 1969. An analysis of the inequalities suffered by women in America.

Ellman, Mary. *Thinking About Women*. New York: Harcourt Brace Jovanovich, 1969. A good collection of analytical essays on the women's movement.

Friedan, Betty. *The Feminine Mystique*, 2nd ed. New York: Norton, 1974. A groundbreaking analysis of the malaise of American women which contains concrete suggestions for improving their lot. The book paved the way for the resurgence of the feminist movement in America.

Millett, Kate. *Sexual Politics*. New York: Doubleday, 1970. Another germinal work that claims male machismo in politics and the culture conspire to deprive women of their rights.

Morgan, Robin. *Sisterhood is Powerful: An Anthology of Writings From the Women's Liberation Movement*. New York: Random House, 1970. An anthology of angry feminist writings of the early days of the new feminist movement.

U.S. National Commission for Manpower Policy. *Women's Changing Roles at Home and on the Job*. Washington, D.C.: Special Report No. 26, September 1978. An official document analyzing perhaps the most important effects of the new women's movement: increasing participation in the labor force and the changing nature of the family.

## VIETNAM WAR

Baker, Mark. *Nam: The Vietnam War in the Words of the Men and Women Who Fought There*. New York: Morrow, 1982. Includes the memoirs of one hundred servicemen and women who served in Vietnam, in oral history format.

Bourne, Peter G., M.D. *Men, Stress and Vietnam*. Boston, Mass.: Little Brown and Co., 1970. Valuable reading, especially for showing how predetermined one-year tours affected American soldiers.

Braestrup, Peter. *Big Story: How the American Press and Television Reported and Interpreted the Crisis of Tet 1968 in Vietnam and Washington*. Garden City: Anchor Press, 1978. Thorough case history of media coverage.

Capps, Walter. *The Unfinished War: Vietnam and the American Conscience*. Boston, Mass.: Beacon, 1982. Another attempt to analyze the lasting effects of the war on American society.

Fitzgerald, Frances. *Fire in the Lake: The Vietnamese and the Americans in Vietnam*. Boston, Mass.: Little, Brown and Co., 1972. Examines the cultural differences between Americans and Vietnamese, and analyzes the United States failure there.

Gelb, Leslie H. with Betts, Richard K. *The Irony of Vietnam: The System Worked*. Washington, D.C.: Brookings Institution, 1979. An analytical history of United States policymaking in Vietnam.

Karnow, Stanley. *Vietnam: A History*. New York: Viking, 1983. A comprehensive history of the war, written with authority by a journalist who covered the American involvement from the beginning.

Kovic, Ron. *Born on the Fourth of July*. New York: McGraw-Hill, 1976. An angry memoir by a Marine sergeant who became paralyzed in the war.

Lewy, Guenter. *America in Vietnam*. New York: Oxford University Press, 1978. Examines United States military policy in the war, and contains many useful official statistics.

Podhoretz, Norman. *Why We Were in Vietnam*. New York: Simon and Schuster, 1982. Includes a forceful case for the morality of American involvement.

Powers, Thomas. *The War at Home*. Grossman, 1973. A detailed account of the antiwar movement in the United States.

Santoli, Al. *Everything We Had: An Oral History of the Vietnam War*. New York: Random House, 1981. A history of the war telling the stories of thirty-three American soldiers who fought in it.

U.S. Dept. of Defense. *The Pentagon Papers.* The New York Times edition. New York: Quadrangle, 1971. An abridged version of the official history of the war as compiled by the Defense Department.

## SHAPING EFFECTS OF
## VIETNAM ERA EVENTS

*Anglican Theological Review* LXIV (January 1982). Special issue on the spiritual effects of the Vietnam Era on America.

Barone, Michael and Ujifusa, Grant. *The Almanac of American Politics.* Washington, D.C.: The National Journal. This annual book presents a comprehensive overview of American political developments.

*The Century Generation.* Available from: The Century Generation, Inc., Suite 9, 1000 Connecticut Avenue, N.W., Washington, D.C. 20036. Brief monthly report on how events of the Vietnam Era are shaping America. Also provides research and clearing house service.

Horne, A.D. ed. *The Wounded Generation: America After Vietnam.* Englewood Cliffs, N.J.: Prentice Hall, 1981. Analyzes the effects of the war in a collection of essays and focuses on the present and future of both the soldiers and the resisters.

U.S. Congress. House Subcommittee on Education, Training, and Employment of the Committee on Veterans' Affairs. *The Vietnam Veterans Leadership Program,* 97th Congress, 1st Session, October 22, 1981. Serial No. 97-42. Explains the Vietnam Veterans Leadership Program.

U.S. Congress. Senate Committee on Veterans' Affairs. *Legacies of Vietnam: Comparative Adjustment of Veterans and their Peers.* 97th Congress, 1st Session, March 26, 1981. Committee Print No. 6. Presents thorough study, based on field research.

———. *Myths and Realities: A Study of Attitudes Toward Vietnam Era Veterans.* 96th Congress, 2d Session, July 1980. Committee Print No. 29. Presents comprehensive national survey results.

Vietnam Veterans Memorial Fund. *The Vietnam Generation and Reconciliation: Men and Women Together.* Available from: VVMF, Suite 308, 1110 Vermont Avenue, N.W., Washington, D.C. 20005. Transcript of a comprehensive round table discussion on the effects of the events of the Vietnam Era. Participants are a cross-section of the generation.

Wilcox, Fred A. *Waiting For an Army to Die: The Tragedy of Agent Orange.* New York: Random House, 1983. Considers the effects on U.S. soldiers of the toxic defoliant used during the war, and contains other information.

# INDEX

# THANKS

This book is the story of many people, their experiences, friendships, associations and remembrances, which I have recounted. Each person in this book helped build it. I thank them for what they have taught me and for their support, love and counsel. These people are just as much a part of the story:

**Ellen Joseph,** spiritual sister of Max Perkins, who edits in the old-fashioned way.

**Roberta Karmel,** friend and counselor.

**Gerry McCauley,** literary agent, who taught me how to create the book.

**Kathleen Palm,** friend and writer who cares deeply about what is happening in our generation, and who prepared "Events, 1959–1975" and the Further Reading list.

**Tom Shull,** Army officer who embodies duty, honor, country.

**Bill Tully,** who wrote the Episcopal Church resolution on reconciliation after the Vietnam War.

**Jacqueline Walker, Monica Harley, Gail Fortson,** and **Helen Pryor,** who put this book through the word processor and into Ellen Joseph's hands.

**Carol Weisbrod, Rick Tropp, Marsha Williams,** and **Mary King,** friends who made the manuscript better.

**Mary Christy Szarwark, Jacqueline Miller, Rose Blodgett, Carolyn Branch, Jacqueline Seppy,** and **Joan Ward,** pediatric intensive care nurses, who have guarded Katie all her life.

**David Todres, Frank Stroud, Maureen Edwards, William Montgomery** and **Bruce Feldman,** doctors who saved Katie's life.

**The DesPortes family,** who gave me a home in South Carolina, where this book was born.